IMPROVING
CHILD
and
FAMILY
ASSESSMENTS

of related interest

The Child's World
The Comprehensive Guide to Assessing Children in Need
2nd edition
Edited by Jan Horwath
ISBN 978 1 84310 568 8
eISBN 978 0 85700 183 2

Social Work Reclaimed
Innovative Frameworks for Child and
Family Social Work Practice
Edited by Steve Goodman and Isabelle Trowler
Foreword by Eileen Munro
ISBN 978 1 84905 202 3
eISBN 978 0 85700 461 1

**Promoting Children's Rights in
Social Work and Social Care**
A Guide to Participatory Practice
Margaret Bell
ISBN 978 1 84310 607 4
eISBN 978 0 85700 486 4
Children in Charge series

Social Care, Service Users and User Involvement
Edited by Peter Beresford and Sarah Carr
Foreword by Simon Denegri
ISBN 978 1 84905 075 3
eISBN 978 0 85700 264 8
Research Highlights in Social Work series

Good Practice in Safeguarding Children
Working Effectively in Child Protection
Edited by Liz Hughes and Hilary Owen
ISBN 978 1 84310 945 7
eISBN 978 1 84642 894 4

**Child Development for Child Care
and Protection Workers**
2nd edition
Brigid Daniel, Sally Wassell and Robbie Gilligan
Foreword by Professor David Howe
ISBN 978 1 84905 068 5
eISBN 978 0 85700 245 7

IMPROVING CHILD
and
FAMILY ASSESSMENTS

Turning Research into Practice

Danielle Turney, Dendy Platt,
Julie Selwyn and Elaine Farmer

Jessica Kingsley *Publishers*
London and Philadelphia

Crown copyright material is reproduced with the permission of the Controller of the HMSO and the Queen's Printer for Scotland.
Box 4.2 on pp.67–8 is reproduced from Thoburn *et al.* 2009 with permission from the Centre for Excellence and Outcomes in Children and Young People's Services (C4EO).

First published in 2012
by Jessica Kingsley Publishers
116 Pentonville Road
London N1 9JB, UK
and
400 Market Street, Suite 400
Philadelphia, PA 19106, USA

www.jkp.com

Library of Congress Cataloging in Publication Data
Improving child and family assessments : turning research into practice /
Danielle Turney ... [et al.].
    p. cm.
Includes bibliographical references and index.
ISBN 978-1-84905-256-6 (alk. paper)
1. Family social work. 2. Social work with children. 3. Family assessment.
4. Social service--Research. I. Turney, Danielle.
HV697.I47 2012
362.82'53--dc23
                                    2011032658

British Library Cataloguing in Publication Data
A CIP catalogue record for this book is available from the British Library

ISBN 978 1 84905 256 6

Printed and bound in Great Britain

CONTENTS

List of Tables, Figures and Boxes
Tables

Figures

Boxes

ACKNOWLEDGEMENTS

This book is based on a research review funded by the Department for Education. In the course of the project, we contacted a number of researchers who had been involved in key government-funded research initiatives and one overview study and would like to thank them for their generous responses to our requests for information and access to published and unpublished reports. The review cannot fully reflect all the work that was undertaken in the studies we have reported but it is clear that there is a wealth of information about assessment to draw on. We were well supported by Jenny Gray, Julie Wilkinson and Isabella Craig at the Department for Education throughout the project. We would like to thank them and other colleagues who were particularly helpful in accessing currently unpublished work. Excellent research assistance was provided by Valerie Bramwell, Gillian Macdonald, Hilary Saunders and Joanne Abbott.

We would also like to thank all the members of our Advisory Group – Marian Brandon, Hedy Cleaver, Isabella Craig, Jenny Gray, Colin Green, David Jones, Helen Jones, Lorraine Radford, Rosemarie Roberts and Julie Wilkinson – for reading and commenting on the report.

Chapter 1

INTRODUCTION

This book draws together information gathered in the course of a review of research, commissioned by the Department for Education (DfE). The review was intended to provide a better understanding of the relationship between the quality of assessments and outcomes for children in contact with children's social care services. More specifically, the purpose of the review was to increase understanding of:

- how information collected and analysed during an assessment has both a short- and long-term impact on future planning, choice of interventions and of placements and psycho-social outcomes for children

- how variations in local authority policies and practices affect decisions about whether initial or core assessments should be undertaken and whether thresholds for intervention have been met.

The period covered by this research review (1999–2010) has been framed by a number of high-profile cases of 'preventable' child deaths.[1] It is also a period where there has been considerable central government investment in services and in research aiming to deepen understanding of the impact of policy and practice changes.

Indeed, during this period the Department of Health and the then Department for Children, Schools and Families (DCSF) funded six research initiatives and a substantial review of government-funded research into different aspects of foster care. Each of the research initiatives had a particular focus: the impact of the Children Act 1989, supporting parents, costs and outcomes in children's social care, 'Quality Protects', adoption and safeguarding. The research studies in each of these research programmes provide a rich source of material on the assessment of children in need from which our review has drawn.

Background

The assessment of children in need and their families is an aspect of social work practice that has attracted considerable attention over the past decade. Poor-quality, incomplete or non-existent assessments have been of particular concern. Five areas have been repeatedly identified in the literature as problematic: a failure to engage with the child, inadequacies in information gathering, differential thresholds, shortcomings in critical analysis and shortcomings in inter-professional working.

Policy and practice context

The period covered by this review starts with the transition from the 'Orange Book', the Department of Health's (1988) *Protecting Children: A Guide for Social Workers Undertaking a Comprehensive Assessment*, to the *Framework for the Assessment of Children in Need and their Families* (Department of Health, Department for Education and Employment and Home Office 2000), which followed the introduction of the Children Act 1989. The new Assessment Framework was designed to provide 'a systematic way of analysing, understanding and recording what is happening to children and young people within their families and the wider context of the community in which they live' (Department of Health *et al.* 2000, p.viii). The decade following its introduction has seen a number of significant additional policy initiatives.

The death of Victoria Climbié in 2000 received substantial media coverage and put the perceived failings of the child protection system under a very public spotlight. Following Lord Laming's inquiry and report (Laming 2003), the then government moved swiftly to accept Lord Laming's recommendations and to initiate substantial policy and practice changes through the *Every Child Matters: Change for Children* programme (HM Government 2004). These were described as 'the biggest changes in a generation' (Gupta and Blewett 2007, p.142). Measures that were intended to have a particular impact on assessment practice include the Integrated Children's System and the Common Assessment Framework, which were introduced against a backdrop of wider service reorganisation and moves to strengthen inter-professional and multi-agency working.

Reconfiguring the social care workforce and the role and task of social work was given further momentum by the again very public furore surrounding the death of Peter Connelly ('Baby P') in 2007 (Haringey Local Safeguarding Children Board (LSCB) 2008, 2009). In this case, the then government responded by commissioning a second report from Lord Laming, *The Protection of Children in England: A Progress Report* (Laming 2009). It added a further 58 recommendations to the 108 presented in the 2003 Victoria Climbié Inquiry Report. The Social Work Task Force was established 'to undertake a comprehensive review of frontline social work practice to...identify any barriers social workers face in doing their jobs effectively and to make recommendations for improvements and long-term reform in social work'.[2] The Task Force reported towards the end of 2009 and its recommendations have been taken forward by a newly constituted Social Work Reform Board whose strategies for implementing the recommendations are likely to have far-reaching implications for education, training, practice, regulation and management of social work.

More recently, the coalition government which took office in May 2010 launched a review of child protection services, undertaken by Professor Eileen Munro. That review was designed to build on the work of both Lord Laming's Progress Report and the Social Work Task Force, and to link to the continuing work of the Social Work Reform Board and other relevant reviews, such as the Family Justice Review. The government identified three principles to underpin its approach to reform of child protection in England: 'early intervention; trusting professionals and removing bureaucracy so they can spend more of their time on the frontline; and greater transparency and accountability'.[3]

Objectives

The key objectives of our research review were to identify and analyse findings from published studies relating to:

- the thresholds operated by local authorities for responding to referrals, and the implications for outcomes
- the quality of the data populating initial, core and other types of assessments carried out for children in need, including looked after children and children placed for adoption
- the variation in the quality of assessments by local authorities and for different groups of children (for example, disabled children, black and minority ethnic children)

- the extent to which professionals engaged with children, young people and their families to produce effective assessments
- the factors that assisted or acted as barriers to good-quality assessments of children in need
- the impact of the quality of assessments on decision making, planning, interventions and ultimately on children's and young people's short- and longer-term outcomes.

Method

Drawing primarily on social work-focused literature, this review covers UK research findings published between 1999 and 2010. Not many studies during this period had assessment as their primary focus and consequently the task of the review was to draw out findings on assessment from a wide range of different research reports, journal papers and other documents. These were identified through detailed searches of a range of databases and through consultation with academic researchers in the field. Overall, material relating to over 100 studies was included in the review. (Full details of the methodology adopted can be found in Appendix A, and a full list of the empirical studies reviewed is included in Appendix B.)

Having offered a brief account of the background to the review and outlined the approach undertaken, we move on to consider the findings, starting in Chapter 2 with a discussion of 'thresholds'; here we look at the thresholds that were used in recognising children's difficulties, in making assessments and those that prompted intervention. Chapter 3 considers the process of information gathering that underpins assessment and what the research evidence indicates about the content of social work assessments, and Chapter 4 addresses assessments undertaken in different practice contexts. Chapters 5, 6, 7 and 8 look at a range of factors that can contribute, or act as barriers, to the production of good-quality assessments. We present some key messages on the links between assessment and child outcomes in Chapter 9 before drawing together our conclusions in Chapter 10.

Notes

1 Starting with the death of Victoria Climbié in 2000, the decade closed with the cases of 'Baby Peter' and Khyra Ishaq; although the deaths of these children occurred in 2007 and 2008 respectively, the cases came fully into the public domain in 2009 and 2010.

2 See www.swap.ac.uk/policyregulation/taskforce/implications.html, accessed August 2011.

3 For further information about the Munro review, see www.education.gov. uk/munroreview, accessed April 2011.

Chapter 2

THRESHOLDS FOR RECOGNITION, ASSESSMENT AND INTERVENTION

Thresholds act as the 'gateway' to the provision of services or interventions, including assessment. This chapter considers research evidence addressing what they mean, where they are set and how these factors have an impact on the assessment of children in need.

Threshold: A contested concept

Before examining the difficulties in defining thresholds for assessment or intervention it is important to acknowledge the contested nature of the concept. The term threshold implies a continuum along which children's difficulties can be arranged in order of seriousness. An agreed degree of seriousness is then determined, and is used to define the conditions (or minimum threshold) for provision of a particular service or initiation of a particular action. Arguably, children's welfare and the risks to it cannot be measured in this way. Not only is it impossible to compare, for example, a child suffering neglect in terms of accessing available health care, a child who has been witnessing domestic violence for several years and a child who has been a victim of repeated, non-penetrative sexual assault, but the point at which services or action are needed cannot be simply defined. The experience of each child is different, and to reduce their needs to a point on a simple yardstick is, at best, likely to be an oversimplification and, at worst, runs the risk of failing to understand the meaning and impact of the experience for that individual. The term threshold, however, persists because decisions still have to be made about entry to services, and to date no convincing alternative approach has been put forward.

It would be unhelpful, clearly, to abandon the language of thresholds without providing a better way of thinking about the issues involved. We will therefore continue to use the concept of threshold here, acknowledging that the discussion is based on an imperfect idea. We would emphasise, however, that there will never be absolute clarity of definition, and in practice it may be difficult to determine when the threshold for formal assessment or intervention has been reached. Both decisions require good assessment skills. The most important thing is that the wide range of circumstances and how they affect any given child are fully assessed and the individual child's situation is adequately understood in relation to decisions about offering services or intervening in some other way.

Where thresholds are set

> [A threshold] is commonly used to refer to a judgement about the seriousness of the child's need using Children Act definitions about actual or likely harm or impairment and moreover, is linked to priority categories established within an individual authority which determine whether a service which may be needed will actually be provided. (Tunstill and Allnock 2007, p.128)

Whilst, as we have indicated, there are significant conceptual and practical challenges associated with the notion of thresholds and no absolute clarity in terms of definition, what thresholds mean and where they are set becomes particularly critical in periods of resource shortage.

What happens when thresholds rise?

Linked to eligibility criteria, setting a high threshold for receipt of services clearly has implications for who gets what, when, and may lead to a situation where children and families are not referred at an early stage in their difficulties, but only later when problems are more entrenched and potentially more serious. Various inspection reports in recent years have raised concerns about thresholds. For example,

Brandon and colleagues (2008) cite the Joint Chief Inspectors' (JCI) Report of 2002, which was based on an examination of eight local authority Area Child Protection Committees in England and found that 'pressures on resources in children's social care had led to a tightening of the thresholds for services for children where there were concerns about their welfare' (Brandon et al. 2008, p.21). In that Report, the JCIs also noted that the local authority response to safeguarding children was felt to be inadequate by many referring agencies, with the 2005 Report observing that 'there remain significant issues about how thresholds are applied by social services in their child protection and family support work' (JCI 2005, p.7, cited by Brandon et al. 2008, p.21). More recently, Sheppard (2009a) drew attention to an inspection report by the Commission for Social Care Inspection (CSCI 2006) in which worries were expressed about the level at which thresholds were operating in children's social care services and suggested that professionals responded to high thresholds by tailoring their referrals 'in the light of their knowledge that only the very highest-need families are liable to get a service' (Sheppard 2009a, p.1429). The issue here would presumably be that access to services could then depend more on the worker's ability to 'read' the system and their skill in framing their assessments than on need alone, and/or that some families with moderately high levels of need would not be referred at all.

The consequences of a high threshold to access services may be considerable. For example, a recent study by Biehal (2005) examined the effectiveness of specialist adolescent support teams that had been set up to offer intensive short-term preventive services to young people at risk of entering the care system. She noted that thresholds for receiving help from either a mainstream social work service or a specialist support team were high and that in most cases a service was only offered when the family had reached crisis point. A similar concern was identified by Farmer and Lutman (2009) in their study of case management and outcomes for neglected children who had been returned to their parents from local authority care. They found that some children experienced abuse and/or neglect over long periods before a child protection plan was made. This varied by local authority, suggesting that the threshold for children being assessed as in need of a protection plan was too high in some authorities. In addition, in the researchers' view 28 per cent of the children were left too long with their parents in adverse circumstances before care proceedings were initiated.

Similarly, although they were by definition looking back at situations that had 'gone wrong', the first two biennial analyses of serious case reviews conducted by Brandon and her colleagues (Brandon *et al.* 2008; Brandon, Bailey *et al.* 2009) both identified concerns about thresholds for access to services which had left children 'hovering on the borders' in a number of cases (Brandon, Bailey *et al.* 2009, p.60) – a point endorsed in the later overview report (Brandon, Bailey and Belderson 2010). The dilemma for practitioners and managers of whether and how to respond to families who 'bump along' and appear to offer adequate child care some of the time, but interspersed with periods of neglect and inadequate levels of care, was highlighted by the review of the case of Shannon Mathews, conducted by Kirklees Safeguarding Children Board. Shannon, a nine-year-old girl, 'disappeared' from home but was subsequently found to have been abducted by her mother and uncle. The Serious Case Review that looked into the circumstances of this unusual case found that the mother's care of Shannon and her siblings had caused concern over a long period of time. A number of agencies had been involved with the family over the years but the Review noted that the threshold for removing Shannon and her siblings from their parents' care had not been reached (Kirklees Safeguarding Children Board 2010).

Where local authorities raise thresholds for access to assessment and to services, this also has a knock-on effect on the way that other services for children and families operate. For example, a study carried out by Tunstill, Aldgare and Hughes (2007) examined, amongst other things, 'the potential of family centres to act as a gateway to family support services'. The researchers noted various changes in the way the family centres they studied were operating, and observed that findings from their review study 'indicated a trend towards higher thresholds, with an increase in reactive, crisis work, and an emphasis on the prevention of family breakdown' (p.125), rather than earlier, more preventive work or involvement in less crisis-driven work.

As can be seen, the implications of local authorities setting high thresholds for access to services have been discussed by a number of researchers and a range of concerns identified. However, other views were also found in the studies included in this review. A series of recent papers by Sheppard (2008, 2009a, 2009b) reported on different aspects of a study investigating the use of social support as a parental coping strategy; the study focused on a sample of families who were referred, or who referred themselves, to children's social care services but did not receive a casework intervention. Sheppard's starting point was the concern he had identified in policy and other documents (for example, CSCI 2005, 2006) about the effects of high thresholds within children's services, particularly the implications of lack of access to services for families whose circumstances demonstrated significant need. His study set out to test the assumption implicit in these documents, that, without access to services, 'families will be referred later with more serious problems that will require intervention, and use more resources' (Sheppard 2008, p.1268).

The first stage of the study involved a sample of 102 mothers who were interviewed within three weeks of their referral to children's social care services; this number had reduced to 69 by the follow-up, six months later. The sample was drawn from families referred to children's social care services in one local authority. The focus was on families who received an initial assessment but whose problems, on examination, were not considered severe enough to warrant allocation for further intervention. Sheppard's intention was to test the hypothesis that 'outcomes would be more positive for mothers who felt they received social support. Specifically, the greater the adequacy of support provided at the time of crisis, the better would be the outcomes' (2009a, p.1431). 'Social support' broadly consists of 'social relationships that provide (or potentially provide) material and interpersonal resources that are of value to the recipient, such as counselling, access to information and services, sharing of tasks and responsibilities' (Thompson 1995, cited by Ghate and Hazel 2002, pp.106–107) and may be provided through formal and/or informal means.

Sheppard's conclusions were interesting in that he found that high thresholds were not automatically problematic for all of these families. While all the families had significant problems and high levels of need, a 'large majority show a marked improvement in their circumstances over the six months following application' (2008, p.1279). However, a 'notable minority of families experienced either no change or a deterioration in their circumstances' (p.1279), which led Sheppard to suggest that a particular challenge may be how to identify which families are likely to fall into which group: 'The problem is, how do we identify them? The data here do not provide a clear answer, but it may be that it lies in the availability and adequacy of support from the informal support networks' (p.1280) provided through family, friends and acquaintances. These findings were not definitive – the follow-up study suffered a reasonably high attrition rate on what was already quite a small sample, drawn from referred families in just one authority. However, they did suggest a variable that might warrant further investigation – the support, and in particular the informal support, networks that the individuals had available – and that the absence of social support may be a key factor to include in eligibility criteria to improve targeting of vulnerable families.

The role and significance of both informal and formal support is addressed more fully in the studies included in the *Supporting Parents* overview report (Quinton 2004) and some complexities are identified, particularly in relation to targeting formal support services. For example, Quinton (2004) noted that parents or carers who attracted formal support may actually be those with the best informal support networks. For this reason, Farmer, Moyers and Lipscombe (2004) and Farmer and Moyers (2008) suggested that assessing foster and kin carers' informal support networks is vital, in order to identify those with the weakest informal support systems who may be in greatest need of formal services. Further research into the role and meaning of informal support and its relationship with formal support may therefore be fruitful.

Ghate and Hazel also noted that for families, being allocated a service did not always or only have beneficial effects and in some situations was perceived negatively. They identified downsides for parents in receiving both formal and informal social support:

> Accepting informal social support, for example, could lead to loss of privacy, loss of control over what happened in one's own home and, if friends or neighbours were involved, immediately involved the recipient in a chain of reciprocal favours that could be stressful to maintain. Semi-formal and especially formal support potentially exposed one to social stigma as well as the risk of professional interference. (Ghate and Hazel 2002, p.179)

The possibility that intervention can have negative consequences may have implications for an understanding of the role of early or 'earlier' intervention, which we discuss below.

Early intervention

The apparent raising of thresholds for receipt of services may be in tension with the current emphasis on early intervention. This may be particularly significant in relation to child neglect where problems may have been identified at an early stage but not pursued:

> It is important to highlight the fact that concerns were voiced about these children from early in their lives, providing the potential for early intervention to help them, with over half (56%) of the children having been referred to children's services before the age of two, including a third referred before birth. Three quarters (76%) had

been brought to children's services attention by the time that they started school. Yet, as we will see, quite often children's services involvement continued over many years without any effective action being taken to protect children. This in turn had a direct relationship with poor outcomes for children at the five year follow-up point. (Farmer and Lutman 2009, p.335)

Farmer and Lutman (2009) have here identified the importance of early intervention for children known to have been experiencing neglect and in some cases it is clear that significant harm or distress could have been avoided had services intervened at an earlier stage. Early/'earlier' intervention has the potential to encourage a different approach, which may impact on understandings of the notion of threshold – with a shift in emphasis from 'significant harm' to 'vulnerability'.

However, Statham and Smith's detailed review (2010) of both the theory of 'earlier' intervention and its application in practice suggests how complicated this can be. They define the concept of 'earlier' intervention as 'intervening early in the life course of a problem, or with children and families at risk of developing a problem, rather than intervening once difficulties have become entrenched and severe' (p.21). A complication immediately arises though: early intervention assumes that additional need can be clearly identified at an early stage and that risk of particular harms can be accurately assessed. But this may not always be straightforward. As Statham and Smith explain, there is a danger of 'false positives' – inappropriately labelling or targeting particular children or families, which is potentially both wasteful of resources and stigmatising for the groups concerned – and of 'false negatives', that is, missing children who did not fit an existing risk 'profile' but who were, nonetheless, vulnerable to a particular harm. Difficulties of this kind suggest that a mixed approach, using both early and later interventions, will continue to be necessary. Indeed, Staham and Smith (2010) caution against viewing early intervention as a 'magic bullet' and their findings have suggested that earlier is not always better. They have identified the need for further research in order to understand better 'what works', why and for whom, as well as what does not work in supporting children with additional needs and their families, who is best placed to offer these support services, how children with additional needs can be identified earlier, and what encourages parents to engage with support services.

The Common Assessment Framework

One of the key purposes of the Common Assessment Framework (CAF) is to 'shift thresholds downwards and change the focus from dealing with the consequences of difficulties in children's lives to preventing things from going wrong in the first place' (Brandon *et al.* 2006, p.47). Studies investigating the early implementation of the CAF have suggested mixed experiences and outcomes. For example, in Brandon and colleagues' (2006) evaluation of the use of the CAF and Lead Professional working in the 12 authorities that trialled the new systems, some interviewees thought that thresholds were being lowered, whilst others reported that thresholds were rising. The researchers noted that 'there was also a perception of taking on social services type work appropriately and that this was how thresholds would move downwards so that help could be offered at an earlier level before problems became entrenched, as anticipated by these initiatives' (Brandon *et al.* 2006, p.48).

Pithouse (2006) reported the findings from one study funded by the Welsh Assembly Government to design, pilot and evaluate a common assessment for children in need in Wales.[1] For the purposes of the pilot, the framework devised was limited to the assessment of children between 0 and 9 years old and did not include urgent child protection referrals; it was trialled in a sub-division of one urban local authority and results were compared with a matched sub-division of a nearby authority that did not have a common assessment protocol in use. Although there are differences between the framework developed by Pithouse and colleagues and the system in use in England, the results of the pilot have some relevance for the use of the CAF in England. In the pilot authority, Pithouse found that there were fewer referrals that received no further action, more referrals moved to initial assessment than previously, and there was 'an increase in allocation of referrals to other social work teams within the authority for action' (Pithouse 2006, p.213). He also reported 'a reduction in referrals that simply came in and went out again to other agencies' (p.213).

Pithouse himself was cautious about the results and speculated, for example, that the increase in referrals 'converting' to initial assessment could have occurred simply because more pressing or concerning referrals were being presented. Commenting more broadly on the changes noted above, he observed that it was:

> ...a matter of some conjecture that these changes are evidence of a positive outcome and a direct consequence of the CAF, for example, the Assessment Framework itself might underwrite some of these

changes (see Cleaver, Walker and Meadows 2004, p.183) and new preventative schemes funded by central and local government targeted at younger children (e.g. Sure Start) may influence referral activity. (Pithouse 2006, pp.213–214)

However, the findings overall did suggest that the CAF process may have had an effect in bringing more focus to assessment and referral, 'thereby introducing a downwards pressure on referral-making by participating agencies' (Pithouse 2006, p.207) and eliciting a more focused response from social services. He noted that there had not been an equivalent increase in child protection referrals alongside the reduction in CAF-linked referrals, which suggested that children's needs were not being overlooked because of reluctance amongst practitioners to use the CAF process, '[n]or was there any increase in self-referrals by adults and children that might have occurred for similar reasons' (pp.207–208).

However, other processes may intervene so that decisions about whether or not to initiate an assessment using the CAF may not be a true reflection of need in a locality. Gilligan and Manby (2008) draw on material collected in the course of a (largely qualitative) evaluation of the early use of CAF processes in two locations in northern England over a six-month period. Practitioners in the pilot areas estimated that 'between a quarter and a third of children and young people in the area could potentially benefit from CAF assessments and the provision of services which may follow them' (Gilligan and Manby 2008, pp.180–181), but the researchers found that the number of CAF assessments completed in the two areas studied was well below the number expected by local service managers. Gilligan and Manby note that practitioners saw 'time spent on CAF assessments as additional to their core activities' (2008, p.181) and, with little expectation of increased staffing, were therefore less likely to instigate such assessments, despite awareness of high levels of need.

Thresholds for decision making: From 'concern' to referral to assessment

In this section, we move on to consider the factors that influence the way concern about a child or family is translated into a referral and how referrals are then processed either to become active cases or to be screened out of the local authority children's social care services system. For those referrals that cross the threshold and become 'live' cases, the trajectory through the assessment process and the various 'exit points' will be considered.

When is a referral not a referral? Managing the referral process

Managing demand within children's social care services involves identifying some contacts/communications as 'referrals' and screening others out or in some way redesignating them. Different studies show that different strategies are used and therefore there is variation in terms of decisions about what actually constitutes a referral, which requires some level of response. Cleaver et al. (2007) found that this was the case in relation to notifications from the police about domestic violence. In some areas a notification of this kind was construed as a referral, whereas in other authorities three such 'contacts' had to occur before a response (in the form of a letter to the family offering an interview) was triggered. Cleaver and colleagues found that these different strategies had a significant impact on the rate of initial assessments in each area and concluded that '[a] clear understanding of what constitutes a referral is required' (2007, p.29).

A later study by Stanley and colleagues (2010a, 2010b) looked in some detail at police notifications to children's social care services of domestic violence incidents. As with the Cleaver et al. (2007) study mentioned above, there appeared to be some confusion about what was a referral, with notifications resulting in provision of a new service in only 5 per cent of the sample:

> The failure of so many of these notified cases to reach children's services' threshold for intervention was attributed by social workers to the low level of seriousness of the incidents and 60 per cent of the cases following a 'no further action pathway' were classified by the researchers as verbal altercations only. (Stanley et al. 2010b, p.6)

However, this finding should perhaps also be viewed alongside the following observation that sheds light on the thresholds with which some social workers appeared to be working:

> 55 per cent of the cases in the sample in which an adult was injured followed a 'no further action pathway' (although all those that involved a child being injured did receive a service) and, similarly, eight of the thirteen cases in which the notification conveyed information about the use of weapons in an incident followed a no further action pathway. (Stanley et al. 2010b, p.7)

Once a number of agencies are involved, the situation becomes more complex. In their study of Sure Start Local Programmes (SSLPs), Tunstill and Allnock (2007) found that 'discrepancies between different agencies around what constituted a referral and what did not' were a key challenge for the eight programmes they worked with, and that 'confusion and/or disagreement about the threshold at which child protection services would be triggered...represented the greatest threat to making appropriate and/or timely referrals' (p.35). Sinclair and Bullock (2002) address a similar point in their analysis of serious case reviews, where they raise the question: 'Is there a common understanding, within and between agencies, of what instigates an assessment of need or risk of significant harm? Is there common understanding, within and between agencies, of the appropriate responses to such an assessment?' (p.29).

Tunstill and Allnock (2007) found that the SSLPs developed practical strategies to manage this, for example by ensuring that they had access to any information or guidance in use in the local authority setting out procedure and practice in relation to thresholds for safeguarding, so they knew what level of need the local service considered important for intervention and could therefore make more informed referrals.

The issue of shared understandings emerged at a later stage in the decision-making process in Daniel's (2004) review of multidisciplinary child protection arrangements in Scotland. Her team found evidence of different expectations from different agencies in relation to the decision about whether a child should be placed on the register at child protection conferences:

> Social work decisions [about registration] were usually based on assessment of the level of risk. Other agencies tended to see registration as a key to resources and therefore pushed for registration for children to be seen as 'in need'. They viewed registration as a marker that 'something needed to be done' for this child and family. (Daniel 2004, p.125)

From referral to assessment: Managing cases in and out of the system

As noted above, not all referrals to children's social care services result in the provision of a service (including assessment), so are decisions being made accurately and appropriately about which cases require a response? In a study of cases involving risk of significant harm, prior to the introduction of the Assessment Framework, Brandon and colleagues

(1999) found that social workers were successful in identifying potentially dangerous situations in 24 out of 24 cases (although the researchers later considered some of these to have been false positives – that is, cases identified as dangerous that later proved not to be). This could suggest that social workers were not missing too many serious cases, although there are significant methodological difficulties in arriving at this conclusion.

Families who did not 'cross the threshold' and received little or no input were the focus of a slightly later investigation by Forrester (2007 and 2008). He collected children's social care data from three local authorities in London on 400 consecutive referrals where cases were closed rather than being allocated for further intervention. File studies were carried out in 2002, and related to cases that had been referred and closed in early 2000. The aim was to identify how many cases were subsequently re-referred, whether there was any pattern to the re-referrals and whether there were any factors statistically associated with re-referral. Forrester suggested that:

> Looking at what happens to referrals that are not allocated is essential if we are to evaluate initial assessment processes and answer questions about whether the right families are receiving services... [and that] it is only possible to provide a full picture of the services provided for children allocated a social worker if we understand the process by which allocation is achieved. For instance, the very substantial number of referrals closed provides a crucial context for understanding the serious nature of the issues in families allocated a social worker. (Forrester 2008, p.297)

He identified some limitations in relation to the design and findings of the study – including the fact that policy and procedures had changed substantially since the research was carried out, with the implementation of the Assessment Framework and the CAF. Nonetheless, the data shed an interesting light on the process of case closure and re-referral. He concluded that:

> This research, in common with a number of other studies, suggests that prior to the Assessment Framework, the Common Assessment Framework and other reforms – whatever the other strengths and weaknesses of the assessment processes – social workers were tending to identify comparatively accurately children at high risk of re-referral involving serious harm. (Forrester 2008, p.298)

Although Forrester's findings indicated that social workers had generally not closed very concerning cases inappropriately, he advised against complacency at the apparent success of that stage of the assessment process, and commented that even if predictive accuracy for the identification of risk of significant harm was high, given the sheer weight of referrals to children's social care services each year, this would still mean that a substantial number of children were being 'missed'.

He noted, in addition, that a small proportion of families (8.5%) accounted for over half (52%) of all re-referrals and asked whether it was possible to identify factors associated with re-referral on the grounds that this might lead to better services for the families concerned and might also help to reduce the number of re-referrals and hence the demand on initial assessment teams. He found that four factors were associated with increased likelihood of 're-referral of actual or potential significant harm':

- previous referrals
- neglect
- family/child relationship problems
- where parental capacity was of concern, particularly where substance misuse was involved.

However, these factors only appeared to become useful as indicators in combination. 'For instance, where two or more were present the likelihood of a closed case being re-referred rose to 59%' (Forrester 2007, p.20). He suggested that this finding might have implications for the design of initial assessment and intervention systems, and that 'policy makers might wish to consider whether some of these families might benefit from periods of allocation or from the development of specialist interventions aimed at neglect, parental capacity issues (particularly drug misuse) or families with parent/child relationship difficulties' (p.20).

In their study of the implementation and early impact of the Assessment Framework, Cleaver *et al.* (2004) audited 2248 referrals across 24 local authorities. They found that of the 2248 total, 866 (38.5%) referrals proceeded to an initial assessment. Further, only 68 referrals (3% of the total number of referrals and 7.8% of initial assessments) led to a core assessment being undertaken.

Factors associated with the decision to recommend initial assessment were the age of the child and the reason for assessment. Referrals were more likely to result in an initial assessment where a child under 15 was involved. Child protection referrals, along with referrals for parental drug or alcohol use or parental mental health problems, and referrals involving a disabled child were more likely to have an initial assessment recorded as the recommended action than referrals related to financial problems and police referrals for domestic violence (Cleaver *et al.* 2004, p.177). However, the relationship between reason for referral and response was not clear-cut. Child protection concerns accounted for almost a third of all referrals (30.3%), but Cleaver and colleagues identified that less than half of these (46.5%) proceeded to an initial assessment – which, as they pointed out 'raises questions over what happens to the remaining child protection referrals made to social services' (Cleaver and Walker 2004, p.85).

Following an initial assessment, a decision to proceed to a core assessment was most likely where child protection concerns had been identified, or where there were concerns about parental drug or alcohol misuse. Reviewing the files, Cleaver and colleagues identified a group of what they termed 'multi-problem cases', where the initial assessment had identified severe difficulties in all three domains of the Assessment Framework. Worryingly, of the 61 cases thus identified, a quarter of the children concerned (n=15) did not receive a core assessment.

Platt's findings (2005, 2006a, 2006b) from a small-scale study of local authority social workers' decision making in 'situations involving concerns about children that came close to the child protection threshold' (Platt 2006b, p.7) throw some light on the way cases are managed into or out of the assessment system. He found that practitioners adopted particular reasoning devices to manage these borderline situations and to decide which cases should receive an assessment, basing their evaluation of referral information on five key factors:

1. Specificity of harm to the child/ren – how clear and detailed the allegation was.

2. Severity of the likely harm – the degree of seriousness attached to the referral by the receiving team.

3. An assessment of the risk of future harm.

4. Parental accountability – whether the parent might be responsible for the harm.

5. Corroboration – social workers drew on two sources of corroboration: information about previous social services involvement, and referrals appearing in clusters with more than one referring agent providing similar information at the same time.

These factors influenced decision making in different ways. Cases that crossed the threshold between no further action and initial assessment typically involved concerns about the wellbeing of a child for which the parent could be held accountable, that could be interpreted as constituting a possible risk of harm to the child, and was corroborated by other professionals or by previous social work involvement (Platt 2006b, p.13).

But to cross the next threshold – from initial assessment to section 47 enquiry – two additional factors came into play:

1. Either the *specificity* of reported harm to a child (e.g. an injury or specific allegation of sexual abuse).

2. Or the workers' interpretation of particular *seriousness*, based on either current information or a pattern that had emerged over time.

(Platt 2006b, p.13)

Platt notes that social workers are under considerable pressure to make the right decision but are working in situations of uncertainty. Indeed, uncertainty is 'an integral feature of the referral stage where information, by definition, is limited and resources are stretched' (2006b, p.14). In such circumstances, the use of 'a limited range of reasoning devices' becomes an understandable response, providing a way of 'transforming the uncertainty into a set of manageable decision-making tasks' (p.15).

Platt's study, discussed above, focused on social workers' thinking processes in situations where both time and personal resources were limited. A different, but complementary, perspective is afforded by a more recent study (White 2009) that focused more explicitly on issues about the 'front door' to services and the way 'front line' practitioners manage the referral process. This investigation of decision making and risk management in children's social work services identified and analysed sources of 'latent error' within agency practices. This qualitative study included an ethnographic approach that allowed for the emergence of rich descriptions of the details of everyday working practices. A number of papers have been published from this study, including one by Broadhurst, Wastell *et al.* (2010). In this paper, the researchers suggested that decisions were made that reflect 'the exigencies of managing workflow dictated by performance timescales' (Broadhurst, Wastell *et al.* 2010, p.360) and that pressure of work and the level of bombardment experienced by social workers encourages the development of 'speed practices' to cope with the demand. This article identified 'well-established "general deflection strategies" that included:

strategic deferment, namely sending the referral back to the referrer to ask for more information; and signposting, deflecting the case to a more "appropriate" agency' (p.360). Other ways of deflecting or downgrading the significance of a referral included routinely treating referrals from family members or friends/neighbours as potentially malicious. If a case did get through the first stage of filtering and was identified for initial assessment, further short cuts were identified, for example by using information from other agencies/professionals (for instance, rather than going and seeing a child themselves, relying on the fact that the health visitor had seen the child recently).

The researchers noted the impact of performance indicators – for example, the requirement to complete an initial assessment within seven working days[2] – on the management of the referral process. They commented on what they considered to be creative – and possibly safer – 'work-arounds'. For example, in situations where the seven working days had not allowed enough time to be confident about a child's welfare, cases would be held open for 'review' while logging the initial assessment as completed, so as to meet the target. The researchers noted that the review period allowed further information to be gathered. Building in this extra space also helped the local authority manage another performance indicator, in relation to the number of initial assessments that 'converted' to a core assessment. But, overall, the pressure to move cases on by whatever means, including designating them for no further action (NFA), appeared to be driving practice in often unhelpful ways:

> Whilst in many cases, an 'NFA' decision may be quite appropriate, our file analysis of open cases did find a common pattern of repeated initial assessments of escalating severity before the case eventually found its way through the front door. (Broadhurst, Wastell et al. 2010, p.362)

Thresholds for responding to re-referrals

In their study of looked after children who had been returned to the care of their parents, Farmer et al. (2011) identified specific concerns about the apparent lack of protection offered to a proportion of children (16% of those studied) who remained at home with their parents despite experiencing abuse or neglect. They found that different thresholds for response seemed to be applied depending on the age of the child: where a baby or child under five was considered likely to suffer harm, great care was taken to assess the parents and monitor the child's return home but 'practice was much less consistent as children became even a little older' and they provide the example of a seven-year-old girl who was returned to her mother who misused alcohol, smacked the child and neglected her. Even after the child received an injury as a result of violence between her parents, and was assaulted by her mother on a subsequent occasion, a further return home was planned.

In a follow-up study examining the case management and outcomes of a sample of children who had experienced neglect prior to coming into care, Farmer and Lutman (2009) noted a concerning pattern of response to referrals following the children's return home:

> After the children were returned to their parents for the study return, children's services departments received referrals expressing concern about the safety and welfare of almost three quarters (73%) of them. In as many as three-fifths of the families such referrals about risks to the children, mostly about maltreatment, were not adequately followed up or appropriate action was not taken to make them safe. (Farmer and Lutman 2009, p.138)

The researchers suggested a number of reasons why the child protection concerns were not taken more seriously in these cases, reasons that chime with other analyses and reflections on practice in relation to child neglect (see also Chapter 6). They included:

- (excessive) caution over initiating care proceedings in neglect cases
- children left too long before being removed from parents as result of responses geared to family support
- supervision orders were in place that were largely inadequate to protect the child.

Variations between local authorities and between professionals

In an earlier section of this chapter, we discussed Cleaver and colleagues' (2004) analysis of referrals in 24 English local authorities. Amongst their findings, they reported that the percentage of referrals defined as child protection varied considerably between local authorities, and that there was a reciprocal relationship between an authority having a low percentage of cases defined as child protection and higher percentages of cases defined in terms of domestic violence and other parenting issues. The researchers suggested that the councils 'may be operating different thresholds for accepting referrals which influences the way in which other professionals describe their concerns when making a referral to social services' (Cleaver and Walker 2004, p.85).

Statistical information published by the government sheds further light on the variation between local authorities, from which it may be possible to infer differences in threshold. In England, in the year ending 31 March 2010, referrals receiving an initial assessment ranged from 100 per cent to 25 per cent by authority (DfE 2010a). This level of variation is not unusual. *The Children Act 1989 Report 2004–2005* noted that '[t]his variation does not follow any obvious pattern by region or type, which appears to reflect councils' policy stances and the extent of implementation of the *Framework for the Assessment of Children in Need and their Families*' (Department for Education and Skills (DfES) 2006, p.43).

A marked level of variation between local authorities was also identified in relation to the number of core assessments completed. Again, it seems likely that this is a reflection of local policy and practice and particular definitions and emphases in terms of the way data are collected and recorded, rather than level of need (DfES 2006, p.44).

Variations between local education authorities in the frequency of assessments and statements of special educational needs for children were noted by Berridge *et al.* (2002) in their analysis of the costs and consequences of services for 'troubled adolescents'. This exploratory study employed a variety of methods to gather information from social services and education departments in four contrasting local authorities about the experiences of groups of 'difficult to manage' adolescents living apart from their families, in residential homes, foster placements and residential special schools for pupils with emotional and behavioural difficulties (EBD). As Berridge and colleagues noted:

> Sociologists highlight the considerable variation between education authorities in the rates of assessments and statements of special educational need, suggesting that the EBD label is more a function of professional decision making, the distribution of power, and the performance and availability of local resources than reflecting any social or psychological problems intrinsic to the pupil. (Berridge *et al.* 2002, p.22)

Major differences in the way in which adults' and children's services interpreted thresholds for referral of children have also been noted, particularly in the context of parents with learning disabilities (Cleaver and Nicholson 2007) and parents with mental health or substance misuse problems (Cleaver *et al.* 2007). In their study reviewing the implementation of the Integrated Children's System, Cleaver and colleagues (2008, p.106) suggest that the introduction of the Common Assessment Framework could help 'to establish a common language to describe children's needs', which in turn should 'ensure more specific referrals and should result in greater clarity over the thresholds for services'. We return to this point in Chapter 7, where the contribution of the CAF to inter-professional working is considered.

In the final part of this chapter we turn to an area of practice that has been particularly affected by some of the difficulties associated with thresholds – work with child neglect and emotional abuse.

Thresholds relating to neglect and emotional abuse

The prevalence of neglect and emotional abuse and increasing awareness of the damage to children caused by such maltreatment make these significant areas for consideration. While government statistics for Child Protection Plans (CPPs)[3] indicate that the numbers of children who are the subject of a CPP as a result of physical or sexual abuse have declined, the numbers of children with a Plan because of neglect and emotional abuse have increased year on year. In 2005 neglect accounted for 13,200 (43%) registrations on the Child Protection Register but by 2009 this had risen to 16,900 (45%) (DCSF 2009b); in 2010 the number of children who were the subject of a CPP for neglect had risen to 19,300, though this accounted for a slightly smaller percentage (43.5%) of the total (DfE 2010a). For emotional abuse, the equivalent figures are 5700 (19%) in 2005, rising to 9700 (25%) in 2009 (DCSF 2009b). At the end of March 2010, the figure stood at 12,300 children and that constituted 27.9% of all children who were the subject of a CPP (DfE 2010a). These figures are likely to be an underestimate of neglect and emotional abuse as they only identify children who are within the child protection system and do not take account of families who are being provided with family support services under section 17 of the Children Act 1989 – or, indeed, those who have not actually 'hit the radar' at all.

A significant issue with neglect and emotional abuse is at what point these forms of abuse are recognised as problematic by professionals in the different children's services and by the general public. Daniel and colleagues' (2009) systematic review of the literature on neglect examined the evidence about the ways in which children and families signal, directly or indirectly, their need for help and the extent to which practitioners are equipped to recognise and respond to these needs. They found that in terms of recognition of, and responses to, neglect, the evidence confirmed a discrepancy between professional and lay judgements, with professionals tending to operate higher thresholds for identifying neglect (Daniel *et al.* 2009, p.59).

While formal descriptions of neglect and emotional abuse exist (see, for example, HM Government 2010a), there are nonetheless significant problems with operationalising them (see, for example, Farmer and Lutman 2009) and coming to a consensus (within and between professions) about common standards for identifying these forms of maltreatment, particularly neglect. In a paper discussing assessment practice in cases of neglect in three Scottish social work departments, Daniel and Baldwin (2001, p.28) noted that 'good assessment takes considerable time and possibly requires two workers, one to work with parents and one with the children. A recurring theme is the difficulty practitioners experience in pinning down when "enough is enough", gathering evidence and in setting thresholds of neglect.' Different perceptions about what constitutes 'good enough' parenting make this a particularly difficult issue for both assessment and intervention.

Level and nature of response to referrals for neglect

Sinclair and Bullock's analysis of 40 serious case reviews highlighted a critical recurrent question: 'How does a professional decide on whether a significant harm threshold has been passed, especially in cases where there is an accumulation of low level concerns?' (2002, p.56). Deciding where the threshold should be set in such cases has been a significant determinant in response to concerns about neglect.

Thoburn, Wilding and Watson (2000) reported on the ways in which cases were managed prior to the introduction of the Assessment Framework and noted that in their study 25 per cent of referrals to social services departments were for neglect, but many resulted in little or no intervention; further, when assessments were undertaken they tended to be 'low key' and to concentrate on 'risks' rather than on the needs of the children. More recent studies tend to confirm that responses to referrals for neglect have often been unsatisfactory. Brandon *et al.* (2008) noted that amongst the serious case reviews they analysed, many of the cases where neglect had been an issue had been known to children's social care services for some time – sometimes for many years – but that 'agencies appeared to avoid or rebuff parents through closing the case, re-assessing, referring on, or through offering a succession of workers' (Brandon *et al.* 2008, p.324). Rose and Barnes (2008) also found that in the cases they reviewed, 'the severity and impact of neglect was not identified by practitioners. The children and their family circumstances were not the subject of careful and co-ordinated multi-agency assessments, nor did they have developed for them coherent and monitored multi-agency children in need plans' (p.20).

The second biennial analysis of serious case reviews by Brandon, Bailey *et al.* (2009) suggests that there have continued to be difficulties in agency response to cases involving neglect and a lack of attention to the neglect of adolescents (also see Hicks and Stein 2009; Stein *et al.* 2007). At the other end of the age spectrum, Ward *et al.*'s (2010) study of decision making in cases where very young children were suffering or likely to suffer significant harm raised 'considerable questions concerning the threshold for significant harm' (p.13), particularly where neglect was the major issue.

While the needs of neglected children have been identified and documented in recent years, the particular difficulties of working with chronic neglect have continued to challenge practitioners. A recurrent concern has been the way that practitioners and other professionals have felt unable to act decisively in the absence of a 'trigger' incident (Dickens 2007). Selwyn and colleagues (2006) identified different factors that could operate in this way:

- A particular event or crisis.

- Clear evidence becoming available (for example, a child being seen to have a bruise).

- The child developing language and being able to communicate with others, and/or entering the school system.

But other difficulties have also been charted by a number of authors (for example, Farmer and Lutman 2009; Horwath 2007; Stevenson 2007; Tanner and Turney 2003): workers can get drawn into complex family dynamics and lose focus on the needs of the child/ren; practitioners become 'de-sensitised' with the result that a persistently low standard of care becomes acceptable; the 'rule of optimism' allows practitioners to attach more significance to (often small) changes than is warranted; a change in worker or in family circumstance (for example, the birth of another child) means that previous history and events are overlooked and it is as if the assessment starts from scratch – what Brandon *et al.*

(2008) referred to as the 'start again syndrome'. This range of difficulties has been elaborated not to criticise practitioners – indeed, Farmer and Lutman have called them 'inevitable errors' – but to draw attention to the particular dynamics and difficulties associated with long-term involvement in cases of neglect and to highlight the need (discussed in more detail in Chapter 5) for focused supervision to support thinking and purposeful practice.

Use of the Child Protection Register/Child Protection Plan

Significant variations have been noted between local authorities in terms of patterns of registration. For example, Farmer and Lutman (2009) found that in one of their target authorities 42 per cent of children whom they judged to be clearly at risk of harm were not registered, but in two others no children were deemed to be in this position. They conclude, as previously noted, that thresholds were set, or were perceived to be, too high in a number of authorities, leaving some children insufficiently protected (see also Daniel and Baldwin 2001; Daniel *et al.* 2009).

Use of care proceedings and supervision orders

Findings from Farmer and Lutman's study on neglect (2009) supported earlier evidence that supervision orders were not particularly effective in these cases. In most of the cases they analysed where a supervision order had been made, the local authority had wanted a care order but either the guardian's recommendation or that of a specialist assessment had supported the granting of the lesser order. Farmer and Lutman (2009) suggested that the poor outcomes for children returned to their parents on supervision or care orders 'calls into question the decision-making in these cases in the court arena' (p.164), a point we return to in Chapter 7.

Other studies have also identified either that care proceedings were not initiated or were left too late in neglect cases (for example, Dickens 2007; Iwaniec, Donaldson and Martin 2004; Masson *et al.* 2008). Defining the threshold at which significant harm is deemed to have been reached is of course critical for decisions about whether and when to start care proceedings. Dickens' (2007) finding that local authority lawyers typically needed a 'catapult' in order to initiate proceedings was supported by Farmer and Lutman, as the following comment illustrates. It is taken from the report on their follow-up study of case management and outcomes for a sample of neglected children who had been returned to their parents from local authority care:

It was relatively rare for entry to care to take place because of an accumulation of concerns about children. Decisive action in cases of neglect often awaited a trigger incident of physical or sexual abuse or a particularly serious incident of domestic violence. (Farmer and Lutman 2009, p.137)

Conclusion

Thresholds are used to set the terms for access to a range of services, including assessment. However, there are significant conceptual and practical challenges associated with the notion of thresholds and no absolute clarity in terms of either definition or application, within or between local authorities. Where and how thresholds are set depends on the interaction of a number of factors. These include:

- the nature and quality of the information about the individual child/ren and family who are the subject of a referral

- the reasoning devices employed by practitioners to manage referrals

- systemic and organisational factors (for example, the level of resources available and perceived pressures to ration demand for services, time constraints and systems requirements).

Many of the conceptual and practical difficulties of working with thresholds are exemplified in practice concerning child neglect and emotional abuse. While higher thresholds may mean that some families with significant levels of need do not receive a service, in some circumstances failure to receive a service does not appear to lead to deterioration in the family's situation. Current research findings do not fully explain this but suggest that the area of families' informal support networks would merit further study. Early intervention approaches and use of the Common Assessment Framework may contribute to lowering thresholds and broadening access to services at an earlier stage. Having considered some of the issues in relation to setting and managing thresholds for assessment and intervention, we turn in the next chapter to consider the content of assessments.

Summary

- 'Threshold' is a contested concept and raises significant conceptual and practical challenges in terms of both definition and application. Considerable variations have been noted between local authorities in terms of where thresholds for access to different services, including assessment, are set.

- As local authorities come under increasing pressure to deliver more for less there are concerns that tight eligibility criteria are being used to ration increasingly limited resources and that therefore the entry level to children's social care has shifted upwards. There is some evidence that the CAF may help to lower thresholds.

- High thresholds for access to children's social care services may mean that children and families with substantial problems and high levels of need do not receive timely help, resulting in continuing distress and/or increased harm to children and families. However, in some circumstances, it appears that failure to receive a service does not lead to deterioration in the family's situation. This may be because informal or other supports are available and/or because some difficulties resolve over time. But further research would be helpful to learn more about which kinds of families cannot function adequately without access to formal services.

- Early or 'earlier' intervention refers to a range of approaches that aim to intervene early in the 'life course' of a problem, before difficulties become established and potentially more severe. While the importance of early intervention has been highlighted in the research, it is nonetheless not entirely straightforward in practice to ensure that the right individuals or groups are identified for intervention. Further research may be needed to understand better what works, why and for whom, in supporting children with additional needs and their families.

- Managing demand within children's social care services involves identifying some contacts/communications as 'referrals' and screening others out or in some way redesignating them. Different studies show that different strategies are used and therefore there is variation between and within local authorities in terms of decisions about what actually constitutes a referral that requires some level of response.

- The rigour of the current system in terms of timing for initial and core assessments may encourage the development of short cuts or 'work-arounds' in practice, some of which have the effect of deflecting, or minimising the importance of, particular kinds of referrals. Pressure to meet targets and timescales may have the unintended consequence of leading to the downgrading of good clinical judgement and of affecting whether or not a case goes from initial to core assessment.

- Deciding where thresholds for intervention should be set has proved to be particularly problematic in cases of neglect and emotional abuse, and a number of studies have identified that this has resulted in delay or failure to act decisively in such situations, leaving children in homes where they are at risk of continuing to be maltreated. Research evidence suggests that cases of chronic neglect typically require an additional 'trigger' event – for example, an injury – before court proceedings are initiated to remove children.

Notes

1   This project was undertaken alongside a larger process, piloting a version of the CAF in four areas in Wales, as reported in Brandon *et al.* (2009b). At the time of writing, a common Assessment Framework has not been implemented in Wales.

2   This was changed to ten working days in the 2010 version of *Working Together* (HM Government 2010a) but the change was implemented after the studies discussed in this review had been completed.

3   The 2005 figures refer to children whose names were on the Child Protection Register (CPR); in 2008, the CPR was phased out and all children whose names were on the Register became the subject of a Child Protection Plan (CPP). Since then, any child whose name would have been added to the Register has become the subject of a CPP.

Chapter 3

THE CONTENT OF ASSESSMENTS: WHAT INFORMATION IS COLLECTED?

This chapter examines research that informs our understanding of the content of an assessment. We look at the information gathered as part of assessment processes, using research that drew data both from written reports in case files and from the professionals involved. We are concerned primarily with the 'raw' information collected for assessment by social workers and other relevant professionals, rather than how they analysed it, which is the subject of a separate chapter.

Our concern in this chapter is with research that examined the quality of the content of assessment reports. The discussion is organised using the three domains of the Assessment Framework. In the following chapter, we move on to explore particular types of information gathered, specific assessment contexts and the implications of the research findings for practice. We begin by addressing the question of the variability of the content of assessment reports both between and within social work agencies.

Variability of content

Describing and analysing shortcomings in social work assessments has been a feature of research and reviews of practice over a number of years, and there is little doubt that there is considerable room for improvement. A degree of caution, however, should be applied in relation to some of the findings. Clearly, within any profession there will be a range of ability and competence. This range of worker skill is applied in a context that is often messy and unpredictable, which in turn exacerbates practice difficulties, including difficulties in undertaking and recording assessments. There are also variations in the ways in which research findings are reported. Some researchers may highlight a minority of cases where there are shortcomings, and indicate that these cases give cause for concern. Other studies give clear messages based on the, often mainstream, examples of good practice. For example, if 15 per cent of assessment reports were reported as poor, this might receive particular attention in one research report. Another report might, however, celebrate the fact that 85 per cent were of moderate or good quality. In the case of serious case reviews and their overview reports, clearly, by definition, the findings are based purely on instances where serious outcomes occurred for the children involved, a factor that limits the generalisations and conclusions that may be drawn from them.

Length and completeness

A key message from the studies reviewed concerned the variability of information contained in assessments. Selwyn and colleagues (2010), for example, in their study of white and minority ethnic children's pathways through care, commented on the absence (38%) or incompleteness (11%) of core assessments in their sample. Similar findings were presented by Cleaver *et al.* (2004) in relation to the use of the Assessment Framework. They commented on the lack of logic in the way core assessment forms were completed and, importantly, found a tendency to treat the summary sections, in relation to each domain of the Assessment Framework, in isolation from other sections in the document. Thomas and Holland (2010), in their study of core assessments based on data collected in 2006, identified variations in length, style and formatting of reports that ranged from 7 to 86 pages in length. These variations occurred within a single authority. They noted that the reports were 'generally narrow, negative and relatively impersonal' (p.2618). This point was particularly important in relation to child development, and we expand on the issues in the next section.

The relevance of these findings lies in the assumption that where an assessment is completed fully and comprehensively, any subsequent intervention is likely to be more appropriate and more carefully targeted at the needs of the child and family. Indeed, Farmer and Dance *et al.* (2010) in relation to adoption, for example, found that having good-quality information about children in the Child Permanence Reports was key to later successful matching.

There is a growing body of information about positive steps social workers can take to build on existing good practice in assessment. Bentovim *et al.* (2009), for example, provide a helpful commentary on the assessment of each domain of the Assessment Framework, as does Horwath (2009). The remainder of this chapter, together with the following chapter, considers findings that help identify and support important elements of good practice. Much of what follows (in both chapters) involves consideration of the risks of poor outcomes for children, in relation to certain key decisions: decisions that would normally be based on prior assessments. In this chapter we will consider information about the assessment of child development, parenting capacity, and family and environmental factors.

Child development

There is a substantial literature available on child development and on methods of assessing developmental progress. Consequently, we begin this section by examining the importance of keeping the child at the centre of the assessment. This is followed by a very brief overview of the relevant knowledge base before moving on to a number of pointers for practice that arose from the present review.

The invisibility of the child

A repeated problem identified by research and inspection reports is that of the invisibility of the child in some social work assessments, or the failure to put the child at their centre (for example, Daniel 2004). Cleaver and colleagues (2004, 2007, 2008) noted that social workers often did not record information covering all areas of child development and in a small number of cases (Cleaver *et al.* 2007) no such information was recorded at all. It is vital that the child is at the centre of the assessment process and we will be returning to this critical point, particularly in the section on child development (below), and in a discussion of the child's voice in Chapter 6.

The knowledge base

Holland (2010, p.105) observed that social workers 'need to know what the usual developmental trajectories for children are, the research evidence about what affects development immediately and in the long-term, and the theories that underpin the developmental assumptions they are making'. Importantly, she also emphasised that practitioners need to be able to exercise judgement in their assessments (referring particularly to core assessments, although with obvious implications for a range of assessment types). She placed particular importance on taking account of the *individual* child, their needs and situation, in addition to using evidence about child development in general, in other words, about the needs and circumstances of *any* child.

Understanding child development is an essential component of an assessment (see, for example, Aldgate *et al.* 2006). We cannot here review the progress made in developmental research in recent years. Instead, we flag up some of the areas with which social workers should be most concerned. One interesting development for social workers has been life course research, which has examined how some children grow up to be adults without any substantial difficulties, even though their childhoods were marked by adversities in their families or environments. We are still some way from understanding the processes that are involved, but both risks and protective factors, discussed briefly below, need to be part of any assessment.

Risk and protective factors

Social work assessments tend to focus on adversities facing a child, and less is known about protective factors. There is, however, research evidence that points to the importance of positive relationships of children with parents, peers, teachers and other adults. Nurturing relationships and positive role models can provide buffers against many of the known risk factors including the effects of poverty (Furstenberg and Hughes 1995; Laub, Nagin and Sampson 1998; Laub and Sampson 1993). Other protective factors for children are school achievement (especially good literacy skills), activities outside school, good self-esteem and the development of coping skills. It is important, in any assessment, that the inter-relationships between the different risk and protective factors is understood.

Lack of stable role models, heightened family stresses, weak emotional bonds between parents and children, lack of parental involvement, low levels of parental control and discipline and an inability to provide an environment conducive to positive development are all known risks to normal child development. In particular, there is considerable evidence that social adversities, frequent parental disagreements and punitive parenting styles are linked to the development of anti-social behaviours (Campbell *et al.* 1991; McGee *et al.* 1991; Webster-Stratton 1990). We also know that children singled out for rejection by their parents (Rushton and Dance 2005) and those neglected for long periods have poorer outcomes than other maltreated children (see, for example, Iwaniec 2006; Stevenson 2007).

Multiple and long-lasting adversities are of particular concern. The duration of adverse events and the timing of experiences in a child's life will determine the effect on the child. For example, the death of a close family member may affect a pre-verbal child differently from one who has the language to ask questions and the cognitive ability to understand what has happened. Studies also show that the number of adverse events is important in assessing risks of harm (Coleman 1974; Haveman, Wolfe and Spaulding 1991). They suggest that multiple changes in family life such as household moves, parental separations, remarriages/changes of partners, particularly during early childhood, are associated with stress in children and are predictive of doing poorly educationally. Children seem much more able to cope with a single event rather than ones that are multiple and simultaneous.

A good knowledge of child development is therefore essential for assessing risks to healthy development, and examining the inter-relationship between positive and negative factors in the child's life. It is also important for understanding how interventions might be tailored to increase resilience. For example, a simple intervention designed to improve looked after children's reading ability (Pallett, Simmonds and Warman 2010) by enabling foster carers to read regularly *with* their foster children saw not only their reading age increase, but also an improvement in the quality of the child/carer relationship, which in turn may act as a buffer against future adversity.

Research has shown that young people who seem to be on course for a maladaptive path can be diverted. For many young people there are opportunities or turning points where positive change can occur (Masten and Powell 2003; Rutter 2000; Quinton *et al.* 1993). While empirical knowledge about turning points for children in the looked after system is currently limited, social workers need to be alert to these opportunities during assessment.

Research findings regarding assessment of child development

Our review identified various shortcomings in the understanding of child development in social workers' assessments. The problem has been recognised over a number of years, and attempts have been made to address it through, for example, the provision of additional post-qualifying learning opportunities that include child development as integral to the curriculum (General Social Care Council 2005). Cleaver et al. (2008), in their study of the Integrated Children's System, found a trend towards more information than previously being recorded on all three domains of the Assessment Framework. However, there was still room for improvement, particularly in relation to children's family and social relationships, their social presentation and their self-care skills. A key area where improvements in recording information on children's development appeared to have occurred was in relation to health and education. It may be that this has occurred as a result of the improved resourcing and awareness of the importance of these areas over the past decade (see, for example, Berridge et al. 2009).

Other researchers have identified limitations in assessments related to attachment behaviours (Holland 2010), children's identity (Thomas and Holland 2010) and their self-esteem (Walker, Hill and Triseliotis 2002). Problems with assessing attachment included misinterpretation of clingy behaviour as evidence of strong attachment (Selwyn et al. 2006) and assessments based on observation of an insufficient number of different situations (Holland 2010). Holland (2010) and Thomas and Holland (2010) identified a problem of core assessment reports describing children's development in almost identical language to that of child development charts. Citing White (1998), Holland argued that to do so produces a prescriptive account of a 'standardised child'. This meant that the information was depersonalised and did not relate clearly to the particular child whose needs were being assessed. Findings from various studies related to identity and to emotional and behavioural difficulties including self-esteem were of particular interest and are summarised in the following sub-sections.

Identity

Thomas and Holland (2010) found that the identity sections, in a sample of 26 core assessments covering 32 children, often concentrated on family relationships and self-esteem. This discussion of family relationships often presented information that was core to a child's identity, such as knowledge of who's who in the family. However, they found a tendency for the analysis of relationships to focus on the parents' actions rather than the child's perspective. Regarding self-esteem, none of the 32 core assessments in their sample commented on the child's self-esteem positively, and a picture of the child's sense of self was notably absent. Despite these findings, the study found that social workers' *verbal* accounts of children's identities were much richer than was reflected in the written assessments. They suggest that this discrepancy may arise from two particular interacting factors. First, social workers may be frustrated at the amount of time they have to spend using information systems and inputting data, although this conclusion relies on other published research related to the Integrated Children's System, which we review in Chapter 8. Second, the purpose of the assessment may lead them to highlight negatives in order, perhaps, to secure services or to gain a legal order. The value of making improvements in the assessment of each child's identity would be in enabling relevant interventions to be planned, so as to build the child's sense of who they are and where they come from. This might assist in promoting the child's self-esteem and self-confidence and a greater sense of belonging.

Emotional and behavioural difficulties

In relation to emotional and behavioural difficulties, Skuse and Ward (2003) make the case for systematic collection of information using standardised measures, such as the *Strengths and Difficulties Questionnaire* and the *Adolescent Well-being Scale* included in the *Family Assessment Pack of Scales and Questionnaires* published to support the use of the Assessment Framework (see Department of Health, Cox and Bentovim 2000). They based this recommendation on the shortcomings of file information encountered in their study, and the prevalence of such difficulties amongst the population of looked after children. Similarly, Quinton (2009) argued that the three behavioural problems (conduct disorders, hyperactivity and attachment disorders) that are known to be commonly associated with placement breakdown are rarely systematically assessed. It should be noted that there is now an expectation that the *Strengths and Difficulties Questionnaire* is used with children aged between 4 and 16 who have been looked after for more than 12 months (DCSF 2009a, paragraph A.20, p.139).

Self-esteem

Other authors have reported on social workers' lack of confidence in assessing children's self-esteem (Walker *et al.* 2002). The tendency was to underestimate levels of self-esteem compared with those obtained using a standardised measure. In contrast to this, McMurray *et al.* (2008) found that social workers had a tendency to overemphasise resilience: 'all children and young people in the sample were described as being resilient by social workers...irrespective of the presence or absence of behavioural or emotional issues' (p.308). They also identified what appeared to be difficulties in articulating and conceptualising resilience. Schofield and Beek (2005) confirmed that the notion is difficult to conceptualise, both in research and in its application to individual cases. Daniel (2006) presented a positive exploratory study of the application of an assessment of resilience based on the author's own workbooks, which suggested positive effects from training staff in working with resilience. Again, interventions of this kind, based on more effective assessment of resilience, may prove helpful.

Whilst in many instances social workers are probably more reflective about children's needs than appears to be the case from a reading of written reports, there seems to be a need for ongoing training and support in relation to understanding and assessing children's emotional and behavioural problems, identities, self-esteem, resilience, attachment, as well as the skills of presenting a meaningful picture of the child on paper. Quinton's review (2006) of identity and self-esteem is a good starting point.

As indicated, some authors have advocated the use of more systematic tools to assess key areas and, as previously noted, materials were published alongside the Assessment Framework for this purpose (Department of Health *et al.* 2000). However, use of such scales and questionnaires appears to be rare in social work practice in the UK (Cleaver *et al.* 2004), although, as noted, the use of the Strengths and Difficulties Questionnaire (SDQ) has now been incorporated into routine practice with looked after children (DCSF 2009a).

Parenting capacity

The assessment of parenting is a core task, both in the context of assessing parents' capacities to protect each of their children from harm and enhance their developmental experiences, and in deciding whether to remove and/or restore children to the care of their parents. Assessments of parenting capacity can occur at a number of decision-making points. There are some key differences between assessments of parents' capacities to meet the needs of each of their children that are conducted to determine which children and families are in need of a service (initial and core assessments), and those conducted specifically for court purposes (often using the core assessment process) (Reder, Duncan and Lucey 2003). In the former it is expected that only a small proportion of children in need and families are likely to require a Child Protection Plan, but families without a Child Protection Plan will also require services. Appropriate services should therefore be provided concurrently with the ongoing assessment. Parenting capacity assessments for family court proceedings differ in that they take place when families are already identified as having major problems (Reder *et al.* 2003).

There is widespread agreement that effective parenting assessments rest upon the accurate identification of the needs of the child and of the parents' capacity to meet their needs. Assessing parenting capacity should be based on an evaluation of the parents' *abilities to parent a particular child or each of the children in their family*. Assessments involve ascertaining whether the child's needs are being met, appraising the impact of any parenting difficulties or parental problems on the child's functioning and development, describing the nature and likely origins of the adult's difficulties in fulfilling their parental roles, and considering whether change is possible (Jones 2009; Reder *et al.* 2003). Thus parenting capacity assessments are 'a planned process of identifying concerns about a child's welfare, eliciting information about the functioning of the parent/s and the child, and forming an opinion as to whether the child's needs are being satisfied' (Reder *et al.* 2003, p.3).

There is consensus that effective parenting needs a mixture of warmth, control and stimulation of children's development. For parents to do this most effectively, they need to be adaptable. This involves the ability to be perceptive, responsive and flexible in addressing their child's needs as they change over time. In the ecological model (Belsky and Vondra 1989) the ability to parent is determined by a range of factors and relationships, and is not seen as fixed, but as undergoing constant change dependent on the circumstances facing parents and their children at any given moment (Woodcock 2003). Parenting capacity is dependent on the family's context, such as their socio-economic situation, housing, culture and societal values, as well as family skills and relationships. This complexity makes it very unlikely that any single assessment tool will be adequate. Rather than examining a checklist of factors influencing parenting, it has been suggested that parenting capacity can only be assessed adequately by exploring the parents' abilities to recognise and meet the particular child's current and anticipated needs, in the context of their capacity to empathise with the child (Donald and Jureidini 2004).

Whilst recognising that assessing parenting capacity is difficult, it is important to conduct such assessments as effectively as possible. As Budd points out:

> At their best, parenting assessments can provide an informed, objective perspective that enhances the fairness of child welfare decisions. At their worst, they can contribute inaccurate, biased and/ or irrelevant information that violates examinee's rights and/or impairs the decision-making process. (Budd 2005, p.430)

Current approaches to assessing parenting capacity are often based on the use of clinical judgement, and are subject to problems associated with the use of such judgements. These problems include a:

- lack of recognition of known risk factors

- focus on the immediate present or latest episode rather than considering significant historical information

- failure to revise initial assessments in the light of new information.

(Based on Munro 1999)

There is also evidence that research findings on the assessment of parenting are underutilised. Woodcock (2003) found, in a small study of social workers, that they hardly ever referred to psychological evidence derived from the literature as a way to structure their understanding of a case or to inform their intervention strategy. The exception to this was when they used instruments that were part of the Looked after Children system. This led to what Woodcock (2003, p.100) called a 'surface-static' notion of parenting, an approach that had a number of elements:

- The workers' surface response meant they did not deal with psychological factors underlying the parenting problems (even where they had identified such factors).

- Workers tended also to rely on exhortation to change, rather than responses informed by psychological observations.

- This was then often associated, when change did not occur, with perceptions by the social worker of 'parent resistance'.

Woodcock cautioned that the sample was small, but similar findings have been reported in other studies. For example, as mentioned above, some studies have highlighted the lack of understanding of attachment theory and/or its misapplication, such that maltreated children were described as 'securely attached' to their parent when they actually displayed clingy behaviour (Selwyn *et al.* 2006; Ward, Munro and Dearden 2006).

There are, however, some particular difficulties in the linking of parenting research to social work practice. Many of the journals in developmental psychology and mental health, where findings are published, are not read by, nor are easily accessible to, social workers. Bentovim *et al.* (2009) have presented a brief review of research related to limitations in parenting capacity, linked particularly to mental illness, substance misuse and domestic violence, to which readers may refer for further information (see also Chapter 9 in HM Government 2010a; Cleaver, Unell and Aldgate forthcoming).

Use of standardised assessment tools

As indicated, there is debate in the literature on the use of standardised questionnaires and tools. Farmer and Dance *et al.* (2010), in their survey of adoption agency practice, found that a few adoption agencies (occasionally) used the Attachment Style Interview (Bifulco *et al.* 1998) or the Adult Attachment Interview (George, Kaplan and Main 1985; Steele *et al.* 1999) to assess attachment style in prospective adoptive parents, either drawing on skills from within the adoption team acquired through training, or relying on external professionals, such as clinical psychologists, to conduct these interviews.

Some questionnaires and scales can assist by helping workers gain a better understanding of how much or how often a concerning behaviour is occurring. For example, studies of social work have noted that parental alcohol and substance misuse is one of the commonest problems that children's social workers are trying to work with (Cleaver, Unell and Aldgate 1999). There was no evidence from any of the children's case files read by Selwyn and colleagues (2010) that social workers routinely collected a history of alcohol and substance misuse. Nor did they find any use of relevant screening tools such as TWEAK or T-ACE (British Medical Association 2007) (the acronyms are derived from key issues covered in each screening tool). See also Department of Health *et al.* (2000) for the Alcohol Scale.

Barlow and Schrader-MacMillan (2009), in a review of 'what works' in safeguarding children from emotional abuse, suggested that tools such as the CARE index (Crittenden 2005) be utilised. However, there can be a temptation to rely more heavily on measures than is warranted, and Munro (2004) has pointed out that practitioners may mistakenly believe the reliability of such tools to be greater than is often the case (see Department of Health *et al.* 2000 for further guidance on the use of questionnaires and scales).

As noted in the previous section, although there are a range of tools to support practitioners undertaking assessments using the Assessment Framework (discussed in Bentovim *et al.* 2009), the impression from the research is that they are underused. Barlow and Scott (2010), in a review examining future directions for child protection policy and practice, suggested that resistance to the use of such tools is based on the belief that they represent a 'tick-box' mentality. Given the limitations of *both* formal and informal assessment methods, however, they argued for a 'third generation approach' in which less formal professional judgements *combined* with validated, structured methods. However, the existence of widespread variations in the use of validated tools suggests that the introduction of more systematic methods would require investment in additional training. Further discussion of these points is presented in Chapter 5.

Overall, the message from research is that instruments and tools can be helpful, but that caution is needed. Standardised tools may be useful, particularly, in gathering information, in checking out opinions of other people involved with the child and in stimulating discussions with the child or parents. They should be balanced with information from a range of sources. The importance of using different sources was reinforced from a different perspective in a review of research into effective practice with 'highly resistant' families (Fauth *et al.* 2010), which concluded that 'There is an urgent need to review practitioners' tendency to rely almost exclusively on *interviewing* parents about their parenting skills to assess capacity' (p. 49). Comprehensive parenting capacity assessments (usually as part of a core assessment) should be based on the integration and synthesis of information from multiple sources and should use multiple methods of information gathering. Methods may include:

1. interviews with the parents together and separately

2. interviews with the child or children

3. psychological testing

4. observation of parent/child interaction

5. review of documents held by the local authority, other agencies and those the parent may have

6. consideration of parental acceptance of responsibility and readiness to change.

Clinical studies have suggested that, where there are significant concerns about parenting capacity, assessments need to consider parental acceptance of responsibility for past acts and any damage done, resolution of previous trauma, management of the parents' own emotional feelings and their capacity to recognise and respond healthily to feelings in their children (Donald and Jureidini 2004). The capacity for change within timescales that will enable parents to meet their child's needs at a sufficiently early age is a difficult area of assessment. One method that social workers have used is that of assessing parental insight and cooperation (see Chapter 6), although there are considerable limitations to this (see, for example, Holland 2010). Others have considered factors such as problem recognition and intention to change, although research into this approach is limited (Barlow and Scott 2010; Turnell and Edwards 1999).

Farmer and Lutman (2009), in their study of social work involvement in cases of neglect, found that expert assessments, often by professionals outside social work, were very valuable in making the case for a child not to return home where change was unlikely. Selwyn *et al.* (2006), similarly, found that social workers tended to overestimate parents' levels of intelligence, a factor, we suggest, that might well be linked to the ability to understand and make changes. Again, an expert psychological assessment was found to be valuable in assessing intelligence. Social workers may be further assisted by input from psychologists in understanding the ability of parents to change, but there are also findings to support the idea that change can be assessed by giving parents the opportunity to change. Subsequent decisions can then be made based on the success or otherwise of these attempts and, where relevant, tools or instruments may be used to measure change over time.

An example of addressing capacity to change comes from the reunification literature (see also Chapter 4). Outcomes for children were better if, before a return home took place, there was a clear plan of action, a written agreement or contract, and ongoing monitoring, thus enabling the parents to demonstrate their abilities (or otherwise) to make a go of the return (Farmer *et al.* 2011; Harwin *et al.* 2003). There are also considerable lessons from the substance misuse field, where motivational interviewing techniques have helped address the abilities to change of alcohol or drug users (Forrester and Harwin 2007; Harwin 2009). Ward *et al.*'s (2010) findings are instructive in this context. In a prospective study of social work and related decision-making processes affecting very young children subject to a core assessment or section 47 enquiry, they found that parents who had overcome their difficulties all did so within the first six months of the child's life, and experienced a 'defining moment' when they realised that they would have to take significant steps to ensure the future wellbeing of their baby.

The role of fathers

A particular aspect of parenting that is covered in the research is the role of fathers. Recurrent shortcomings have been identified, amongst many groups of professionals, in taking account of men in the households with which they were working. There is an extensive literature on fathering, and within that a considerable range of research findings indicating how social workers and other professionals can fall into the trap of ignoring fathers, of dismissing their contribution or of loading responsibility onto mothers to protect children from any dangers coming from the father (for example, Scourfield 2003). These responses are often attributed to gendered patterns in the division of labour, with women predominantly taking responsibility for child care, and, indeed, the majority of social workers are women. In addition, not infrequently, the child's father is absent from the family and information on such fathers may be in short supply. Professional vigilance is necessary to ensure that information about fathers is available whenever possible, especially as fathers may exert a considerable influence even when they are not living with their children.

Summary

In summary, key findings related to the assessment of parents' capacity to meet the needs of their children included the importance of understanding the basic requirements of the parenting task, of considering parents' ability to change, and the need to take account of the role of fathers as well as mothers. Improving the content of the assessment of parenting capacity requires a combination of approaches: better collection of information on which decisions will be made, including using validated tools, interviews (including history taking), observation, reports and demographic information. Assessment needs to be done on a 'child by child' basis as a parent may be able to care for one child but not another within the family. It is important to ensure that the assessment of parenting capacity is not 'generalised' and is based on an understanding of the particular individual's ability to parent a specific child.

Family and environmental factors

The assessment of family functioning is important, as it has been suggested that the best predictors of multi-type maltreatment are poor family cohesion (family members feeling disconnected from one another), low family adaptability (rigid roles and inflexibility in relationships and communication) and the poor quality of the adult relationship (Higgins and McCabe 2000). An assessment of family functioning is essential in any assessment of parenting capacity and can provide a basis for a strengths-based approach. This approach accepts that all adults and children possess strengths that can be tapped to improve the quality of their lives. A strengths-based approach is also associated with recruiting parents into programmes designed to assist them with their parenting. For example, a key to recruiting parents to positive parenting programmes is to assure them that the programme will help them improve skills they already possess (Long *et al.* 2001). We found few studies that examined the way these key qualities had been assessed within the family as a unit rather than within individuals. Nonetheless, Pithouse (2006) reported improvements in the extent to which family strengths were recorded, following the piloting of a common assessment in Wales. In the first part of this section we examine how family and environmental factors may affect parenting capacity.

Family and environmental factors and their effect on parenting capacity

Beyond more general parenting issues, three specific family and environmental factors emerged from the literature within the context of parenting capacity: the issues raised by substance misuse, domestic violence and parental learning disabilities. While none of these factors predicts child maltreatment, they make parents more vulnerable to impaired parenting capacity.

In the context of substance misuse, Harwin and Forrester (2002), found that social workers had difficulty estimating levels of parental alcohol or drug consumption, which, again, may lend support to the value of using more formal instruments such as the Alcohol Scale (Department of Health *et al.* 2000). Forrester and Harwin (2006) showed that, in these types of cases, 'the parents have more difficulties, the families have more social problems and the children are considerably younger than children in other cases allocated a social worker' (p.332). Farmer *et al.* (2011) also found that parental substance misuse, particularly alcohol misuse, was underestimated by social workers, and that it was linked to higher levels of maltreatment during reunification. Both sets of researchers commented on the need for easier access to treatment for parents with alcohol and drugs misuse problems, and on the adverse impacts of drugs and alcohol misuse on parenting capacity and on the child (Farmer *et al.* 2011; Farmer and Lutman 2009; Forrester and Harwin 2006, 2008). Several studies concluded that there is a need for social workers to have a good understanding of how to assess and work with substance misuse (Farmer *et al.* 2011; Farmer and Lutman 2009; Forrester and Harwin 2006, 2008; Harwin and Forrester 2002; Harwin and Ryan 2007). Forrester and Harwin (2008) estimated that substance misuse issues may affect a third of the children social work practitioners work with. Given this level of prevalence, arguably substance misuse should feature prominently in social work education at both qualifying and post-qualifying levels.

A considerable body of research has demonstrated the adverse effects on children of living with domestic violence (see for example Hester *et al.* 2007). The importance of understanding the significance of domestic violence and its effects on children's wellbeing was underlined in Rose and Barnes' (2008) report. Their analysis of 40 serious case reviews undertaken between 2001 and 2003 found that although overview reports often drew out the association between domestic violence and a range of behaviours exhibited by the children (poor school attendance, bullying, aggression and offending), the reviews 'also note the lack of significance attributed to the domestic violence…and the impact this may have been having on the child or children of the family' (Rose and Barnes 2008, p.26). Similar points were made in subsequent analyses of serious case reviews (Brandon *et al.* 2008; Brandon, Bailey *et al.* 2009). A number of studies have noted this apparent 'tolerance' of domestic violence (see, for example, Farmer and Lutman 2009). And in relation to the language of assessment reports, Holland (2010) has drawn attention to a tendency partly to blame women in situations involving men's violence. Use of language in assessment reports such as *volatile* and *incident*, she suggested, risks diluting the message in an assessment report, and may shift responsibility away from the perpetrator. Cleaver *et al.* (2007), in their study of families experiencing domestic violence and substance misuse, highlighted the importance of a holistic approach: in their sub-sample of 17 cases where the parents were interviewed, they found that problems of domestic violence and substance misuse rarely existed in isolation. Other problems that they cited included health problems (mental or physical), learning disabilities, financial and housing problems, and prostitution. It was clear that the parents struggled to protect or shield their children from these difficulties, and consequently an assessment of the impact on the children of these types of problems is vital.

In relation to parents with learning disabilities, Cleaver and Nicholson (2007), in their study of social work with children living with a parent with learning disabilities, found problems with basic care, keeping children safe and providing adequate stimulation, guidance and boundaries. Parenting difficulties were also more likely to be associated with other problems such as drug misuse or domestic violence, and the study reflects the vulnerability of some young women with learning disabilities in relation to their male partners. Mothers with learning disabilities were also potentially vulnerable to being targeted by paedophiles who gained access to their children through providing emotional and practical support. It is important, however, not to make automatic assumptions about parenting deficits amongst this group: in Cleaver and Nicholson's sample, two-thirds of cases where an initial assessment was undertaken did *not* have multiple problems. Further discussion of the assessment of parents with learning disabilities is included in Chapters 7 and 10.

Chapter 9 of *Working Together* (HM Government 2010a), 'Lessons from research', provides a useful summary of current research knowledge in relation to the effect of different forms of maltreatment on children's health, development and welfare, the different sources of stress that can impact on children and families and their effects on children's wellbeing; this latter section includes messages from research addressing social exclusion, domestic violence, parental/carer mental illness, problematic parental drug or alcohol use and parental learning disability.

Other family and environmental factors

With regard to the use of the Assessment Framework, Rushton and Dance (2005), in their study of the service response to children singled out for rejection, suggested that least attention was paid, in social workers' assessments, to environmental influences. Cleaver and Walker (2004), reporting on their study of the Assessment Framework, suggested that the *impact* of environmental factors on children's welfare was not fully appreciated by many practitioners. They based this conclusion on the finding that 'referrals involving children over the age of 15 years, police referrals for domestic violence or referrals relating to financial or housing problems' (p.85) were the least likely to result in social workers undertaking an initial assessment. However, in the same study, Cleaver *et al.* (2004) found a relatively high level of recording in core assessment reports of family and environmental factors that were likely to impact *negatively* on the child. Although these findings appear contradictory, they relate to different parts of the process (i.e. response to referrals and recording of core assessments respectively). Selwyn and colleagues (2010), similarly, in their study of minority ethnic children in care, found that little attention had been paid to family issues such as how and why parents had become dislocated from their country of origin and the impact this had had on them. They speculated that this difficulty arose partly because of lack of availability of interpreters.

Others have suggested that this problem of variable attention to the three domains of the Assessment Framework is more widespread. Assessments based on the use of the 'triangle' can become 'lopsided' if there is a focus on one side of the triangle at the expense of the others (Horwath 2002). This may happen, for example, if an overemphasis on parenting capacity occurs, and professionals perceive child neglect in terms of an act of omission or commission on the part of the carers, without any consideration of the impact of the act on the child's health and development. A lopsided triangle can also occur if professionals are measuring 'good enough' parenting in terms of carers doing their best, even if they fail to meet the needs of their children.

To help counteract the tendency for environmental issues to be missing from an assessment, Jack and Gill (2003) offered a range of practical suggestions. Drawing on messages from both research and practice, their prompts and guidelines provide an aid to social workers in incorporating these issues more fully into their assessments. Others have emphasised the need to have knowledge of the case history, an awareness of key past events (Farmer and Lutman 2009) and the ability to understand the possible relationships between past experiences and present situations and behaviours (for example, understanding the 'meaning of the child' to the parent in question: Reder, Duncan and Gray 1993). In this context, the importance of chronologies – a point recognised in his first report by Lord Laming (2003) – was re-emphasised by Brandon *et al.* 2008.

Understanding the interaction of factors affecting the child's development and the capacity to parent is important. We will examine the skills of analysis more fully in a later chapter, but Woodcock summed up the task of assessing parenting capacity in the context of wider environmental factors as follows:

The assessment of parenting will not simply involve appraising the development of the child to assess how well the parenting task is carried out, but also the way other determining factors of the ecological parenting model influence the parental capacity to carry out that task... Under the Framework (for Assessing Children in Need and their Families), the emphasis will be on 'judgement' and to facilitate this social workers will need to have an understanding of how the different factors fit within a framework, rather than existing as individual attributes of 'vulnerability'. It is this careful analysis of interacting factors that is considered to provide an insight as to the effects upon children in families. (Woodcock 2003, p.101)

Conclusion

This chapter presented an overview of research findings concerning the content of children in need assessments, based on the three domains of the Assessment Framework. In doing so, we were very much aware that the Assessment Framework provides an overarching scaffold for social work assessments of children in need, and that many specific aspects of children's needs require special attention within that. Skilled use of a wide range of knowledge, and of specific relevant materials, tools and so on, enables social workers to drill down into particular issues facing particular children and their families. In the next chapter, we continue this theme in relation to some of the particular areas of assessment or contexts of decision making that social workers can be expected to focus on.

Summary

- The content of local authority assessment records varied, both between and within local authorities. At one end of the spectrum, social work records can be short and impersonal, with significant gaps in information and a tendency to present a rather limited picture of the child. At the other end, there was evidence of high standards of practice.

- The presentation of information regarding children's developmental needs in assessment records was variable, with some reports characterised as presenting a 'standardised child'.

- Social workers' knowledge of child development continues to be a vital area, and the research highlighted a need for further professional education in relation to identity, resilience, self-esteem, attachment and the identification of the specific behavioural problems which contribute to poor placement outcomes for looked after children.

- The assessment of parenting capacity appeared to suffer from an absence of agreed understandings of the standards and expectations that are deemed acceptable, in order for parents to be meeting the needs of each of their children. There was evidence of a rather superficial approach in some cases that did not fully assess the underlying reasons for parenting difficulties.

- Assessing parents' capacities to change presents challenges for social workers, and a multi-faceted approach including observation, use of standardised measures and use of multiple informants appears to be most effective. In terms of practice, simple exhortation of parents to change was noted as unlikely to succeed.

- There were variations in the extent to which assessments addressed the effects of family and environmental factors on children's health and development and parent's capacities to meet their children's needs.

- Greater use of standardised measures for assessment was advocated by some commentators. To put such a recommendation into practice has implications for social work training in terms of building up the necessary expertise, for developing supervisory capacity and for the additional time needed for social workers to collect and analyse information from children and families.

- There was a need for social workers to have a greater understanding of the impact of substance misuse on children's development, particularly when estimating the levels of alcohol or drug use of parents they are working with.

- It is important to ensure that the assessment of parenting capacity is not a 'generalised' parenting assessment, but is based on an understanding of the particular individual's ability to parent a specific child.

Chapter 4

ASSESSMENTS IN PARTICULAR CONTEXTS

In this chapter we turn to specific practice contexts where focused assessments are considered of particular importance. The range of contexts examined was determined by the areas covered by the research reviewed, and as such cannot be considered exhaustive. The areas include analysing likelihood of abuse and neglect, reunification, placing and matching children, working with ethnic differences, unaccompanied asylum-seeking children and young people, and disabled children. The research findings provided some limited information on how these assessments should be addressed, and whilst it was not possible to undertake a further literature review of each specialist area, we have tried to incorporate pointers to good practice where available within the terms of our review.

Assessing the likelihood of child abuse and neglect

Assessing whether a child is suffering, or likely to suffer, significant harm may take place in a variety of contexts. Typical situations are initial assessment, core assessments, section 47 enquiries or other types of assessments connected, for example, with reunification decisions. Government guidance (HM Government 2010a) notes that assessments will draw on a range of information, including the outcomes of specific types of risk assessments (para 5.49). The brief of our review focused on assessments relating to *children* and excluded the detailed examination both of risk assessment tools and of assessments focusing on adults where a specific child is not involved. Consequently we do not discuss risk assessments relating to adult perpetrators of abuse or violence, but acknowledge the significant literature and greater use of formal methods in these fields.

In this section we examine how to use information about risk factors intelligently, within a holistic assessment. Some of the best-known forms of risk assessment are actuarial methods, which involve, typically, the identification of the presence or absence of standardised risk factors, and often incorporate a cumulative scoring system. A number of criticisms of actuarial methods were put forward by studies in our sample (Barlow and Scott 2010; Daniel *et al.* 2009; Statham and Smith 2010), and readers may wish to refer to these sources for further analysis. The significant point made in the studies was that actuarial methods should never be applied in isolation. They should be combined with a holistic assessment of the child's situation and used as an aid to professional judgement rather than a substitute for it. Indeed, the National Society for the Prevention of Cruelty to Children (NSPCC) has responded to this issue with a research review that identifies key pitfalls facing practitioners in the initial assessment of need and risk (Broadhurst, White *et al.* 2010). This publication highlights key areas where attention to good professional practice (and thereby making good judgements) is vital in ensuring appropriate responses to children who may be suffering or likely to suffer significant harm.

Notwithstanding the criticisms of standardised risk assessment methods, it is important for practitioners to know of risk factors that may be indicative of poor future outcomes for children. The operation and interaction of these factors can then be assessed comprehensively in an individual case, in conjunction with other relevant strengths and difficulties, with a view to establishing the severity of risk of harm for the child in question (see also Horwath 2009). The importance of examining the *interactions* between ecological factors in a child and family's situation was emphasised by Brandon *et al.* (1999, 2008). Whilst this is a theme we will return to, their analysis included an individual case that illustrates the point more fully, and is reproduced below.

Box 4.1 Case study: Carly (age nine weeks)

Theme of case and background

Carly suffered a head injury (thought to be a shaking injury) when she was nine weeks old. At the time of the injury the family had not been receiving any services beyond universal health services. Carly lived with her mother (aged 19), and her father (aged 20) in rented accommodation. During her pregnancy, Carly's mother presented four times to Accident and Emergency, twice reporting assaults to her abdomen.

(i) *Child's needs/characteristics/behaviour.* Carly was born at term with a normal delivery. In her early weeks she fed well, gained weight and responded well although she was also reported to have colic and to cry persistently at times. There were two recorded attendances at Accident and Emergency by the time she was four weeks old, one for a viral infection and the other with a rash.

(ii) *Mother's history/profile/parenting capacity.* Carly's mother was known to children's social care and child and adolescent mental health services when younger. She had Special Educational Needs and left school early and was reported to be 'self contained and withdrawn' at school and aggressive at home. Police were regularly called to the family home during Carly's mother's adolescence to respond to reports of violence among family members. She moved frequently between family members during her childhood and adolescence.

(iii) *Father's history/profile/parenting capacity.* Carly's father had a history of mental health problems, and behavioural problems throughout childhood. He had taken a number of overdoses and was reported to have poor anger management and poor self control. There was domestic violence in his household when he was younger and his mother had long term depression. The health visitor noticed that both parents' emotional reaction to Carly was immature and exaggerated in comparison to other young parents.

(iv) *Family environment.* The family suffered harassment by neighbours. There were financial difficulties in the household and police had been called to an incident of violence between parents. The parents did not feel supported by extended family.

(v) *Professional involvement/engagement.* Both parents had high levels of contact with a range of health professionals, including the health visitor, the GP, NHS Direct out of hours service and attendances at Accident and Emergency in the early weeks of Carly's life. Although parents sought help actively, pre-arranged appointments, for example with the health visitor, were often missed or cancelled. No health professionals were aware of the high level of contact with different branches of the service, nor of the pattern of contact (for example repeat attendances at A & E).

(vi) *Analysis of interacting risk factors.* There were many interacting risk factors in this case namely: high levels of domestic violence in pregnancy including blows to the mother's abdomen, mental health problems, frequent moves, lack of family support, financial worries and poor anger control for both parents. The combination of these issues signal that stress levels in these young parents were high and the capacity to deal with the demands of a new baby would be likely to be compromised. 'Persistent crying' and colic provided markers that this baby was at a high risk of injury from these parents whose emotional reaction to their baby had been noted as 'immature' and in whom a distressed baby would prompt high levels of anxiety, distress and agitation (Howe 2005, p.71).

What could have been done differently in Carly's case?

- **Information sharing**. There was a need for information to be shared within and across health services in the ante and post natal period so that the risks to the baby could have been properly considered. Given the parents' frequent moves this information needed to be widely accessible.

- **A holistic assessment**. A holistic assessment during the ante-natal period could have incorporated an understanding of the parents' history and the expertise of key professionals who knew the parents to consider the impact of parental history, mental illness and domestic violence on their parenting capacity.

- **Taking account of the parents' responses**. When the baby was born the early responses of the parents were a significant clue to their coping capacity. Had the parents' pattern of seeking help been logged, their mounting panic at times of stress would have been evident.

Source: Brandon *et al.* 2008, pp.131–132

In addition to the interaction of risk factors, Brandon, Bailey *et al.* (2009), in their second review of serious case reviews, showed that family/environmental problems in families with significant difficulties can become mirrored by equivalent difficulties amongst the professionals working with them. This tendency has been highlighted as a feature of serious child abuse cases and has been described previously, for example by Britton (1981). Brandon and her colleagues painted a picture of chaotic, overwhelmed families alongside overwhelmed professionals, children being overlooked within their own families being mirrored by professionals not taking sufficient account of the child, and a general impression of multiple family problems mirrored by multiple organisational and professional difficulties. Whilst this was based on a sample of serious case reviews, and the conclusions have not been tested prospectively, it emphasises the importance of standing back and understanding how professional systems interact with family and environmental factors when a professional is assessing a child and family.

Turning to more systematic identification of factors associated with child abuse, a number of reviews have been undertaken in recent years. For present purposes, we are particularly concerned with children who have often already been referred to social work services, and for whom problems, even as significant as child abuse, have already begun. In these circumstances, there is a need for professionals to be aware of factors that are linked with repeat abuse, or other ongoing adverse outcomes.

In this context, Hindley, Ramchandi and Jones (2006) undertook one of the few systematic reviews of research into risk factors for recurrence of maltreatment. Although the studies that met their inclusion criteria were all from the US or Australia, the factors they identified were consistent with a range of other reviews, and are set out in Figure 4.1. We would emphasise that these factors are based on statistical analysis and must be subject to detailed assessment in individual circumstances. They also suffer limitations common to many such lists, with broadly defined items such as 'parental mental health problems' that offer little assistance to the practitioner in evaluating the effects of particular manifestations of the factors concerned on the assessed child's health and development. Such lists cannot and must not be viewed deterministically, and no one factor on its own is likely to lead to maltreatment. However, professionals will come across cases where numbers of these factors appear. In such instances, they should examine carefully the ways in which the factors interact with each other (see the case study in Box 4.1 from Brandon *et al.* 2008) and consider the extent to which they are likely to produce negative outcomes for the child in question.

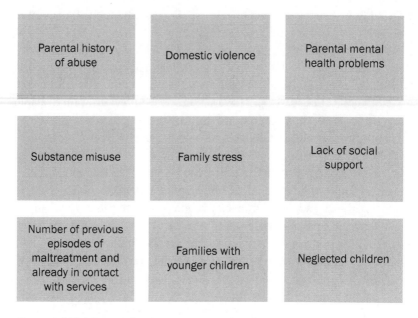

Figure 4.1 Risk factors for the recurrence of maltreatment
Source: Hindley *et al.* 2006

Several recent studies in the present review also demonstrated that children who return to a parent following more than a short period of planned care are more likely to be re-abused than those who remain in permanent foster care, are placed with relatives or are adopted (Brandon and Thoburn 2008; Farmer 2009; Sinclair *et al.* 2007).

In addition to the Hindley *et al.* (2006) review, Thoburn and Making Research Count Consortium (2009) drew up a list of features of families who, research indicates, are likely to find it hard to change (Box 4.2). Whilst this list was *not* derived from a systematic review of research, it presents a perspective that is complementary to that of Hindley *et al.* (2006) and includes items that are widely supported in the research literature. Use of the list has not been evaluated prospectively in actual assessments of children and families.

Box 4.2 Children who are likely to experience maltreatment and their parents

'Hard to change' parents

Parents who become known to the social care services because their children have been harmed or are considered likely to be harmed, but who are particularly difficult to help in a way which achieves and maintains the necessary change for the child, are referred to in this briefing as *'hard to change' parents*. These parents usually have one and often several of the following characteristics:

- are isolated, without extended family, community or faith group support
- were abused or emotionally rejected as children, or had multiple changes of carer
- have a mental illness, personality disorder and/or a learning disability
- are particularly vulnerable if no other parent or extended family member is available to share parenting, and if this is combined with having a child who is 'hard to parent'
- they have had children by different partners, often involving an abusive relationship
- they have an alcohol or drug addiction and do not accept that they must control the habit for the sake of their child's welfare
- they have aggressive outbursts and/or a record of violence, including intimate partner violence
- they have obsessional/very controlling personalities, often linked with low self-esteem
- they were in care and had multiple placements or 'aged out' of care without a secure base (mitigated if they had a good relationship with a carer, social worker or social work team who remained available to them through pregnancy and in early parenting)
- they are especially fearful of stigma or suspicious of statutory services; this includes those from communities which consider it stigmatising to seek state assistance, immigrants who have

experienced coercive state power before coming to the UK, or people with poor childhood experience of services.

Children most at risk of continuing harm

Some children and young people have characteristics, which make them 'hard to engage', or 'hard to help/change' and, when combined with one or more of the above parental characteristics are most vulnerable to continuing harm. These children and young people can have one or more of the following characteristics:

- born prematurely, under-weight and/or suffering the effects of intrauterine drug and/or alcohol misuse, which can make children fretful, hard to feed and unresponsive

- with disabilities or other characteristics which make them hard to parent or 'unrewarding' in the eyes of parents who lack self-esteem and confidence

- individual members of sibling groups 'singled out for rejection' (Rushton et al. 2001) and/or targeted for abuse

- children returning home from care, especially if they suffer the loss of an attachment figure (usually a foster carer). Several recent studies have demonstrated that children who return to a parent following more than a short period of planned care are more likely to be re-abused than those who remain in permanent foster care, are placed with relatives or are adopted (Sinclair et al. 2007; Brandon and Thoburn 2008; Farmer 2009)

- teenagers (who have often suffered from unrecognised or unresponded-to abuse or neglect) who engage in risk-taking or anti-social behaviours (Stein et al. 2009).

Source: Thoburn et al. 2009, pp.3–5

As with the material from Hindley et al. 2006 we suggest that the information in Box 4.2 may be utilised by practitioners as an aid to thinking in undertaking an assessment, rather than as a 'tick-box' rating. Neither list draws attention to the importance of identifying and addressing enmeshed professional systems (see discussion of mirroring on p.65). Nevertheless, other material in the present review complements the above extracts. Cleaver et al. (2004) categorised cases as having multiple problems if there were severe difficulties in all three domains of the assessment triangle. However, Horwath (2002) has drawn attention to practitioners' difficulties in giving equal attention to all three domains (see Chapter 3).

Summary

In summary, key findings regarding the assessment of whether a child is suffering or likely to suffer significant harm were that there is a degree of agreement about the features of families who may be most difficult to help or are likely to continue to harm their children. Even with this knowledge, 'scientific' or actuarial prediction of dangerous families is complex and difficult, and formal methods should only ever be used in conjunction with professional judgement. Nonetheless, since a number of these risk factors may be present in a considerable number of families known to children's social care services, judgements about when to intervene are not always easy to make and will depend on the impact on the child of their current and previous adversities (from observation and using research knowledge) considered within the context of the whole history of the case. Two central features of professional judgement should be an analysis of interacting risk and protective factors, and honest appraisals of whether professional systems have become enmeshed.

Reunification

Reunification of children from the looked after system to their parents' care has been identified, over a number of years, as an issue that has received much less attention in research, practice and policy than many other aspects of social work (Biehal 2006; Farmer 2009). Although assessing the likelihood of further maltreatment, or of placement breakdown, will often be a key aspect of planning a child's return, we found a number of specific features in the research that might assist social work decision making in this area. They need to be considered within the context of research findings about poor outcomes for children returned 'home', which have already been noted and which will be discussed further in Chapter 9. Important aspects of assessment for reunification provide the focus for this section. It is expected that an assessment will be undertaken using the core assessment as a framework when contemplating the return of a child to his or her parents' care (DCSF 2009a; HM Government 2010b).

In relation to the presence or absence of an assessment, in Farmer *et al.*'s (2011) study of reunification, 43 per cent of the children returned to a parent from care or being looked after without any assessment of their situation, or after only an initial assessment, and a third were never assessed before or during the return. Where an assessment took place, it appeared to lead to better service provision. After assessment, two-thirds (65%) of the parents and over half (55%) of the children received specialist help from children's social care services, compared with only a third of the parents and children whose circumstances had not been assessed. In addition, when multi-agency assessments had been undertaken, children were more likely to be returned home to an improved situation and to experience return stability. Wade, Biehal *et al.* (2010), in their study of the care pathways of maltreated children returned home compared with those who remained looked after, presented a slightly more optimistic picture, with assessments occurring in 72 per cent of cases where children were returned home. Variations in practice between local authorities were particularly evident in relation to the purposefulness of social work planning, and the assessment of likelihood of the recurrence of harm. Where children were formally 'placed with parents' under a care order, rather than simply discharged home, assessment and planning were more thorough. Farmer *et al.* (2011) found that issues (such as drug/ alcohol problems or continuing domestic violence) with the potential to jeopardise the success of reunification frequently remained unresolved or hidden from children's social care services. In addition, where there had been no assessment, these children were among those who were least likely to be monitored adequately.

A set of practice points (Table 4.1) were compiled for the present review, based primarily on Farmer *et al.* 2011, Harwin *et al.* 2003 and Wade, Biehal *et al.* 2010. As with the preceding section on analysis of risk factors, our view is that the factors identified by these questions need to be analysed carefully to consider how they may interact if the particular child returns home, and thus how they might lead to positive or negative outcomes for this child.

Table 4.1 Assessing children and young people where reunification home is being considered

Questions the assessment should address	The research base
1. *Was the child maltreated prior to separation?* Consider for each child: • age of the child • whether parents have mental health problems • how long the child has been in care or looked after • does the return involve a group of siblings (generally, children returned home with siblings do better than those returned alone but see opposite)? • if a lone parent, what support is available?	Re-abuse rates for reunified children are between 25 and 46%. Under 12 years old are more at risk of re-abuse, and babies under one year are most at risk of re-abuse. Re-abuse is also more likely where: • parents have substance misuse difficulties or mental health problems • the child has been looked after for three or more years • where the return is specifically to a lone parent, and involves other siblings.
2. *Has a return home been tried before?* Consider: • what has changed to make this return home work where previous attempts did not?	Previous failed returns are strongly related to later breakdowns of a return home. Parental ambivalence relates to return home disruption. Higher risk of return home disruptions where there have been no changes in family composition (for example, the abusing parent is still living in the household).

3. Assess the family and environmental conditions, and how they will support or otherwise the return home.

Consider:

- what risk factors are in family environment and how support might alleviate them?

The following factors appear to be related to breakdown of reunification:

- continuing parental alcohol or drug misuse
- continuing parental mental health problems
- continuing domestic violence
- parent/s living in poverty or on benefits
- inadequate housing
- lone parents
- social isolation
- older age of child
- child has problems related to schooling
- tensions between siblings
- poor parenting skills
- child's tendency to self-harm.

4. Analyse the child's looked after experience to date.

Consider:

- the child's wishes and feelings
- whether the child retains a sense of place and of belonging in the family home.

The following child factors are linked to breakdown of reunification:

- longer periods being looked after
- more movement whilst looked after (e.g. changes of placement, changes of school).

Retaining a sense of place in the family home, possessions remaining untouched and so on are also associated with a positive outcome.

Children's wishes and feelings, about whether they want to return home and when, are important. Their reservations need to be taken seriously.

5. Assess changes in the home situation.

Consider:

- are the changes likely to have a positive impact?
- what is the child's relationship with, for example, a new step-parent?
- have the child and parent/s faced up to difficult issues that led to separation?

Returning a child is as complex as separation, and needs to be addressed sensitively.

In cases where parents misuse substances, there should be clear expectations that parents will be required to address their misuse before children are returned and that their use of substances will be closely monitored and reviewed before and during return. Substance misuse is linked to higher levels of abuse and neglect, poor parenting and domestic violence during return.

6. Assess changes in the birth parent/s and/or child

Consider:

- how far have the original problems been resolved?
- if there is substance misuse, how is this being managed?
- does the parent want the child home?
- does the child want to return to this parent?

Assessment and planning should specify, from the outset, what needs to change, over what timescales (having regard to children's developmental needs) before return is possible, and how this is to be supported and monitored.

Using written contracts that agree clear goals with parents, and are regularly reviewed, can be effective, alongside the provision of tailored services addressing parents' and children's difficulties.

7. Plan the support the family will be offered.

Parent/s need access to treatment for their substance misuse problems alongside more training for practitioners in how to work with substance-misusing parents.

Good preparation for the return, plus good-quality social work support and monitoring following the return, are associated with higher chances of success.

Source: Based on the work of Farmer *et al.* 2011; Harwin *et al.* 2003; Wade, Biehal *et al.* 2010

Note: These practice points were compiled by the present authors from the research cited above, and have not been evaluated prospectively in a practice context.

Placing and matching

Quinton's (2009) conceptual and research review of matching in adoption practice found that assessment of *prospective adopters* had received much more attention in the practice literature and in official guidance than the *assessment of children*. Research reviews (for example, Rushton 2003, 2004; Sinclair 2005) on disrupted placements and placement outcomes have consistently shown the characteristics and behaviours of children that are the most strongly predictive of placement difficulties in adoptive or foster families. Age at placement is one of the strongest of these, but this is substantially because of its association with emotional and behavioural problems, notably difficulties in making and sustaining relationships ('attachment problems'), oppositional and conduct problems, and overactive and restless behaviour ('ADHD'). However, Quinton found that these difficulties were rarely systematically assessed in practice (see also Quinton and Murray 2002). He was also unable to establish how many social work training courses had substantial, practice-related training in normal and abnormal child development and its assessment.

The assessment of these developmental needs, as well as those related to educational progress and attainment, is difficult with young children. Quinton found that judgements based on the hypothesised consequences of the child's prior experiences, as well as on the capacities of adopters to deal with these, were used for young children. Much of the judgement on needs was based on clinical/practice hunches and experience. Quinton concluded that assessment as it is done in current practice may be as good as we can get and the notion of specific matching of parents 'capacities' to children's 'needs' may be unachievable at present. Whilst this is almost certainly true, Farmer and Dance *et al.*'s subsequent empirical study of family finding and matching in adoption (2010) found that researcher judgements about the quality of the match at the time it was made (which considered the extent of compromise on the children's needs or the wishes of the adoptive parents, excluding consideration of ethnic matching) were closely associated with placement outcome. In two-thirds (63%) of disrupted or continuing but unstable placements, the match had been categorised as poor, whilst disrupted or continuing but unstable placements occurred in only 5 per cent of good or fair matches. Similarly, only 31 per cent of poor matches were rated as positive placements for children, as against 93 per cent of good or fair matches.

In Selwyn and colleagues' (2010) sample of children with adoption recommendations, all types of assessment were poorer in quality for minority ethnic children than for white children. Matching assessments for minority ethnic children were dominated by the need for a 'same race' placement and children's other needs such as permanency or care for significant health and developmental delays were often omitted from reports. The majority of the children had complex multiple heritages and the availability of an 'exact match' was remote.

The York foster care studies (Sinclair 2005) highlighted a key feature of successful placements, and one that was almost certainly related to the child's willingness to be in placement and that was 'click' or 'fit' – some carers and children simply took to each other and had a personal chemistry. There is some evidence that the 'fit' between adopters or foster carers and children can be assessed at quite a refined level and that this can make a difference (Kanuik, Steele and Hodges 2004; Quinton et al. 1998). New approaches such as 'adopter-led' matching, are trying, with some success, to bring the otherwise unknowable element of personal chemistry into play. Well-evaluated accounts are lacking, although Farmer and Dance et al. (2010) found that there was no difference in children's outcomes six months into the adoptive placement whether the adoptions were adopter-led or made by professionals. These approaches may, in due course, have the effect of increasing the number of matches and lead to outcomes at least as good as those produced by more traditional methods. The use of discussions around a particular child, such as child appreciation days, as part of the assessment process, is another way of trying to bring some reality testing into the assessment process.

Working with ethnic and cultural differences

Section 22 (5) (c) of the Children Act 1989 requires that when making decisions in respect of a child, a local authority 'shall give due consideration...to the child's religious persuasion, racial origin and cultural and linguistic background'. However, the research evidence suggests that these issues were not always well understood or addressed in assessments (Ofsted 2008, 2009; Selwyn et al. 2010). Selwyn and colleagues' (2010) 'pathways to permanence' study found that social workers typically did not assess these areas but assumed that culture was the same as ethnicity. In addition, in this study of permanence/

adoption the quality of assessments was especially poor for black and Asian children and there was more delay in permanence decisions for these children. The profiles of black and minority ethnic children too were sometimes poorly written and often stressed the complexity of a child's ethnicity. Black and minority ethnic children were less likely than others to be placed for adoption because of a concentration on 'same race' placements combined with social worker's pessimism about the likelihood of finding a placement and limited promotion. For children with complex ethnicities or additional needs it was unlikely that an adoptive family could be found that would meet *all* the child's cultural needs (see also Farmer and Dance *et al.* 2010).

We do not have the space here to discuss the complex conceptual issues around defining notions such as ethnicity and culture. However, it would appear that more sophisticated understandings of both these concepts would allow for more effective assessment, as the statement below from Sinclair and Bullock suggests:

> Within a case file the record of ethnicity needs to move beyond a simple uni-dimensional categorisation, such as that used for database purposes, and include a more sophisticated description of the several aspects of ethnicity. Further, this should be based, as far as possible, on self definition, asking the child or family how they describe their own ethnic identity. Information on a child's ethnicity allows for a fuller description of the child, just as with age and sex. Similarly, as with age and sex, it may or may not give rise to particular needs but it alerts the practitioner to such a possibility.
>
> In undertaking an assessment, practitioners need to give careful consideration to any needs that arise in relation to any aspect of the child's ethnicity, ensuring these are clearly articulated. For example, the child and family's ability to speak and understand English; their familiarity with services in order to gain access to them; the impact of racism or uprooting from their country of origin and the significance of cultural or religious practices. (Sinclair and Bullock 2002, p.20)

In addition, if part of the point of an assessment is to build a full picture of the child – and in the case of fostering and adoptive assessments, to ensure the best placement match – then a range of factors become relevant, for example the kind of food a child is used to eating, celebrations and festivals they are familiar with and whether they have attended a place of worship.

In their discussion of the effects of children's ethnicity on case management in neglect cases, Farmer and Lutman (2009) highlight the need for social workers to have a level of 'cultural competence' to support their assessments and work with families from black and minority ethnic backgrounds. Drawing on Korbin and Spilsbury's work (1999) they note that:

> Cultural competence puts child protection first but that this is understood within a cultural context, including identifying culturally appropriate interventions and sorting out which aspects of a family's difficulties are 'cultural', which are 'neglectful' and which a combination of these. (Farmer and Lutman 2009, p.155)

Misunderstandings about different cultural practices and/or an attitude of cultural relativism may leave a child at risk of suffering serious harm. Farmer and Lutman identified a small number of cases in their sample where a reliance on cultural explanations meant that concerns about a child's safety or welfare were not taken as seriously as they might have been. Again, this suggests the need for a more nuanced understanding of culture – and of the limits of cultural explanations.

Elsewhere, a lack of understanding and validation of different cultures and experiences was noted, with similar implications for assessment. For example, Cemlyn et al. (2009, p.130) found '[a] lack of understanding and validation of Gypsy and Traveller culture and experience [that could] lead to inadequate responses and to the pathologisation of families'. They found that there was an emphasis on explanations that drew on culture and lifestyle rather than, or with less attention to, environmental factors such as the experience of poverty or discrimination. The researchers emphasised that assessment needed to use all three domains of the Assessment Framework to ensure holistic assessment that also considered the structural factors that impacted on the family (Cemlyn et al. 2009; see also Selwyn et al. 2010).

Unaccompanied asylum-seeking children and young people

One study identified for this review (Wade, Mitchell and Baylis 2005) included an exploration of the role of social work assessments in relation to unaccompanied asylum-seeking children and young people. The study involved analysis of the files of 212 unaccompanied children/young people from three authorities, 31 interviews with children and young people and 27 interviews with support workers. The situations of children and young people seeking asylum are complex, with interacting effects of often very traumatic experiences in their home country, the shock of entering a new country and the formalities of immigration procedures, age assessments, and so on. Initial referral was often a crucial point at which to gather basic information about a child or young person. Additionally, the initial or core assessments examined in the study attempted to collect information on: placement needs, health and emotional wellbeing, education and training, family and social relationships, development, immigration, and risk of exploitation, offending or substance misuse.

The initial assessments were often confined to basic information gathering, and in a high proportion of cases there was an urgency about practical tasks such as arranging an immediate placement. There were also notable issues facing the young person, such as thoughts and worries about relatives in the home country, networks and links to relatives or other young people in the UK, and the effects of traumatic experiences such as witnessing family members being killed or taken away. Some of this information took a long time to emerge, and many young people would not be ready to address their experiences in a therapeutic sense for some time to come, if at all. The study found variations in assessment practice, with regard to the amount of information recorded at referral and as to whether an initial assessment was undertaken. The vast majority (88%) of children and young people did receive an initial assessment, although variations in the proportions of initial assessments between authorities were statistically significant. Where initial assessments did not take place, this appears to be explained by young people being referred directly to another agency (for example, for urgent housing), assessments being planned but delayed until a specialist team had been established, or, in a very small number of cases, loss of documentation. Core assessments were only undertaken in a very small number of cases, and usually in situations where more complex needs were becoming apparent.

Disabled children

There was limited information on assessing disabled children in the studies that met the criteria for this review. Where included, the key point that emerged was to question the Integrated Children's System exemplars for recording core assessments, on the basis that the same formats apply to both disabled and non-disabled children. Cleaver et al. (2004) found that social workers thought the core assessment recording format was unhelpful for assessing disabled children. Mitchell and Sloper (2008) reported a similar finding, that social workers found the ICS exemplars (which were based on the core assessment format explored in the Cleaver study) to have a number of aspects that were inappropriate for assessing disabled children. An example was the mismatch between chronological age and cognitive development for some disabled children, because of the reliance of the exemplars on standard developmental milestones.

Cleaver *et al.* (2004), however, found that social workers' concerns about the Assessment Framework were not supported by parents' views. Parents of disabled children were as positive or more so about the assessment process as parents in other situations. Some social workers in this study appeared to view the parents of disabled children as 'heroic carers' or to feel sorry for them. These reactions could inhibit the practitioners from expressing concerns and, if necessary, confronting parents, and the assessment consequently focused on the child's disability, when in fact the research suggested many parents appear to welcome engagement with social work services over these issues. More holistic assessment, including, for example, parenting capacity, was seen by some social workers as unnecessary and insulting. From a policy and practice perspective, the concern is that genuine difficulties, even including possible child abuse or neglect, might be overlooked if assessments are overly focused on the needs of parents of the disabled child. Further guidance on safeguarding disabled children is available in Murray and Osborne (2009).

Conclusion

This chapter identified some of the key contexts of social work assessments. Reviewing them highlights the diversity of assessment tasks and the way in which the Assessment Framework was neither intended to nor could be expected to give detailed guidance on all the elements it might be necessary to assess in every type of case. A range of materials are available to help practitioners address key aspects of an assessment (see, for example, Horwath 2009), and other suggestions were made in the body of the current chapter. As indicated in Chapter 3, it is important to remember that the Assessment Framework is a scaffold for an assessment, rather than an instruction manual, a point to which we will return. In the next chapter, we examine how the information collected during an assessment is pulled together and analysed.

Summary

- There is a level of agreement from research about the features of families who may be most difficult to help or who are likely to continue to harm their children.

- Predicting which parents are most likely to re-abuse children is difficult, and formal methods should only be used in conjunction with professional judgement.

- Professionals working with complex family problems should develop strategies to ensure that inter-professional dynamics do not mirror the family's difficulties.

- When reunification of children with their families is planned, quality assessment contributes to better decision making and service provision.

- Little is known about exactly how best to match children with specific adoptive families. However, serious compromises in matching children's requirements or adopters' preferences have been shown to be related to poorer outcomes.

- A number of practice issues were identified in relation to assessments of minority ethnic children. They include the need to distinguish between culture and ethnicity, ensuring that interviews are conducted in the users' first language. Social workers could also misunderstand cultural practices, which could leave children at risk of suffering harm.

- Assessment practice with regard to asylum-seeking children and young people, in terms of developing a full and detailed assessment, was variable. The majority of children and young people received an initial assessment.

- In relation to disabled children, social workers often believe there is a mismatch between the core assessment exemplars and the needs of disabled children and their families. Parents of disabled children, however, were appreciative of the core assessment process.

Chapter 5

ANALYSIS, CRITICAL THINKING AND REFLECTION IN ASSESSMENT

Assessment requires more than just the collection of 'facts'. It must, of course, involve systematic and purposive gathering of information, but this then needs to be 'processed' in some way – synthesised, analysed, reflected upon, interpreted – to allow the practitioner to come to a view about the meaning of the material. But, with few exceptions, research and practice literature have consistently identified shortcomings in relation to this analytical process (Bell *et al.* 2007; Brandon *et al.* 2008; Brandon, Bailey *et al.* 2009; Cleaver *et al.* 2008; Cleaver and Walker 2004; Munro 1998, 1999; Ofsted 2008; Rose and Barnes 2008; Sinclair and Bullock 2002), drawing attention to repeated examples of absence or failure of analysis. Analyses of serious case reviews, in particular, highlight difficulties that have arisen in terms of collecting information and then, perhaps more importantly, in interpreting it.

In this chapter we consider what is known about the significance of critical and analytical thinking for effective assessment work, the difficulties associated with this way of thinking, and the factors that promote its use in practice. However, there are significant practical difficulties in researching people's actual thinking processes, rather than what they *say* they think or do. Studies have tended to draw on self-reports (with the limitation noted above) and/or retrospective analysis of files and other documentary evidence from which inferences are made about the underpinning thinking processes. But there is a broader theoretical and practice-based literature that addresses some of the issues associated with critical, analytical and reflective thinking in social work (see Turney 2009 for a review of relevant literature) which supplements and informs the empirical data and from which we also draw in this chapter.

Before addressing these issues, we look briefly at the way language is used in recording and how well reports are written.

Recording and writing skills

The ability to present clear, full and accurate information in written form has been identified as a key part of the assessment process and some of the practical and systems-based constraints have been mentioned.

The importance of the way language was used to draw attention to, or minimise, aspects of a situation was noted by Holland (2010), in relation to the presentation of information about domestic violence (see Chapter 3). She also found that, in some cases, practitioners adapted their style of writing depending on the use they expected to be made of the assessment report and the audience to whom it would be presented. Interview data from the study conducted by Thomas (2010, cited by Holland 2010), for example, showed social workers making a distinction between assessments for court and those destined for non-judicial arenas. She quoted one social worker who described her court reports as 'very factual' and carefully backed up with evidence and her non-court reports as 'more "free-flowing"'.

Selwyn and colleagues' study of the costs and outcomes of non-infant adoptions (2006) also identified issues to do with reporting and writing. The research team found that both the profiles that were produced for black and minority ethnic children and some of their assessment reports were very poorly written and the latter reports contained significant gaps. They concluded that particular skills and training were needed to write an effective profile for a child who is to be placed for adoption. In terms of the Child Permanence Report (CPR), Farmer and Dance *et al.* (2010) observed that adoption workers were likely to be more familiar with the style and formats required for this and other reports, even if they have less knowledge of the child than the child's social worker. So they suggested that, since children's social workers usually do few CPRs, they would benefit from the assistance of their managers or from adoption workers in completing them. We return to recording in more detail in Chapter 8.

Adopting an 'assessment mindset'

Effective assessment does not consist simply of 'static, events-based description' (Brandon *et al.* 2008, p.63) but moves from an account of *what* happened to consideration of *why*; it requires the social worker to analyse and evaluate the information collected and to come to a decision about how to proceed. What the idea of an 'assessment mindset' suggests is that the nature and quality of social work thinking is a critical part of that process.

In their analysis of the report into the death of Victoria Climbié, Reder and Duncan make the point that, from the outset, assessment should be a purposeful and focused process and that this requires a particular approach:

> Practitioners need to adopt an assessment mindset, in which they automatically embark on an assessment in order to inform them how they should respond to a referral and regularly review their assumptions and formulations in the light of new information. Assessment would then become a thoughtful process rather than a mechanical exercise or a procedure whose parameters have been pre-selected. (Reder and Duncan 2004, p.105)

They emphasise that, rather than simply reinforcing the procedural or managerial control of assessment, there is a need for social workers to think about, and understand the reasons for, what they do; for example:

> Practitioners who understand why they need to speak to the child alone, speak to the child's carers, visit their accommodation and seek the views of other professionals...[as specified in Recommendation 40 of the Laming Report] are much more likely to do so meaningfully and then make sense of the information that they have obtained. (Reder and Duncan 2004, p.106)

Thus, the ability to manage what they refer to as 'the more "thinking" aspects of professional practice' (p.99) is seen to be critical for effective assessment and safer practice. This emphasis on the nature and quality of thinking is reflected in the framework proposed by Brandon *et al.* (2008) for 'case formulation' (Box 5.1).

Box 5.1 Framework for case formulation

The Framework for the Assessment of Children in Need and their Families (Department of Health *et al.* 2000) provides 'a systematic way of analysing, understanding, and recording what is happening to children and young people within their families and the wider context of the communities in which they live' (p.viii). Ideally therefore, the ecological description should form the basis of a detailed assessment, analysis and formulation of the problems, vulnerabilities and risks of harm. Their origins, possible causes and interactive effects should also be considered.

Case formulation

A case formulation should summarise, integrate and synthesise the knowledge brought together by the assessment process. The formulation, drawing on developmental and psycho-social theory, should provide a coherent framework for:

   (i) describing a problem,

   (ii) examining its genesis, development and maintenance, and

   (iii) planning an intervention.

It is out of this formulation that hypotheses emerge about the causes and character of the problem/concern. In turn, provisional hypotheses guide future observation and data collection. In the light of new evidence and practice outcomes, hypotheses are under constant review, evaluation and revision.

It is within the context of the analysis and formulation that new facts might be allocated or pursued. Each new piece of evidence should help confirm or modify the working hypothesis of the nature of the caregiving environment and the developmental risks and protections afforded by that environment for the child. Or as Reder and Duncan (1999) put it, 'it is the meaning of individual attributes in the context of interpersonal functioning that gives the valid clues to the risk' (p.74).

Source: Brandon *et al.* 2008, p.66

So a priority for practice should be to promote the development of reasoning skills and an understanding of the different elements of hypothesising, testing, reflecting, planning and evaluating that make up the broader process of analysis.

The use of reasoning in assessment

Munro (2008, 2010) has drawn attention to two different forms of thinking in social work: analytical and intuitive reasoning. These are often presented as competing and mutually exclusive approaches:

> At one extreme, analytical reasoning is formal, explicit and logical. It is associated with mathematics and rigorous thought, where every step in the argument is spelled out. In contrast, intuition is non-verbal, swiftly reaching a conclusion on the basis of largely unconscious processes. (Munro 2008, p.2)

Munro argues, however, that rather than seeing them in 'either/or' terms, analytical and intuitive thinking can more usefully be thought of as different points on a continuum. So it may be more constructive to develop both kinds of thinking, as each has something important to contribute, a view that is also endorsed by Reder and Duncan:

> Different permutations of reasoning and different types of information are required, depending on the context, so that an integration is needed. Integration is also necessary because both styles are fallible, as exemplified by the limitations of either risk protocols or professional judgements in accurately predicting risk of child abuse. (Reder and Duncan 2004, pp.109–110)

A similar case is made by Holland (2010) in her discussion of the approaches she calls 'scientific discourse' and 'reflective evaluation'. She shows how practitioners move between these different modes of thinking in the course of the assessment process.

Theoretical frameworks

Brandon et al. (2008) draw attention to the importance of practitioners being able to make use of a clear theoretical framework for analysing material gathered during assessments. But research evidence suggests that practice is not routinely supported by, or grounded in, an explicit theoretical understanding or, at least, that this is generally not evident from the study of case files and reports. Drawing on information from a range of sources, including content analysis of the records of 152 families who had received help from a Child and Family Support Service in England, Macdonald and Williamson's (2002) evaluation of this service found that reference, either explicit or implicit, to a theoretical framework was rare in the assessments reviewed. As part of a study of outcomes for children in need, commissioned by one social services department, Preston-Shoot (2003) undertook an analysis of case files to provide information about the nature and quality of social work assessments and of young people's experiences of professional intervention. He too noted that 'files did not contain much direct or explicit evidence of theory-informed or research-informed practice in terms of assessment, planning or methods of intervention' (p.43), but also made the point that absence of written reference to research or theory did not necessarily imply that social workers lacked the relevant knowledge or were unaware of current research. However, he advised that the models on which particular practice are based should be made explicit in file notes, when formulating and completing assessments and in supervision discussion.

Brandon and colleagues (2008, 2010; Brandon, Bailey et al. 2009) recommend a transactional-ecological approach, and explain this underpinning framework as follows:

> The ecological transactional perspective requires a dynamic, not a static understanding and assessment of children and their families. Central to this approach is the need to take account of carers' experiences of being parented themselves and the history of their own relationships with family, peers, partners and professionals. All of these dimensions of experience influence carers' sense of themselves and how they see others. Parents' and carers' emotional histories, cognitive models and current life stressors, like poverty, domestic violence and ill health, affect their states of mind and the way they understand and interpret the needs and behaviour of any children in their care. The past, present and future need to be understood through this lens. Understanding will be limited if this does not happen. (Brandon, Bailey et al. 2009, p.110)

They refer back to the theoretical underpinning of the Assessment Framework, which was based on an ecological model that 'understands the importance of recognising the presence of multiple risk and protective factors *and their possible interactions*' (Brandon et al. 2008, p.63; emphasis added). As we have seen, the Assessment Framework identifies three inter-related 'domains' – the child's developmental needs; parenting capacity; and family and environmental factors – and represents these in a triangle to emphasise the connections between the different aspects of people's lives and experiences (Brandon et al. 2009; Daniel 2006;

Horwath 2002; Jack and Gill 2003). It requires a move from a linear approach (where the three domains are addressed separately and sequentially) to a more circular or systemic way of thinking where the inter-relationships between different aspects of people's lives and experiences are explored.

Impediments to critical and analytical thinking

Effective thinking in social work – making use of an assessment mindset – involves the careful use of a range of different 'thinking approaches'. We have identified that practitioners need to be able to draw on both analytical and intuitive modes of thought. In addition, these need to be accompanied by an ability to think both critically and reflectively (Gambrill 1990; Munro 2008; Turney 2009).

However, a number of factors – practical, emotional and psychological – appear to impact on the individual's capacity to think effectively. In their analysis of a sample of 'Part 8' Reviews into cases of fatal child abuse, Reder and Duncan refer to the *Beyond Blame* study of 1993, and note that there were:

> a series of factors in practitioners' working contexts that had a profound impact on their handling of cases. These included gaps in training and experience, agency reorganisations, stressful working conditions, excessively heavy workloads and fixed beliefs about particular families or the nature of child abuse in general. Absent or inadequate supervision was also highlighted as an important contributory factor. (Reder and Duncan 1999, pp.101–102)

The research reviewed here suggests that most, if not all, of these factors still pertain and have a powerful effect on practice and practitioners, as we discuss below.

Practical demands

At a practical level, some practitioners seemed to be unsure what was expected from them in relation to undertaking assessments – and how to do them. Cleaver and Walker (2004), for example, found that 'a significant proportion' of the social workers, who completed their questionnaire at the time the Assessment Framework was being introduced, lacked confidence in their ability to manage the assessment process effectively and expressed considerable anxiety about how to analyse the information they gathered.

Critical and analytical thinking is not always easy; it takes time and intellectual energy to do well, both of which may be undermined by workforce issues such as high turnover and low morale. In addition, pressure of work and requirements to meet deadlines or performance targets may encourage a climate of 'busy-ness' and an emphasis on 'getting the job done' that reduces the opportunities for thinking and reflecting.

'Everyday' patterns of thinking

A number of forms of bias and inconsistency can impact on thinking and reasoning. Galanter and Patel (2005) offer a 'selective review' of decision making, drawing on a range of literature within the fields of behavioural and cognitive psychology, with a view to applying their understanding to the decision-making practices of child psychiatrists and psychologists. The focus here is on clinical practice (and this is clearly reflected in the language of diagnosis and treatment used in their discussion) but, while there may not be an exact translation from the medical to the social sphere, many of the errors and biases that Galanter and Patel identify seem equally salient for other forms of practice. For example, they highlight:

- *Availability bias* – which involves 'overestimating the probability of a diagnosis because it is especially memorable or salient' (p.677).

- *Confirmation bias* – where the practitioner selectively gathers and interprets evidence that confirms a diagnosis and ignores or minimises the significance of evidence that contradicts it.

- *Effect of description or unpacking principle* – by which they mean that when more detail of an event is provided, its judged probability increases.

- *Hindsight* – the likely diagnosis seems a lot clearer, looking back, once the correct diagnosis of a condition has been made.

- *Order effects* – 'information presented later in a case given more weight than information presented earlier'.

(Summarised from Galanter and Patel 2005, p.677)

Within social work, similar issues have been explored by Helm (2010), Holland (2010) and Munro (2008), amongst others, and particular patterns of thinking described. For example, the tendency towards 'verificationism' (Holland 2010) and 'fixed thinking' (Brandon, Bailey *et al.* 2009) have been identified. Verificationism refers to the propensity for people to be drawn towards information that confirms their initial view of a situation and to reject that which discounts or challenges it (Holland 2010). Fixed thinking, as the name suggests, describes the tendency again to make up one's mind and then stick to that understanding, resisting alternative explanations or interpretations. Psychologists have suggested that these are general, 'human' habits of thought, rather than being restricted to any particular occupational group but the consequences of both 'verificationist' and fixed thinking are potentially particularly significant for social work.

In the recent case of Peter Connelly ('Baby P') different professionals appeared to form a view of Peter's situation that was resistant to change. Evidence (head injury with no satisfactory explanation, sustained by a baby) that in other circumstances might have alerted practitioners to the dangers of the situation was interpreted in a way that failed to challenge the view of Peter's mother as a concerned parent, apparently working cooperatively with the different professionals involved (LSCB Haringey 2009). As Lord Laming noted in relation to the professional responses to Victoria Climbié and her carers, practitioners need to be able to maintain an attitude of 'healthy scepticism' and 'respectful uncertainty' (Laming 2003, p.322 and p.205) while working with families, and to be open to the possibility that they may need to revise their earlier judgements, despite the fact that 'reviewing judgements is intellectually and emotionally hard' (Reder and Duncan 2004).

Fixed thinking may be a particular concern in work with neglect cases: in their analysis of serious case reviews, Brandon, Bailey *et al.* (2009) identified 'a particular "neglect case" mindset' and note that 'once an assessment has been completed or a child protection plan which focuses on neglect has been made, this may preclude other forms of harm being considered' (p.50). Farmer and Lutman (2009) similarly found that many cases of neglect received passive rather than proactive case management.

The impact of working with chronic neglect can further unsettle practice in a variety of ways: we have noted elsewhere the finding from Brandon and colleagues' review of serious case reviews that professionals in some cases responded to new developments — for example, the birth of another child in a family — in a way that appeared to disregard the previous case history, describing this as '[a] "start again" syndrome preventing practitioners thinking and acting systematically in cases of longstanding neglect' (2008, p.101). More recently, looking at findings that recurred across three biennial reviews (Brandon *et al.* 2008; Brandon,

Bailey *et al.* 2009, 2010), Brandon and colleagues (2010, p.54) found that the 'start again syndrome' continued to provide 'a helpful way of conceptualising practice and decision making especially in cases of neglect'.

It is important, then, to recognise that assessment is a dynamic process within which analysis plays a continuing part. No assessment provides the 'last word' about a family or situation, and the process therefore needs to remain open to review and rethinking. For example, Farmer and colleagues' (2004) study of foster care for adolescents showed that some factors which related to outcome (such as the placed child's impact on other children in the family) only emerged as the placement progressed. So rigorously reviewing placements is essential for ensuring that the child's needs and those of other foster family members are being adequately addressed.

Emotional demands: The impact of fear, violence and stress

In his second report, Lord Laming (Laming 2009, p.4) observed that 'anxiety undermines good practice', a view that has been borne out by a number of studies and commentaries on practice (see, for example, Cooper 2005; Ferguson 2005; Littlechild 2005; Rustin 2005). In their study of social work with parents who misuse alcohol or drugs, Harwin and Forrester identified working with threatening or abusive parents as the third most common difficulty facing practitioners. They gave an example, in the words of one of the social workers in the study:

> It was terrible, it was absolutely terrible, I mean I haven't gone down to the market since this case because of fear of being attacked. They threatened to kill me, they've actually tried to do all sorts of things, they came into the office, they've assaulted staff, and they've damaged property, they've thrown urine in staff's face, and it was a horrible experience and I would never want to go through that again. (Harwin and Forrester 2002, p.37)

They noted that the fear of assault was much more common than actual assaults, but nevertheless this could have a marked effect on both the worker and their practice. The way in which stress clouds thinking is further demonstrated in the following example from Brandon, Bailey and colleagues' review:

> The capacity to understand the ways in which children are at risk of harm requires clear thinking. Practitioners who are overwhelmed, not just with the volume of work but by the nature of the work, may

not be able to do even the simple things well (Cooper *et al.* 2003; Cooper 2005). One health visitor who was reported to have found her contact with one family 'overwhelming,' gave an example of how this affected her feelings, her behaviour and her thinking: with hindsight...she noted that the family focused her attention on the older children and she found (their) aggression and distrust of other agencies difficult to manage. (Brandon, Bailey *et al.* 2009, p.44)

The emotional impacts described here have a demonstrable effect on practitioners' ability to remain alert and focused on the child during assessment and in longer-term work.

The complex emotional dynamics of much social casework invite attention to a number of other psychological processes that may impact on the practitioner's thinking. For example, in Chapter 4 we noted the way professional systems can come to mirror family systems. In addition, an awareness of processes identified within psychodynamic theory such as transference, counter-transference and projection may contribute to a deeper understanding of the interactions *within* a family, as well as between family members and different professionals.

Systems issues

A number of writers have commented on the difficulties practitioners experience in working with formalised systems that appear to constrain thinking, and draw particular attention to the recording formats – which form part of, for example, the Assessment Framework, the Common Assessment Framework and the Integrated Children's System – that now structure significant areas of assessment practice. In his report, *The Protection of Children in England*, Lord Laming noted that:

> Professional practice and judgement, as said by many who contributed evidence to this report, are being compromised by an over-complicated, lengthy and tick-box assessment and recording system. The direct interaction and engagement with children and their families, which is at the core of social work, is said to be at risk as the needs of a work management tool overtake those of evidence-based assessment, sound analysis and professional judgement about risk of harm. (Laming 2009, p.33)

We return to this point about the effects of proceduralisation and the increased reliance on structured electronic recording templates in Chapter 8.

Professional judgement

The quotation from the second Laming report (above) draws attention to the role and use of professional judgement. In this section we consider the issue of professional judgement in more detail – what supports and what hinders its use in practice, and what kind of knowledge and experience it is based on.

Using assessment frameworks

While concerns have been expressed about the more bureaucratic aspects of the Assessment Framework, Millar and Corby (2006) found that it could have therapeutic potential. Findings from their study of the use of the Assessment Framework based on interviews with service users and social workers suggested, for example, that '[i]t was evident that in some cases the use of the assessment framework facilitated open and clear communication between social workers and service users. The framework itself provided a useful tool for this' (2006, p.892) and contributed to a therapeutic outcome, in the sense that it was 'experienced as an enhancement to personal understanding or well-being' (p.897).

Holland (2010) has taken a slightly different, though not incompatible, line and suggested that a structured assessment framework need not necessarily limit the worker's ability to reflect or engage fully with the complexity of family situations. She noted that the Assessment Framework provided 'the *potential* for complexity and reflection' (p.51), and suggested that there was space in the core assessment records where the social worker provides their analysis of the family situation, to 'give a more transparent explanation to service users and other agencies' (p.51). Arguably, using the assessment framework in this way depends to some extent on the knowledge, skills and values of the practitioner and this more positive approach cannot be guaranteed. As Macdonald (2001) observes, an Assessment Framework can still be used in a way that distorts the assessment and discriminates between groups of service users.

In the previous section we noted the different forms of bias and cognitive error that can impact on thinking and reduce the quality of an assessment. Munro suggests that a framework or checklist for assessment can be crucial 'in reminding practitioners of the full variety of sources of evidence they should be considering' (2008, p.145). While this is potentially a useful function, Macdonald and Williamson make a significant point about the role that frameworks can play, pointing out that:

> Telling people *what* information to collect does not enable them critically to appraise it, to make sense of it, or to recognise its significance. Assessment is a skilled activity, inextricably linked to the knowledge base that informs it. The new framework provides pointers to what it considers to be important knowledge in making good assessment, but in and of itself it cannot address the gaps in people's knowledge or in their assessment skills. (Macdonald and Williamson 2002, p.40)

This point was endorsed by Crisp *et al.* (2007) who also argued that use of a framework such as the Assessment Framework was no guarantee of good practice; rather, that depended on the knowledge and skills of the practitioner and their ability to establish an effective relationship with the service user in the course of the assessment. The importance of professional skill and judgement is also drawn out in Daniel and Baldwin's (2001) study of assessment practices in cases of child neglect. The researchers make a similar point to the one drawn by Macdonald and Williamson (above), concluding that a framework cannot do the job of analysing the information collected in the course of an assessment. 'Guidance by paper' is no substitute for skilled and thoughtful practice:

> A good analysis of the information involves professional judgement, something that cannot be set out in guidance. The problem can be summed up simply: a good social worker can be given a blank piece of paper and will produce a brilliant assessment – a poor social worker can be given a book of guidance and will produce no more than description and a collection of information. Currently it seems that there is an attempt to develop professional judgement via guidance by paper. (Daniel and Baldwin 2001, p.35)

Tools, scales and questionnaires

In the previous section, we noted that frameworks for assessment, such as the Assessment Framework, have been subject to critique on the grounds that 'guidance by paper' (Daniel and Baldwin 2001, p.35) does not support the development of professional judgement. A similar debate is evident in relation to the role and use of tools, scales, and questionnaires in assessment and draws attention to the role and use of professional judgement and practice knowledge.

Studies identify an interesting tension: on the one hand, a number of researchers have commented on the fact that practitioners generally make little use of standardised tools, scales or questionnaires to inform their assessment and plans (Barlow and Schrader-Macmillan 2009; Cleaver *et al.* 2007; Selwyn *et al.* 2006). On the other hand, however, it has been argued that checklists, and the type of tick-box mentality they can give rise to, may undermine the exercise of careful professional judgement (see, for example, Brandon *et al.* 2008; Laming 2009).

The role and usefulness of different tools, checklists, questionnaires and scales has already been discussed, so the arguments are not repeated in detail here. The point to emphasise, though, is that it is not an option simply to ignore these instruments or dismiss them as an unwelcome manifestation of a 'tick-box' culture. As previously noted, Barlow and Scott (2010, p.16) identify the need for 'a "third generation" approach, which consists of "empirically validated, structured decision-making" (White and Walsh 2006) or "structured clinical judgement"', where structured clinical judgement involves 'a combination of both standardised tools and clinical skills' (Barlow and Scott 2010, p.53; also see Bentovim *et al.* 2009 and Jones 2007).

So the value of certain tools should be acknowledged, where they are used to *support*, rather than bypass, thinking (see Corby 2003; Gillingham and Humphreys 2009). Selwyn and colleagues have drawn attention to the importance of tools in cases where it may be necessary to get some understanding of, for example, a person's use of alcohol or their level of learning disability. These are areas where social workers will usually have little expertise but a tool could help identify the need for expert opinion early in the process rather than by the time cases get to court and also help the social worker to understand just how able the parent is to cooperate and engage with the assessment. For example, in their study of costs and outcomes in non-infant adoption (Selwyn *et al.* 2006) there were several examples where the parent's ability had been overestimated by the social worker because they were verbally able, only to find later from a psychological assessment that their IQ was extremely low. This additional information was crucial to an assessment of whether the birth parents could or could not change.

Daniel *et al.* (2009) make the point that using tools and scales is no substitute for professional knowledge and judgement and this is reinforced by a number of authors (for example, Brandon *et al.* 2008; Jack and Gill 2003, p.7). The following quotation from Brandon and her colleagues' second review of serious case reviews succinctly summarises the position:

> There are tools which can be used alongside the Assessment Framework (Department of Health *et al.* 2000) that can help workers

understand the neglect the child is experiencing (like the Graded Care Profile, Strivastava *et al.* 2003) or understand more about strengths and risks of harm in the family like Signs of Safety (Turnell and Edwards 1997). But these tools cannot detect feigned compliance; professional judgement, good supervision and a skilled use of multi-agency expertise and knowledge are essential. (Brandon, Bailey *et al.* 2009, p.113)

The point to draw from this, perhaps, is that 'assessment cannot be replaced by "algorithms" for recognition' (Daniel *et al.* 2009, p.40) but that judicious use of appropriate tools and measures may be helpful in some situations (Bentovim *et al.* 2009). It is also clear that effective use of tools, scales and questionnaires in practice depends on the professional skill, knowledge and judgement of the worker (Quinton 2009). And, of course, if practitioners are going to use different assessment instruments and tools competently and confidently, they will need training in their purpose and proper use – and, as previously noted, this may not be included in social work training (Quinton 2009).

Knowledge to support the exercise of professional judgement

The ability and confidence to exercise professional judgement depends on a secure knowledge base that draws together both relevant academic or research-based understanding and 'practice wisdom'. As has been observed (for example, by Schön 1983, 1987) this latter kind of knowledge is often tacit; in Bell and colleagues' study (2007, p.64), social workers sometimes referred to 'implicit modes of analysis and understanding that undergird good practice'.

The research reviewed identified a number of substantive areas of knowledge that social workers need to be able to draw on to support effective assessment and improve decision making (some of which were identified in Chapter 3). In terms of *content* knowledge – drawing on theoretical knowledge and awareness of the research evidence – the following areas have been highlighted:

- child development (Cleaver and Walker 2004; Holland 2010; Quinton 2009; Ward *et al.* 2010)
- recognising potential signs of child abuse and neglect
- patterns of attachment and children's attachment needs (Farmer and Dance *et al.* 2010; Sinclair 2006; Ward *et al.* 2010)
- issues around parental drug/alcohol misuse, including understanding the impact of substance use on parenting capacity

and the effect on the child (Cleaver *et al.* 1999 and forthcoming; Farmer *et al.* 2011; Farmer and Lutman 2009; Forrester and Harwin 2006, 2008; Harwin and Forrester 2002; Harwin and Ryan 2007)

- domestic violence and its effects on children's wellbeing (Cleaver *et al.* 2007; Hester *et al.* 2007; Rose and Barnes 2008)

- the potential impact of parental mental health difficulties on children's development and wellbeing (Cleaver *et al.* 1999)

- parental learning disability (Cleaver and Nicholson 2007).

Each assessment will also require practitioners to build up case-specific knowledge based on an understanding of family history, structure and living arrangements. In relation to family history, research highlights the importance of:

- the case history and awareness of key past events (Farmer and Lutman 2009)

- the use of chronologies (Brandon *et al.* 2008) – a point also recognised by Lord Laming in the Victoria Climbié Inquiry Report (Laming 2003).

In relation to family structure and living arrangements, the research evidence points to the importance of:

- knowing who the key family members are, who is living in or visiting the home

- 'practical looking' – seeing the different rooms in the house, for example the kitchen or bathroom and where the child sleeps: 'these concrete circumstances are part of the child's life and can be very revealing of the nature of their day to day experience. It also generates information that can be used in accessing the nature of the parental response to the child's needs' (Tanner and Turney 2000, p.345).

Professional judgement depends on the skilled use of theoretical knowledge, applied appropriately in light of the understanding of the particular family's situation. This, in turn, is supported by key conceptual processes, including:

- the ability to recognise the possible relationships between past experiences including previous interventions and present situations and behaviours

- an understanding of the 'meaning of the child' for the parents (Reder et al. 1993).

In addition, professional judgement should not be exercised in a vacuum. Practitioners need to be accountable and their judgements open to scrutiny. At the same time, the kinds of decisions that social workers make are often challenging, complex and made in situations of less than perfect knowledge. So the proper exercise of professional judgement also needs support. Typically, the main forum for both scrutiny and support has been professional, case-based supervision. So in the next section, we look at evidence in relation to the role and importance of supervision and consultancy.

Supervision, consultancy and support

The commonly held view that supervision is critical to the development and maintenance of good practice has been reinforced by Lord Laming (Laming 2003, 2009) and the Social Work Taskforce (2009), and expectations about supervision are incorporated into both *Working Together* (HM Government 2010a) and the requirements for newly qualified social workers' (NQSW) first year in practice (Children's Workforce Development Council 2009). However, detailed information about this aspect of practice is not always available and the methodology of many studies precludes knowledge about the nature and quality of supervision provided. Nonetheless, Brandon (1999) identifies a link (though not statistically significant) between social workers receiving 'good or adequate' supervision and families who had positive outcomes. So in this section we consider the role and importance of supervision and other forms of consultation.

The role and importance of supervision

Working Together (HM Government 2010a, p.123) identifies that good quality supervision can help to:

- keep a focus on the child
- avoid drift
- maintain a degree of objectivity
- challenge fixed ideas
- test and assess the evidence base for assessment and decisions
- address the emotional impact of the work.

It also notes that supervision is 'a critical aspect of the support that employers should provide to social workers' (p.124). It should be both 'educative and supportive', playing a key role in supporting the development of the individual's professional skills and knowledge base and offering the practitioner space to explore their feelings about the work and the families with whom they engage.

Supervision has the capacity to introduce a 'fresh pair of eyes' (Burton 2009) and to challenge assumptions. It offers an opportunity to review and re-appraise understandings of cases and to 'disrupt' habitual or settled patterns of thought, which may be particularly necessary in light of the concerns identified earlier in this chapter about fixed ideas, and the tendency to seek confirming rather than dis-confirming evidence to support one's initial assumptions about a case. The supervisor can take on the role of devil's advocate and offer alternative perspectives or hypotheses. This may not always be easy as problems of 'group think' can occur, for example in review meetings where a particular view or plan can become very difficult to challenge (see, for example, Farmer 1999).

Of course, supervision is neither infallible nor always a positive experience (for supervisor or supervisee). The kind of reflective supervision we have discussed here makes practical and emotional demands on the supervisor that may be similar to those experienced by the practitioner they are advising and managing. They too may miss things or not pick up on gaps in thinking, so there may be occasions when supervision can usefully be offered by someone who is 'outside' the case and therefore less prone to being drawn in to the casework dynamics – a similar approach to the one that has been advocated for the organisational audit or health check recommended by the Social Work Task Force.

As noted, supervision can provide a space in which the practitioner can be helped to 'keep thinking alive' in a context that supports the development of reflective practice. Alternatively, though, it may evoke a managerialist response, linked to the need to meet performance indicators. The value of reflective supervision – and the importance of the organisational context within which it occurs – is emphasised by Brandon, Bailey and colleagues:

> Because working with children and families is difficult and stressful, practitioners need to work in safe 'containing' organisations that allow them to be curious and encourage them to puzzle over what is happening in families. Organisations need to deal helpfully and

supportively, not defensively, with the complexity of practice and decision-making. Ruch makes a good case for reflective practice which offers a response to cases, like many of the case reviews in this report, which can appear confusingly 'similar yet different'. Reflective practice:

Acknowledges the uniqueness of each individual and practice encounter and the diverse types of knowledge required to address the complex issues these encounters generate (Ruch 2007, p.660). (Brandon, Bailey *et al.* 2009, p.114)

Different approaches to supporting analytical thinking and professional judgement

Formal supervision is not the only way to encourage practitioners to develop critical, analytical and reflective thinking. Different approaches can be used to support the process of thinking purposefully and clearly about referrals, assessments and decisions; for example, group or peer supervision can become a regular part of a team's programme of meetings, or multi-agency fora can be set up, perhaps on a district-wide basis, to provide advice and/or consultation on particular areas of practice (examples include the Nottinghamshire and Nottingham City LSCB's Multi-Agency Forum for Emotional Abuse; Bristol LSCB Emotional Abuse Multi-Agency Forum; London Borough of Camden's Complexity Forum). While there has been little research into the use of such groups, there is anecdotal evidence that practitioners may find them a valuable source of advice and support in dealing with complex and challenging cases.

Other ways of providing advice and consultancy to practitioners include strategies for using other professionals' expertise. As part of their adoption survey Dance *et al.* (2010) asked local authorities about their use of tools or other specific approaches to the assessment of children and observed that this question also gave the participants a chance to describe any examples of good or innovative practice in this area. Of the 32 agencies that responded on this particular issue, a 'major innovation' (reported by 19 agencies) in relation to assessing children's needs was the involvement of child psychologists. Different arrangements were found: 12 of the 19 agencies provided formal opportunities for social workers to consult with either individual psychologists or multidisciplinary teams; seven agencies reported that these professionals were attached to the adoption team, and other agencies 'mentioned referral of children for psychological assessment when this was felt to be needed' (p.50).

In contrast, issues have been raised in some studies about the knowledge and level of qualification of staff in some agencies, at particular levels of intervention. For example, Brandon, Bailey *et al.* (2009, p.62) note that some overview reports indicated that staff 'working at both levels 1 and 2 and with cases on the threshold of receipt of services from children's social care, were not appropriately qualified to assess or deal with the level of complexity evident in the children who required family support services'. They also found that, in some instances, complex neglect cases were 'left' with less qualified – or, indeed, unqualified – staff. This perhaps reflects a concern noted earlier, by a number of writers that the potentially severe impact of neglect on children's health and development was not widely enough recognised; cases were not given priority and were not seen as sufficiently serious to cross the child protection threshold, or even the threshold for assessment by children's social care services, a point we noted in Chapter 2.

Conclusion

This chapter identified that good assessment involves more than just information gathering; it needs the worker to be able to *analyse* and make sense of the material. So the nature and quality of social work thinking is a critical part of the assessment process and should be informed by a clear theoretical framework. The transactional-ecological approach proposed by Brandon *et al.* (2008; Brandon, Bailey *et al.* 2009) appears to offer a helpful way of thinking about the interconnecting risk and protective factors in families' lives. Critical and analytical thinking is challenging and takes time and energy. A number of factors can undermine the capacity to think purposefully and effectively and these operate at practical, cognitive/psychological, emotional and systemic/ organisational levels. However, there are also factors that may support and promote it, and reflective supervision may be particularly important in this regard. Frameworks and the use of tools can support assessment practice but these should be used in support of, rather than as a substitute for, the exercise of professional judgement – and that depends on the knowledge and skills of competent and confident practitioners.

Thinking and reasoning play a critical part in the assessment process but, to be effective, must be grounded in a thorough understanding of the child and family's situation, needs and strengths. And to gain this knowledge, the social worker needs to engage directly with the child and their family – assessment must be a 'relational activity' (Rose 2009, p.43). So, in the next chapter, we move on to consider this aspect of assessment practice and the research evidence informing an understanding of professional engagement with children, young people and their families.

Summary

- Effective assessment needs to move beyond the simple collection of information (that is, a record of *what* happened) to consideration of *why*; it requires the social worker to understand and *analyse* the information collected and to come to a decision about how to proceed. The ability to think critically and analytically and to convey the results both verbally and in writing is essential for good assessment practice. Longstanding difficulties in relation to analysis have been identified that have had a damaging effect on practice and outcomes for children.

- An 'assessment mindset' draws on a range of reasoning skills and needs to be supported by a clear theoretical framework. The Assessment Framework identifies three inter-related 'domains' as a basis for the assessment of children in need and the transactional-ecological model proposed by Brandon *et al.* (2008, 2010; Brandon, Bailey *et al.* 2009) offers an effective framework for understanding the ways in which different risk and protective factors interact.

- Intuition and analytical thinking have a place and are helpfully seen as complementary rather than as antagonistic or mutually exclusive approaches. While there is little empirical research on social work thinking, there is a wider theoretical and practice-based literature, and Munro's work (2008) in particular provides much food for thought about the use and effects of different modes of reasoning.

- A number of factors can hinder the process of analysis and critical thinking and undermine the exercise of professional judgement, for example: cognitive errors and everyday habits of thought such as fixed thinking and/or 'verificationism'; practical demands, including pressure of work and tight deadlines for the completion of assessment tasks; emotional impacts of the work on the worker (for example, the effects of fear, violence and/or stress); and systemic and organisational issues.

- Assessment tools, measures and checklists can be used to support information gathering and analysis by reminding practitioners of key areas to explore and also providing baseline data on specific issues, such as misuse of alcohol or drugs. Workers need to have a good understanding of when and how to use these tools and the limitations of the various measures – their use cannot be a substitute for sound professional knowledge and judgement.

- Professional judgement must be supported by a sound knowledge base that includes awareness of research evidence. Although there is little direct research evidence, it is likely that analytical and critical thinking can be supported and encouraged in the context of case-based reflective supervision which takes place in an organisational culture that supports reflecting and learning. Other forms of peer/group supervision and consultancy may also contribute to the promotion of effective thinking in practice.

Chapter 6

ENGAGING WITH CHILDREN, YOUNG PEOPLE AND THEIR PARENTS

Over the last 30 years a recurring theme in inquiry reports and serious case reviews has been the way that professionals have lost sight of the child. Reports into child deaths have shown that children were sometimes literally not seen by social workers or, if seen, were not engaged with in a meaningful way (for example, Blom-Cooper 1985; Bridge Child Care Consultancy 1995; Laming 2003; London Borough of Greenwich 1987; London Borough of Newham ACPC 2002). In this chapter we address an aspect of practice that is critical to assessment, namely that of social workers' engagement with the children and young people whose needs are being assessed and with their parents. We look first at why children and young people should be involved in assessments.

Children and young people's voices

Why involve children and young people?

The Children Act 1989 has been described as opening the way for the establishment of principles that have given children an increasing influence on decision making (Thomas 2000). The signing, in 1991, of the United Nations Convention on the Rights of the Child set out a comprehensive set of children's rights. Article 12 of the Convention states that children and young people have the right to express their views freely in all areas that they are involved in, and Article 4 states that that these views should be listened to and respected. Subsequent legislation (for example, the Childcare Act 2006) and the establishment of a Commissioner for Children have confirmed the policy commitment to children and young people's participation.

The legal requirements and policy commitments to ascertaining children's wishes and feelings are underpinned by research. Engaging children and young people in social work assessments is important because it provides information on circumstances and concerns from a different perspective to that of the adults and provides a better basis for planning.

It also enables children and young people to believe that they have the ability to create change and have control over elements of their lives. Young people's belief in their capabilities to exert control over events is a protective factor in the face of adversity and is linked to the development of resilience (Bostock 2004). Better relationships are formed when children and young people believe that their opinions are respected and research has found that placements are more likely to be stable if children and young people are in agreement with the plan (Sinclair 2005).

Excluding children and young people from the processes that affect them may leave them feeling helpless and disengaged and can mean that key information about their needs, or the risks affecting them, has not been obtained.

Research findings on children and young people's voices in assessments

In reviewing relevant material we distinguish between studies that sought children and young people's views about assessment and those that used case files and other documentary evidence to consider how far their wishes and feelings were recorded and reported. Some information about children's views on a variety of topics is available in reports compiled by the Children's Rights Director (see, for example, Morgan 2010). But our review included relatively few studies that had sought children's views directly through face-to-face interviews and where this had occurred the sample numbers were often quite small. In terms of this review, Bell (2002) explored the views of 27 children and young people about their experience of child protection investigations from first contact, through to assessment and subsequent interventions. Whilst the sample may not have been representative, she described as striking the finding that the majority of children and young people had had a positive relationship with one of the social workers they had known. The minority who had not had this experience were those the study identified as having been wary and distrustful throughout the process of professional involvement. Cleaver (2000) echoed this finding in a study of contact arrangements for children in foster care. She found difficulties in establishing the children's wishes and feelings because of an unwillingness or inability 'to talk with social workers about sensitive and emotive issues' (2000, p.272). It should be noted, however, that the success of a child's relationship with their social worker arises from a range of factors, including the skills of the worker involved.

Some studies have captured children's views about whether they were consulted about their needs and the services provided. For example, Butler and Astbury (2005) in their evaluation of a young carers' support service recorded some quite hard-hitting comments from their interviews. Young people's concerns related particularly to local authority social workers not listening to them, not taking account of their needs and fears, breaking promises and being overly concerned with cost-effectiveness. Cleaver's study of contact between children who were looked after and their families (2000) found problems with the young people's involvement in the decision-making process in relation to placements; the findings from the qualitative study of a sample group of children aged 5–12 suggested that 'in two thirds of the cases, children were ill-informed about their forthcoming placement' (Sinclair 2005, p.131). On the other hand, Aldgate and Bradley (1999), in their study of families using short-term fostering arrangements, found that almost all the older children remembered being given information about what was happening, and more than half felt they had been consulted about decisions. However, the authors also highlighted that children and young people felt that they had had little opportunity to disagree with plans or to have plans changed. It is certainly true that social workers often face the dilemma, when consulting children, that there may be limited opportunity to alter the plans that have been made, for example in relation to substitute care placements, where there may be little choice of placement (see, for example, Sinclair 2005).

Turning to the studies that collected data about children's engagement from case files and other records, several identified a failure to consult with children and young people at various stages of their involvement with children's social care services. For example, Brandon et al. (1999), in a sample of 105 new child protection referrals, found no evidence that children or young people's opinions were specifically sought about placing their names on the child protection register,[1] although 45 per cent of the sample were under five years of age. Cleaver et al. (2007), in their study of social work and child protection in the context of domestic violence and substance misuse, reported that the child had been seen in three-quarters of the initial assessment cases in their sample. The rate was higher in cases of alleged domestic violence. Farmer et al.'s (2011) study of reunification showed that in a third of cases of children aged over four, the case files indicated children had been consulted about the return home, although files may under-report such consultation. In addition, they found from interviews that there were a few children who would have preferred to have remained looked after, but had not always been able to make their views known. Ninety-one per cent of the children and young people aged five or over in Wade, Biehal et al.'s (2010) study of maltreated children who stayed in care or returned home were reported as having been consulted during the planning process. Interestingly, Broadhurst, Wastell et al. (2010) found evidence of 'short-cuts' that involved social work teams recording the child as 'seen', at the initial assessment stage, even if they had only been seen by another professional such as a teacher or health visitor. Apart from Broadhurst et al.'s finding, it is tempting to regard this set of findings as indicative of improving practice over time. Unfortunately, the differences of focus and methodology make the studies difficult to compare, and such a conclusion would be difficult to support.

A number of studies have shown that the amount of information recorded on children's views was limited. Cleaver et al.'s (2008) study of the Integrated Children's System found that much less information was recorded about children than about their parents. In studies of Common Assessment Framework assessments and referrals, Pithouse (2006) found minimal evidence of the recording of children's views, nor of children or young people's consent for the assessment to take place (Pithouse et al. 2009). Daniel and Baldwin (2001) suggested a need for more recording of direct quotations from children in assessments and of direct observations of children to address the frequent lack of such information on files. Preston-Shoot (2003) reported on the absence of the child's voice in a range of case file documents, including those relevant to the assessment process, and Thomas and Holland (2010) commented that social workers often relied on the parents' views of the child (in this case on the child's identity) rather than seeking information from children themselves. In addition, as noted in Chapter 3, Holland (2010) showed that children were often described in two-dimensional terms in assessments, with much less analysis of their needs than of those of their parents.

Barriers to the involvement of children and young people in assessment

A number of reasons have been suggested to explain why social workers have difficulty communicating with children and young people. For example, Broadhurst, Wastell *et al.* (2010) acknowledged that seeing and assessing children can be difficult because of trying to complete initial assessments within the seven-working-day timescale. This study predates the change of timescale from seven to ten working days (HM Government 2010a), but the problem of seeing and assessing children adequately is known to have existed before any such timescales came into being (see, for example, Reder and Duncan 1999). Rose and Barnes (2008) noted that observation and direct work with children was time-consuming and emotionally challenging. They argued that greater attention should be given to the emotional impact on workers of extensive engagement with children and their parents, as well as to workers' understandable fears of resistance, hostility or even violence from parents (see also, for example, Stanley and Goddard 2002). This suggests that appropriate opportunities for reflection and support are likely to be needed by social workers to prevent a disconnection from the needs of the child.

Holland (2010) described some of the difficulties of gaining children's views during assessment because of children's concerns about confidentiality, their loyalty to their parents, and anxiety about the consequences for their parents of what they might say. There can even be direct consequences for the children themselves. In an earlier study, Farmer and Owen (1995) showed that one of the possible consequences of a disclosure of maltreatment was that children were sometimes abused by a parent in retaliation. Selwyn *et al.* (2006) made the interesting point that there can be real difficulty for social workers in distinguishing between parenting behaviour that meets the parents' own needs and parenting aimed at meeting the child's needs. This could lead to children and their needs being overlooked.

There is a complex relationship between a lack of focus on the child, and work with the parent/s. Brandon and colleagues (2008), in their review of serious case reviews, suggested that a lack of professional focus on the child may be linked to patterns of parental cooperation. They cited examples where parents made it difficult for children to be seen alone, deflected attention away from allegations of maltreatment, and how the parents' needs sometimes dominated attention to the extent of overshadowing the needs of the child. Farmer and Lutman (2009), too, in their longitudinal study of neglect, noted that at times the number and range of child and family problems made working with the families difficult and sometimes children's neglect was marginalised in favour of other issues.

In their second review of serious case reviews, Brandon, Bailey *et al.* (2009) built on this picture by describing an 'enmeshed interaction between overwhelmed families and overwhelmed professionals [that] contributed to the child being lost or unseen' (p.3). Misunderstandings about what could be done, or about managing confidentiality, contributed to the difficulties, and erroneous assumptions were made about steps that other agencies were taking. They also expressed concern about a strengths-based approach getting in the way of standing back and analysing the risks of harm to the child (although the importance of enhancing families' strengths – in appropriate cases – should not be underestimated). These findings resonate with those of Farmer and Lutman (2009), who found reluctance amongst professionals to act in cases of neglect. They speculated on the reasons for this, suggesting that social workers might not wish to believe that parents with whom they had a relationship could have maltreated their children. They suggested that workers might also want to avoid damaging relationships with the family, avoid stigmatising already disadvantaged families, may be over-identifying with the parents, and that there is a habituation associated with long-term work in this field, which might desensitise workers to the extent of children's difficulties.

Keeping older young people 'in focus'

Keeping the child at the centre of the assessment process can be a particular issue in relation to older young people. A number of studies commented on an apparent unwillingness to intervene with this group, in some cases because of a (possibly misplaced) reluctance to bring young people into local authority care, or in response to perceived pressures to ration resources. This lesser level of engagement (Hicks and Stein 2010; Stein *et al.* 2007) may also reflect a misunderstanding of the vulnerability of older young people and a belief that they will sort things out for themselves, or that practitioners do not follow up contact with the young person if initially rebuffed. However, evidence from serious case reviews undertaken by Brandon and colleagues (Brandon *et al.* 2008;

Brandon, Bailey *et al.* 2009) highlights the vulnerability of this group. In both studies, approximately 10 per cent of cases involved young people aged 16–17; of these over 80 per cent died, reflecting the many suicides in this age group. It is important, therefore, that practitioners are aware of the potentially significant impact of neglect and abuse on these young people and that agencies have appropriate strategies and resources in place to address their needs.

Good practice in engaging children and young people

We turn now to what may constitute good practice in engagement with children and young people. Franklin and Sloper (2005), in a study of the participation of disabled children and young people, identified some examples of ways of involving them in assessment and planning. All the research has shown that disabled children want the same things as any other child. Franklin and Sloper (2005) drew attention to the need for social workers to have the competence and confidence to communicate effectively with children who use alternative and/or non-verbal modes of communication. For example, children's preference may be to express themselves through art or writing. The National Children's Bureau (NCB) have provided a number of tools to help social workers listen to and work with children (Dalzell and Chamberlain 2006; National Children's Bureau undated). There are also practice guides (for example, Clark and Moss 2001; Marchant and Jones 2003) which offer useful help on communicating with children. However, social workers may not have the opportunity to use these skills regularly enough to develop them to an appropriate level, nor the time to spend with the child or young person that would enable them to get to know the child properly and understand their preferred method of communication.

Wade and his colleagues (2005) identified a preference for the exchange model of assessment (Smale *et al.* 1993) amongst social workers working with unaccompanied asylum-seeking children and young people. The exchange model involves engaging the service user in their own assessment, identifying their needs and priorities in their own terms. It contrasts with a questioning model, where the social worker takes more of the role of expert and asks questions determined by a pre-set format. Use of the exchange model implies greater engagement with service recipients and places their definition of their needs at centre stage.

In terms of promoting good practice, Cleaver *et al.* (2004) and Butler and Williamson (1994) found that the children and young people wanted social workers to:

- take time to explain what is happening and why
- listen to them, and respect their views and experiences
- believe what they said
- be honest, reliable and straight talking
- talk to people they think are the important ones to talk to
- give them something to remind them of what was decided.

These findings are reasonably consistent with those of Bell in the study of children's views referred to above:

> The tasks for social workers and other professionals are clearly indicated by the children themselves. They want to be seen alone, they want to have the time and opportunity to build a relationship, they want information that is accessible and appropriate, and they want to be offered real choices about what services are available and the range of ways participation and representation can take place in decision-making forums. (Bell 2002, p.10)

Summary

In this section, on children and young people's voices, we reviewed the importance of focusing on the child or young person and presented key research findings relevant to engagement with children and young people. Giving the child a central place in assessments is not simple and a range of barriers may make good practice difficult to achieve. The research findings suggested a range of systemic difficulties that appeared to contribute to a loss of focus on the child. These points are presented in Table 6.1 as a means of summarising the important issues. Organisations may find it helpful to review these barriers on a regular basis, with a view to developing and maintaining ways of managing them. The points were derived, by the review team, from the studies described above.

Table 6.1 Barriers to maintaining a focus on the child

Organisational	Interpersonal	System
• Lack of time • Short cuts and 'work arounds' • Lack of knowledge and skills needed for observation and direct work with children • Habituation to low standards of parenting	• Understanding children's loyalty to their parents • Concerns about managing confidentiality • Over-identification with parents • Parents making it difficult for children to be seen • Parents diverting attention from concerns • Misusing strengths-based approaches • Fears of violence • Emotional impact of the work	• Pressure to deliver cost effectiveness • Professionals feeling overwhelmed

Relationships between parents and professionals
Conditions for working together with parents

Turning to engagement of professionals with parents, we begin by reviewing the conditions needed for good relationships. A considerable amount of work has been undertaken over the past two decades to try to improve our understanding of how professionals can work with parents and, where possible, work 'in partnership' with them. Arguably, the way social workers engage parents is fundamental to most assessments, an essential building block for planning suitable interventions arising out of the assessment. As long ago as 1995 a set of principles for working in partnership with parents was published in government practice guidance (Department of Health and Social Services Inspectorate 1995), most of which continue to have relevance today. More recently, although not focused specifically on assessments, an international review of research and relevant experimental studies (Trotter 2002, 2008) presented an important set of skills needed for working with involuntary clients. These principles are reproduced below:

- *Role clarification:* Ensure clarity about what the worker can or can't do, what the client's role is, and what each can expect from the other.

- *Collaborative problem solving:* Provide help to address the problems that led to the current situation; the worker needs to take a collaborative approach.

- *Pro-social modelling and reinforcement:* Identify and try to build on pro-social strengths, such as good relationships within the extended family. Worker should model 'good behaviour' by keeping appointments and doing what they said they would do.

- *Challenge and confrontation:* Extreme challenging is generally unhelpful although some level of challenge is appropriate. Better outcomes occurred where clients believed that workers were clear about their own authority and how they might use it.

(Summarised from Trotter 2008)

Our review of assessment-related findings in recent UK research generally supported and complemented the principles put forward by Trotter. Corby, Millar and Pope, for example, in their study of parents' experiences of the implementation of the Assessment Framework, suggested key factors in ensuring that assessments were carried out in a way that was meaningful and helpful to parents. These factors were as follows:

> The knowledge, skill and attitude of the assessor; an ability to tailor the standardised format to the individual situation; a willingness to listen carefully both to children and parents and demonstrate empathy and respect; clarity about the specific purpose of the assessment; a positive belief in parents' ability to change. (Corby, Millar and Pope 2002, p.12)

Whilst several of these points are commonly recognised good practice, the need for clarity about the purpose of the assessment appears to us to be particularly important (as mentioned in Chapter 5). A clear sense of purpose may be not always be easy to communicate to parents and children, but it is important that practitioners are themselves clear about the purpose of each assessment undertaken and that they convey this to parents and children as effectively as they can. And clearly a belief in the parent/s' ability to change will be virtually impossible in cases where change is very unlikely (Thoburn and Making Research Count Continuum 2009, see Chapter 4).

In a similar vein, Platt (2008) examined engagement between social workers and parents mainly in the context of initial assessments of children in need. He characterised workers' skills in establishing and maintaining relationships with parents as 'sensitivity, honesty and straightforwardness, and listening and accurate understanding' (p.306). He confirmed that it was often easier to establish a good relationship with a parent when using a less coercive form of intervention (for example, an initial assessment rather than section 47 enquiry). This degree of *formal* coercion was not, however, the only determining factor. Efforts by a social worker to assess reported concerns that fell short of the section 47 ('child protection') threshold could also affect the relationship adversely. An example of this was a lone parent of a child with emotional and behavioural difficulties who experienced a social worker's questions about her parenting capacity as intimidating, suggesting the importance of worker skill in undertaking such assessments. These findings are consistent with a study of section 47 enquiries by Bell (1999), and with research into Common Assessment Framework (CAF) assessments. Gilligan and Manby (2008) found that parents' levels of involvement were dependent on the skills of practitioners, and parents' appreciation of a 'straight talking' social worker was confirmed by Ward *et al.* (2010). The relationship between coercive interventions and poorer relationships with parents was also evident in a study of children for whom adoption was planned (Selwyn *et al.* 2006), where there were much more significant difficulties in engaging parents, probably reflecting the more serious actions related to adoption.

Parents with learning disabilities

Several studies have given attention to engaging parents with learning disabilities. One concern is for the rights of the parents as disabled people, and how they may be balanced against the rights of their children to good standards of care and nurture. Cleaver and Nicholson (2007) found that parents with learning disabilities were rarely given details about their rights. In only 3 of 26 cases were they given the necessary information, compared with 6 of 14 cases in a comparison group of parents without learning disabilities. In spite of this, there was a fair amount of evidence in the study of social workers' commitment to working in partnership with learning disabled parents. Practitioners were more likely to record the views of parents with learning disabilities than those without and they spent considerable amounts of time explaining things to them.

Unfortunately, in spite of this additional attention, a number of parents with learning disabilities were unable to recall anyone explaining to them why they would be carrying out an assessment, and there were gaps in their understanding of the processes they had experienced. Strategies social workers used in working with parents with learning disabilities included the following:

> Using a close relative or friend in interviews to act as an intermediary; arranging for interviews to take place at the social work office to cut down the distractions and keep parents focused on the task in hand; including other known professionals in meetings to reassure parents and put them at their ease; arranging for families to attend family centres to help with the assessment of parents' capacity to develop and learn relevant parenting skills. (Cleaver and Nicholson 2007, p.106)

The study noted, however, that parents with learning disabilities may find family centres intimidating if, as people with learning disabilities, they are in a minority. Booth and Booth (2005) undertook research into the experiences of parents with learning disabilities going through care proceedings, from the assessment stage through to the courtroom experience and afterwards. They reported on the importance to the parents of the social worker's attitude. This, they suggested, was defined by three qualities (p.115): 'a readiness to listen', 'not being bossy' and 'being helpful'.

Booth, McConnell and Booth (2006), drawing on information from the same study, also identified the problem for parents with learning disabilities of managing time. In this context, difficulties in keeping appointments, attending meetings, keeping a diary or calendar and so forth contributed to professional perceptions of lack of cooperation.

Some of the ideas for good practice from these studies apply to all parents, not just those with learning disabilities. Cleaver *et al.* (2007), for example, highlighted good practice in sharing records and reports with parents and with young people. Their results showed that social workers were particularly appreciated where they went through reports with the parent or young person, reading, explaining and discussing relevant points. The ability of parents with learning disabilities to demonstrate cooperation with professionals is another issue, to which we will return later in this chapter.

Barriers to good engagement with parents

There are, of course, a range of barriers to achieving good relationships between parents and social workers. A number of authors have highlighted the difficulty of working with involuntary clients. In child protection full partnership is achieved in only a few cases (see Thoburn,

Lewis and Shemmings 1995). Clearly, the difficulty in this context is related to keeping the focus on the child at the same time as developing or maintaining a working relationship with the parent, or, put another way, it is necessary to manage the processes leading to coercive decisions whilst maintaining productive involvement from parents. Clifford and Burke, in their study of the variable use made by local authorities of voluntary adoption agencies, found this balancing act to be a significant feature. Their findings related the problem to the context of making a good assessment of the situation:

> In our research, workers knew well that it was '…very important to be sensitive towards the service user, and to make a relationship with them'. Although this question was not the focus of our research, the majority of social workers raised this issue as a matter of concern. They deliberated on the problems of '…managing the inherent contradiction and tensions of working towards rehabilitation whilst simultaneously thinking about permanent placement', and used various strategies to ensure as far as possible continued partnership with the birth mothers, but also to make the best assessment for the child. One interviewee commented that: '…because she became so close to the family, and especially to the birth parent…it was hard to be detached about what was right for the child. Sometimes she would now raise this with her senior, and suggest an additional independent source for assessment such as the psychiatric service.' (Clifford and Burke 2004, p.313)

Millar and Corby's (2006) findings in their research into the use of the Assessment Framework proposed three factors that can work against good communication between social workers and parents. These can be summarised as:

1. a reluctance to voice concerns about the care of the child that might lead to conflict with the parents

2. the difficulty for practitioners of communicating explanations of social work decisions, where those processes are often more intuitive and less consciously formulated

3. shortage of time.

Forrester and colleagues (2008) explored social workers' reactions to case vignettes in the context of discussing child welfare concerns with parents and working with resistance. The research focused on identifying the skills social workers used in response to certain kinds of communication from service users. Their findings indicated (in contrast to Millar and Corby 2006) a high level of confrontation and also a low level of listening, a tendency for workers to impose their own agenda and low levels of empathy. These shortcomings were so pervasive that they suggested there were underlying systemic problems and that social workers might be overusing confrontational approaches because of the 'double-bind' of avoiding collusion with parents, at the same time as needing to use listening skills and show genuine empathy.

A critical issue for social workers in attempting to engage parents is the presence or otherwise of denial of family problems, an issue that can affect initial and core assessments in particular. Working with parents who denied their own substance misuse was identified as the most common problem raised by social work practitioners working with a sample of alcohol- and drug-misusing parents (Harwin and Forrester 2002). Social workers adopted a range of strategies in an attempt to find evidence of substance misuse where they suspected it. Cleaver *et al.* (2007), similarly, suggested that alcohol or drug misuse were key factors in cases where the social workers were finding it difficult to engage the parents. There was continued evidence from research that parents in these and other circumstances sometimes did not tell social workers about their problems out of fear of the children being removed (Farmer and Lutman 2009; Harwin and Ryan 2007).

It is perhaps unsurprising that problems of engagement or compliance on the part of parents were identified in many of the studies reviewed. Farmer and Lutman (2009) in their research on neglect found that there were difficulties in engaging 69 per cent of the mothers and 54 per cent of the father figures. As examples, they cited restrictiveness about the times professionals could visit, refusals to communicate with professionals, selective mutism and failures to comply with key requirements or conditions. Overall, they found that two-fifths (39%) of the parents actively resisted or attempted to sabotage work. Selwyn *et al.* (2006, p.38), similarly, noted that social workers often had to deal with families 'who were hard to support, whose circumstances were complex, or who acted deviously'. Factors of this kind were evident in well over half the cases in their follow-up sample of children for whom adoption had been planned. The existence of these difficulties appears to support the view, expressed in Chapter 3, that a range of tools and other methods should be used in the assessment of parenting.

Good assessment requires a range of effective communication skills, but working across language barriers may be particularly challenging for all involved. Some studies have indicated that service users may not always be offered the option of being interviewed and assessed in their language of choice (Chand 2005; Hatton *et al.* 2004). Given the complexity and sensitivity of the issues being addressed in many social work assessments, this seems a significant loss and may contribute to an additional risk of misunderstanding on both sides, or of deliberate manipulation of the assessment process. We discuss the consequences of not developing a shared understanding in the next section, and will return to the question of deliberate manipulation in Chapter 7.

Each of the studies in this section has given an insight into the tensions and dilemmas involved in much social work with children and young people, particularly where there are significant concerns for the children's welfare. Other research findings on assessment and decision making, which are explored in the next two sections, highlight the link between the working relationship of social worker and parents and the extent of shared understanding of the parents' situation.

Shared understandings between parents and professionals

The relationship which develops between parents and professionals is crucial to obtaining relevant information for assessments, and is a factor that affects all types of assessment process. As the assessment progresses, the degree of agreement between parents and professionals becomes a central feature and may lead to greater cooperation in planning subsequent interventions, which in turn might lead to improved outcomes for the child. Whilst acknowledging that agreement may be based on false understandings, in this section we review research findings that help us to understand the degree of agreement (sometimes referred to as congruence) between parents and professionals in the context of assessments. In the following section we turn to the relationship between this engagement and subsequent events.

Corby and colleagues (2002), in a study based on a mixed sample of cases involving initial and core assessments, showed that it was possible, in some cases, to achieve a shared understanding between professionals and parents about their needs, and that this could lead to improved outcomes for children. Platt (2007), in turn, proposed a simple typology of congruence, based on a study of initial assessments using a sample of families with children in need where the referral information was considered borderline to the child protection threshold, and in a very few cases led to an investigation:

- *Actual congruence.* The assessed needs were perceived as congruent by the parent, and the 'fit' was very close between how the worker described the situation, and how the parent described it.

- *Perceived congruence.* The assessment was perceived as fully congruent by the parent, but the worker's view, whilst including the parent's view, was broader than that presented by the parent.

- *Partial congruence.* There were aspects of the assessment that the parent disagreed with, or they did not fully understand the social worker's view.

- *Incongruent.* The situation of serious and significant differences of opinion between worker and parent.

(Summarised from Platt 2007)

This, and other studies such as that by Aldgate and Bradley (1999), showed that shared understanding can occur on two separate dimensions: agreement regarding the *problems* the family faces, and agreement about the most appropriate *plan of action* to address those problems (i.e. the service response). Aldgate and Bradley (1999) found parents to be most satisfied with the degree of consultation where there was a shared agenda with the social worker regarding their problems.

In an earlier study, Farmer and Owen (1995) identified three dimensions of agreement or disagreement between parents and professionals about problems of abuse or neglect when children were placed on the child protection register. They were agreement regarding commission of the maltreatment (i.e. whether or not it had occurred), culpability for it (i.e. who had caused the harm) and whether the child was still at risk of further harm. They noted that it was important for practitioners not only to consider professional concerns about children, but also to address the parents' views of current risks to their children, which might be different but valid, such as those arising, for example, from the lack of a stair gate or from the activities of local drug dealers.

The role of parental cooperation or engagement in planning and decision making

The discussion so far has shown that agreement between parents and professionals about the nature of child and family difficulties can contribute to a positive working relationship. Cleaver and colleagues (2007), in their study of domestic violence and parental substance misuse, found that where social workers had a good relationship with the parents, the parents 'were more likely to cooperate with the plans for the children' (p.105). The pattern of causation of this effect, however, is complex, and is likely to be bi-directional. For more detailed discussion, see Platt 2007. There was also evidence that social workers *assessed* the current degree of cooperation by parents as part of their overall approach to assessing the needs of the child (Holland 2010; Platt 2005) and that this assessment then contributed to decision making.

Holland (2010) painted a picture of parents being well regarded by the social worker if they conformed to key expectations, such as providing plausible and insightful explanations of their behaviour. She suggested that agreeing a *plausible explanation* of the family's problems between social worker and parents was the most important factor affecting the relationship between the two parties, and ultimately the outcome of the assessment. She highlighted the disempowered position of parents in the assessment relationship:

> The parent was required not simply to co-operate and accept concerns, but to provide an adequate explanation to the social worker of how those concerns arose and to show contrition for past acts. Such interactions can take on a nature that is almost confessional, with the worker rewarded for their sensitive questioning through disclosures made by the parent of feelings of shame, or with the parent changing their story to acceptance and explanation of their wrong-doing. On the other hand, explanations were inadequate if they were made implausible due to inconsistencies and denials. (Holland 2010, p.82)

Even more powerful, perhaps, than this concept of the plausible explanation were those parents who had taken responsibility themselves, irrespective of social work involvement, for tackling the problems they faced. Interventions de-escalated in such circumstances (Platt 2007), and support packages were more limited.

Following assessment, the issue of parental cooperation or engagement is thus likely to make a significant contribution to decisions regarding further action (Brandon *et al.* 2008; Holland 2010; Iwaniec *et al.* 2004; Platt 2007). A review of studies of care proceedings (Brophy 2006) showed that in the majority of cases lack of parental cooperation was a significant factor in being involved in care proceedings (see also Masson *et al.* 2008). This pattern was repeated in relation to emergency protection orders (Masson, Oakley and Pick 2004) and in the decision whether or not to return a child home (Farmer *et al.* 2011; Wade, Biehal *et al.* 2010). Holland (2010), however, identified a small number of parents where, despite their cooperation, reunification did not take place because they had not provided a plausible explanation of their difficulties. Brandon and colleagues' (2008) study of serious case reviews suggested that a questioning mindset was needed concerning the likely reasons for the cooperation (or lack of it), and why parents might be behaving in a particular way with a particular professional at a particular time. At a most basic level, it is frequently the case that engagement with parents is more satisfactory with one parent (typically the woman) than with others, a factor that suggests a need for caution in the way 'parental' engagement is assessed and addressed (see, for example, Ashley *et al.* 2006).

Thus, the issue is not a simple one of poor cooperation leading to coercive state intervention. As Dickens (2007) suggested, paradoxically, parental non-cooperation can be an effective way of deterring court applications, since in certain cases it might prevent professionals from obtaining the necessary evidence to succeed in court. Farmer and Lutman (2009) too, in their study of neglect, noted that very little action was taken by social workers in response to problems such as parental obstructiveness, and in around one-fifth of such families the case was closed *because* of the lack of engagement. Interestingly, of the 40 families examined by Sinclair and Bullock (2002) in their review of serious case reviews, just over a quarter of the parents were categorised as 'fully co-operative and keen to receive help', a category that excluded all cases where there was evidence of non-cooperation including disguised compliance. This finding gives an indication, rendered important by the non-random nature of the sample, that good parental cooperation with professionals does not assure children's safety and many other issues need to be considered. On a similar theme, Barlow and Scott (2010), in a review of research that may have implications for the future of safeguarding practice, cautioned against viewing a parent's commitment to working with individual professionals as indicative of an ability to change. Their view has been echoed in recent findings by Ward *et al.* (2010) in a study of infants identified as suffering or likely to suffer significant harm. They found that the superficial features of parental engagement with services (such as keeping appointments or allowing social workers access to the child) could be misleading and were not indicative of a real willingness or ability to change.

Since social workers assessed parental engagement largely through verbal interactions, those parents who did well in this context shared many of the attributes of being articulate, aware of the social worker's concerns, cooperative, motivated and plausible (Holland 2010). However, as noted in Chapter 5, Selwyn *et al.* (2006) found that social workers often overestimated the intelligence of birth parents, and their capacity to change, because they had good verbal skills, whilst psychological assessments showed much more limited intelligence and understanding.

Cleaver and Nicholson (2007) reported on the tendency of many parents with learning disabilities to agree with things that were said to them, apparently in an effort to please. Booth and colleagues (2006, p.1000) in their study of parents with learning disabilities found that relationships were more negative where the parent was seen as 'inarticulate, inconsistent and passive'. Holland (2010) and Booth *et al.* (2006) both identified the perception of passivity or inarticulacy as potentially disadvantageous to the parent concerned. Holland further noted in her study that all those described as passive were female. The importance of their findings, however, is in recognising that parents with learning disabilities may well lack the skills needed to negotiate the complexity of child protection procedures. Working with parents with learning disabilities demands additional social work time and the use of concrete concepts, to ensure parents understood what is happening (see also Booth *et al.* 2006). Many were bewildered by what was happening to them, a finding that has also been shown with parents who did not have learning disabilities (Cleaver and Freeman 1995; Department of Health 1995; Farmer and Owen 1995). Children's social workers need to be able to work competently with adults in a range of circumstances:

> There is a danger that in the move towards creating Children's Services, we may forget that for most of the children, the difficulties that they have are a result of adult problems in their parents – such as substance misuse, mental illness or learning difficulties. It is therefore essential that social workers for children are skilled in working with vulnerable adults. (Forrester and Harwin 2007, p.16)

However, this needs to be balanced against the difficulty, highlighted in a number of high-profile cases, of keeping the child properly 'in view'. Working with adults who may be extremely needy in their own right is of course key to effective family-focused assessment and intervention, but in complex cases there is a danger of allowing a focus on the adults' needs to mask those of the child. We return to the problems of collaboration between adults' and children's services in Chapter 7. The challenge is to work with parents *and* with children to improve outcomes for the child.

Conclusion

In this chapter we presented two key arguments. First, we reiterated the point that keeping the child 'in view' is fundamental to good assessment, and concluded that the barriers to achieving this should be reviewed organisationally, as systemic issues. Second, we analysed the relationship between professional engagement with parents and the use of coercive forms of intervention. The relationship is complex but, in many cases, poor engagement can lead to more coercive intervention. Taking these two points together, there is sometimes a seemingly contradictory expectation on social workers to establish good engagement with parents, at the same time as maintaining a central focus on the child. In the next chapter we extend our analysis of the complexity of inter-relationships during assessments, by looking at inter-professional working.

Summary

- Keeping the child 'in view' is fundamental to good assessment, and there was evidence of variable practice in this regard. Research suggests that children are not always seen or consulted during assessments. Social workers do not always record the child's words and views, but instead presuppose what the child might say or rely on parents' or other professionals' views of the children. Children have reported feeling that they are not listened to or that they have had little opportunity to affect social work plans.

- Barriers to involving children include time constraints, insufficient skills, lack of confidence in conducting direct work or undertaking child observations and insufficient support. In addition, some parents make it difficult for workers to see the child and/or overwhelm workers with their own difficulties.

- When children are seen, they may find it difficult to be open because of concerns about confidentiality and the consequences of what they say for their parents. Under-recognition of children's difficulties may arise from workers over-identifying with the parents or becoming desensitised to maltreatment. These barriers are determined by a range of factors, not simply the practice of individual workers, factors that it would be worthwhile for organisations to review regularly.

- Good practice in engagement with children and young people includes taking time to build relationships, listening to and respecting them, giving information, providing support for them to understand records or reports, and offering them real choices whenever possible.

- Reviews of research have suggested that the skills and tasks required to promote good engagement with parents include role clarification, appropriate levels of challenge, careful listening and clarity about the purpose of the assessment. Whilst engagement is more difficult with more coercive forms of intervention, parental involvement in all kinds of assessment depends on the worker's communication skills and ability to work with resistance.

- Parents with learning disabilities have been shown to have difficulty in recalling explanations about assessments and understanding procedures, in spite of evidence of social workers spending time explaining things to them. Some evidence suggests that the difficulties that some parents with learning disabilities have in managing time can lead to a professional perception of lack of cooperation.

- Social workers have the very difficult task of trying both to gain and maintain relationships with parents whilst at the same time making a good assessment of their children. There was evidence of variable practice in assessing and working with parents, ranging from over-use of confrontational approaches to, conversely, reluctance to voice concerns and inappropriately closing cases.

- There was also evidence of deliberate efforts by parents in some cases to frustrate professionals' attempts to engage. This was linked to escalation in coercive interventions.

- During assessments and later interventions, the degree to which social workers and parent/s formed a shared understanding of the family problems and the plan of action, affected how far parents were seen as cooperative. It appeared that where social workers had a good relationship with parents, the parents were more likely to cooperate with plans.

- Deciding who was cooperative was affected by whether parents provided plausible explanations of family problems, were articulate and conformed to social work expectations. Whilst parental cooperation was usually thought of as representing reduced risks of maltreatment, this was not necessarily correct, and cooperation was found to be a poor indicator of potential change. Parents (or one parent) may have been outwardly cooperative even in circumstances where a child was being maltreated, or apparent cooperation may actually have been disguised compliance. Moreover, parents who were passive or inarticulate were sometimes thought of as less cooperative than, in fact, they were.

- Parental cooperation was found to be a significant factor in decision making about children's futures, with poor cooperation often leading to more coercive interventions. Sometimes, however, poor cooperation had the opposite effect, resulting in de-escalation or case closure, for example where lack of engagement reduced the possibilities of gathering evidence necessary for legal proceedings.

Note

1   Now referred to as being the subject of a Child Protection Plan.

Chapter 7

INTER-PROFESSIONAL WORKING

Successive child death inquiries and serious case reviews have shown that failures in communication and information sharing between professionals played a critical role in the way parental behaviours were understood and the social work decisions that were made. Analysis of these cases (for example, Brandon *et al.* 2008; Brandon, Bailey *et al.* 2009; Laming 2003; Reder and Duncan 1999; Rose and Barnes 2008) found that: chronologies were only assembled after the serious injury or fatality had occurred; often no single professional had an overview of the case; different practitioners held different pieces of information; the significance of information was not recognised and referrals were not followed up. Concern about the danger of such communication failures has highlighted the need for greater inter-agency cooperation. The Victoria Climbié Inquiry Report (Laming 2003) made a strong case (as had many previous child death inquiries) for improving inter-agency working, with the assumption that communication between different professionals would improve 'if agency boundaries were dissolved and they all worked together within the same organisational structure' (White and Featherstone 2005, p.213).

In this chapter we consider how the research selected for this review of assessment contributes to our understanding of the value of a multi-agency and multi-professional[1] approach and the contribution different professionals can make to assessments in a range of contexts. Research addressing the importance of information sharing and good communication between agencies and between practitioners is also discussed. It was beyond the scope of this review to evaluate wider profession-specific literatures, so the following discussion draws on research and literature that focused explicitly on *inter-professional* working.

Every Child Matters and beyond

Government guidance since the 1970s has emphasised the importance of improved communication within and between agencies that come into contact with vulnerable children and their families. Joined-up working has been promoted as a route to improving services, on the basis that better coordination and less duplication will lead to greater efficiency and effectiveness, and leave less opportunity for children to 'slip through the net'. The drive towards more and better inter-agency working took on a particular impetus in the *Every Child Matters* programme that promoted structural change to improve the quality of cooperation and coordination between services. The requirement for agencies to work together has been set out in legislation and related guidance (HM Government 2010a).

The Labour government (1997–2010) introduced a range of policy initiatives intended to promote multi-agency and inter-professional working, for example:

- moves to align children's social care services with education services

- development of strong local partnerships

- co-location of different professional groups

- introduction of the Common Assessment Framework and Lead Professional working

- the development and implementation of the Integrated Children's System

- commissioning frameworks for service provision.

These initiatives prompted a wave of procedural and practice-focused change, designed to bring about better linked and, in some cases, formally integrated services. Agendas promoting multi-agency working were widespread and the presumption was that social workers would change their ways of working in line with these new directives. However, research (Cameron and Lart 2003; Frost 2005; Glisson and Hemmelgarn 1998; Sloper 2004) has found that inter-professional working is not always straightforward and may not necessarily achieve the objective of improving outcomes for children and families. Improved structures do not necessarily improve inter-professional working and problems have continued.

Barriers to inter-professional working

A number of general features have frequently been identified that have an impact on the success or otherwise of inter-professional working. For example, commonly recognised barriers to multi-agency working include:

- previous history of conflict between individuals and organisations
- competitive relationships between services
- bureaucracy stifling creative planning
- conflicting policies, procedures, priorities and funding streams
- concerns about accountability
- professionals and disciplines insisting on undertaking particular parts of assessments and therapeutic work
- lack of a 'common language'.

(Adapted from Worrall-Davies and Cottrell 2009, p.340)

It is not difficult to see how these different factors would affect the ease with which professionals work together on assessments.

A number of studies and reviews have drawn attention to the complexities and challenges that are raised by multi-agency working. Cameron and Lart's (2003) systematic review of the research evidence on joint working suggested that evidence for improved effectiveness was limited. This view was shared by Sloper (2004) who explored the factors that facilitated or hindered the development of coordinated multi-agency services. She also concluded that 'there is little evidence on the effectiveness of multi-agency working itself or of different models of such working in producing improved outcomes for children and families' (Sloper 2004, p.571). An American study (Glisson and Hemmelgarn 1998) went further and suggested that major structural change and greater inter-agency coordination may not be the best way to promote improvements in service delivery and outcomes for children. This longitudinal study found that *intra*-organisational 'climate' and culture (which included features such as cooperation, role clarity and low levels of conflict) were greater determinants of 'positive service outcomes (the children's improved psycho-social functioning) and a significant predictor of service quality' (p.401). In contrast, increased *inter*-organisational collaboration had 'a negative effect on service quality and no effect on outcomes' (p.401). At a more theoretical level, Luckock (2010) considered some of the barriers to integrated working, adding to the view that this is not an uncontentious topic either conceptually or in practice.

Barry's (2007) international literature review of approaches to risk assessment in social work showed that different professional groups had different perspectives on risk and prioritised different factors in reaching their decisions, for example balancing children's rights against the family's rights in assessing risk of different sorts of harm, a finding repeated in more recent UK research (Boddy *et al.* 2009) which looked at young people on the 'edge of care'. Some of the issues related to shared definitions of 'problems' (for example, neglect) and thresholds have been discussed in Chapter 2. However, an example of different perspectives is given in Daniel and Baldwin's (2001) study of assessment practices in child neglect cases in three Scottish social work departments. They noted that there were 'examples of very effective interdisciplinary working, with schools, health visitors and with voluntary organisations' (p.26). However, they also found that practitioners had:

> mixed feelings about interagency communication; interagency collaboration via core groups appears to work well and to be valued, but in some situations there is a lack of agreement about thresholds and evidence. [One respondent commented]: …if the mother's got mental health problems, there can be a reluctance from medical people to actually say, to divulge the mother's problems, which then can make an impossible situation for the worker to try and do an assessment. (Daniel and Baldwin 2001, p.28)

Refusal to share information between agencies and joint working with adult services have been longstanding concerns. More recent research has continued to identify these two areas as problematic.

Confidentiality and information sharing

Different professions often have different interpretations of confidentiality. Half the GPs who participated in Tompsett and colleagues' (2009) exploratory study identified tensions in their safeguarding role. They reported that patient confidentiality and seeking consent were constraints when dealing with children potentially suffering harm. Health professionals also expressed concerns about information sharing and client confidentiality in Cleaver and colleagues' (2007) study, despite government guidance on these issues (HM Government 2008). The latter study found that there were particular difficulties where health practitioners were unwilling to disclose information about adult service users to children's social care. In some cases mental health practitioners tended to see their (adult) client 'in isolation' and did not necessarily consider the effect of the adult's mental health difficulties on the health and development of the children in the family.

Lack of information or understanding about a parent's mental health status presents a critical barrier to an accurate assessment of a child's needs and is likely to adversely affect planning and intervention, a point we return to below, in relation to working with adult services.

Adult services

Seeing the adult service user in isolation has often been identified as a significant issue affecting different areas of practice. Particular concerns were noted in Cleaver and colleagues' (2007) study of child protection in the context of parental substance misuse and/or domestic violence, with adult-focused services such as drug teams not taking into account the ways in which the parents' problems or lifestyle were likely to impact on their children's development. Similarly, the researchers found that children's health and social care services had their own priorities and maintained a focus on the child, with less attention to the adults' needs. As they note, 'this difference in focus will inevitably lead to situations where priorities conflict' (Cleaver et al., p.66). Cleaver and colleagues have argued that clear local guidelines and procedures are needed to support inter-agency working and inter-professional relationships. Commenting on the involvement or lack of it from adult services, they found only one authority in their sample of six that had a joint protocol between adult substance misuse services and children's social care.

Elsewhere, Cleaver and Nicholson (2007) found tensions and conflicts (in relation to cases involving parents with learning disabilities) between adults' and children's services. Learning disability services typically operated different thresholds and eligibility criteria to children's services. Research has also identified profound differences in professional perspectives between what are often more advocacy-focused and supportive services for parents with learning disabilities and children's safeguarding services (Tarleton, Ward and Howarth 2006).

Although inter-professional working can be difficult in practice, it is now an established feature of the social care landscape. In the following section some examples are given of the research findings in relation to the involvement of particular professional groups in assessment processes.

The role and contribution of different professional groups

Social work-led assessment is typically a complex undertaking, involving vulnerable children and families with challenging, multi-faceted problems. To get a good understanding of the child's needs, strengths and difficulties, a holistic assessment will need to call on the knowledge and perspective of a range of different professionals involved, such as those working in health and education.

Health

Health services deliver universal provision such as the community-based services of health visiting and GPs, and specialised services such as child and adolescent mental health (CAMHS) or adult psychiatric provision. In this review of research on the assessment of children in need, there was evidence to suggest that health-related assessments had a significant part to play in promoting children's welfare. It is well known that children who are looked after have a higher prevalence of mental health problems than children have in the community (Meltzer *et al.* 2003), and that for most children the conditions were pre-existing their entry to care (Sempik, Ward and Darker 2008). Therefore, given the link between emotional and behavioural difficulties, the stability of placements and poorer long-term outcomes for young people, it is important that practitioners are alert to assessing these needs at an early stage. The evidence suggests that such assessment would be beneficial at entry to care so that appropriate services can be accessed and foster carers prepared, a point reinforced by the use of the Strengths and Difficulties Questionnaire with looked after children (DCSF 2009a).

The contribution of the health specialist was also underlined by Hill and colleagues (2002) who conducted a study of the role of the specialist nurse in promoting the health of looked after children. They reported that there was 'positive evidence of improved health outcomes... through nurse-led health assessments' (p.40; see also Daniel *et al.* 2009; Dunnett and Payne 2000; Emery 2006).

Adoption is another area of practice where a good health assessment is crucial in planning. Many of the children placed for adoption will carry genetic risks, have been exposed to pre-birth risks (such as maternal drug/alcohol misuse) and have been maltreated during infancy (see, for example, Farmer and Dance *et al.* 2010; Selwyn *et al.* 2010). Assessment of children's physical and psychological health is essential if appropriate matches are to be made and an adoption support plan developed based on children's needs. As we saw earlier, Farmer and colleagues (2010) noted how some local authorities were involving child psychologists as part of the processes of linking and matching children to prospective adopters. They described this as an 'innovation' in contributing to the understanding of children's attachment history and pattern of attachment and in helping the decisions to be made about the separation of sibling groups. Farmer and Lutman's study of neglect (2009) also noted that a psychologist's assessment in care proceedings could make a major contribution to the decision of whether or not children could be returned to their parents.

Education

Educational assessments play an important part in the range of assessments experienced by children in need. Social workers need to take account of the findings of such assessments for care planning and to participate in the assessments where appropriate. Educational and care planning for children in need should go hand in hand. For looked after children – those with the greatest personal and family difficulties – joint education and care planning have improved over the past decade, linked to the various government initiatives such as *Quality Protects* and virtual school heads (Berridge *et al.* 2009; Brodie 2009).

Assessments in the education system can impinge on children in need in a variety of ways. All school pupils currently undergo teacher assessment and/or standardised assessment tests at the end of school years 2, 6 and 9 to compare progress with peers. Official statistics on test results can be complex to analyse year on year, especially at the local level, as different subjects produce different results, the cohort size can be small, and the age-cohort changes annually, so a particular pupil group may have more or fewer learning problems than the previous year. A main policy target of the previous Labour government was to narrow the social class attainment gap, including the educational achievements of looked after pupils (DCSF 2008). Evidence indicates that the educational achievements of looked after pupils have improved steadily, so policy has had a positive impact to some degree. However, the test results of looked after pupils have not always improved as much as have those of the wider school population, so the attainment gap has not been narrowed by as much as was intended.

Though the overall educational experiences of looked after children have improved, research studies suggest that social workers, foster and residential carers are not always as aware of educational assessment test results as they should be (Berridge *et al.* 2008). The care system, therefore, can replicate the characteristics of a poor home-learning environment. Middle-class parents would generally show keen awareness of their children's test results, and it is important to create and reinforce the same interest and support throughout the care system. Social workers and carers, therefore, need to be more involved in the process, results and consequences of educational assessment tests.

More broadly, interesting issues arise from the different assessment processes of professional groups. Children with difficulties can end up being catered for within different systems: for example, school exclusion, special education, social work services, youth offending or CAMHS. It has long been known that African-Caribbean boys have higher rates of school exclusion, yet proportionally fewer statements of special educational needs for 'behavioural, emotional and social difficulties' (BESD) (Grimshaw and Berridge 1994). It has been suggested that the process of service allocation may be class-based or even discriminatory, or to some degree arbitrary, depending on which professional the child first sees: GPs initially may turn to mental health services and CAMHS, whereas schools may be more likely to consider special education services (Malek 1991). However, a recent study of 'difficult adolescents' showed that the family and background experiences were much more adverse for looked after teenagers compared with those attending residential special schools for pupils with behavioural, emotional and social difficulties, so the populations are not interchangeable (Berridge *et al.* 2008).

A significant minority of children in need will have experienced assessments for a statement of special educational needs, including disabled children. This applies to a quarter of all looked after pupils, compared with about 3 per cent of the wider school population. It was once suspected that entry to care may preclude the assessment of special educational needs, although with the introduction of teams of looked after children education support services ('LACES') and virtual school heads (Berridge *et al.* 2009) this would no longer be true.

One study found that foster placements were less likely to break down when there had been contact with an educational psychologist (Sinclair, Wilson and Gibbs 2005a). However, it was difficult to explain the reasons for this, and the finding could not be considered conclusive.

Disabled children with statements of special educational needs may have posed fewer difficulties in foster placements than the sorts of challenges that other looked after children may bring. Alternatively, it may have been that educational psychologists helped to devise educational plans and supports to enhance children's attendance, happiness at school and educational performance (Sinclair 2005, chapter 9). Whatever the explanation, educational assessments are important for vulnerable children, especially those with special needs, and social workers should be aware of and contribute to these assessments where appropriate. Similarly, relevant information from educational assessments should be incorporated into social work assessments and plans.

Adult substance misuse and domestic violence services

Many of the families that social workers work with have experienced domestic violence and/or have substance misuse problems. Harwin and Forrester's (2002) study of parental substance misuse in two London boroughs found that specialist alcohol and drug advisors and children's social workers could work well together. They noted that social workers valued the advice and assistance that the specialists in substance misuse provided. It enabled them to gain a better understanding of a parent's substance misuse and how they might assess and intervene effectively. Given the prevalence of substance misuse amongst families involved with children's social care services, it is surprising that a number of research studies have raised concerns about the limited training and experience 'mainstream' social workers have for dealing with these issues (Cleaver *et al.* 2007; Farmer *et al.* 2011; Forrester and Harwin 2006, 2008).

Despite the potential benefits, Cleaver and colleagues' (2007) study of children living with domestic violence and/or parental substance misuse raised questions about social workers' willingness to involve specialist adult agencies. Their analysis indicated that, at the stage of initial assessment, the agencies most frequently contacted by social workers were health, education and police services. They found evidence of limited involvement of specialist agencies providing services for domestic violence or substance misuse. Domestic violence services were consulted in only 4 per cent of cases and substance misuse services in 16 per cent of cases at the initial assessment stage. Representation from the specialist services went up to 5 per cent and 18 per cent by the time of the initial child protection conference although these issues were known to feature in 73 per cent and 60 per cent of the cases respectively.

By the time cases in Cleaver and colleagues' intensive sample had progressed to a core assessment, a slightly different picture had emerged. While the involvement of substance misuse services had increased, domestic violence services were still not routinely involved. Cleaver and colleagues suggest a number of possible reasons for this, including social workers not seeing the involvement of domestic violence services as relevant, a lack of resources or insufficient local services. The same pattern continued through to the planning stage following core assessment, with domestic violence services still considerably less involved than might be expected given the prevalence of the problem in the sample cases.

Harwin's (2009) evaluation of the first pilot Family Drug and Alcohol Court (FDAC) in Britain described a different approach to specialist assessment in care proceedings where the parents had substance misuse problems. FDAC is a specialist court that includes a multidisciplinary specialist team that advises the court about parent progress and related issues, assesses and supports the family and links them into relevant services. The emphasis is on support and direct work with parents and children, not just assessment of needs. Harwin found that a distinctive feature of the team's work was 'the speed with which assessments were provided to the court; the regular feedback and link with the court through reviews; and the combination of direct, therapeutic work with parents with assessment and co-ordination of other services' (Harwin 2009, p.26). While this approach was not without teething troubles, it does nonetheless offer an alternative approach to court-based assessment that appears to navigate some of the difficulties around the use of specialist/expert assessment by integrating the different specialists into one main team with tight timetables.

Working with the courts: The use of 'expert' assessment

In her review of research on care proceedings, Brophy (2006) found that 'where cases concern highly vulnerable children and parents with complex multi-dimensional problems – and this is likely to be the majority of cases [involved in proceedings] – they usually demand a range of knowledge, clinical skills and expertise beyond those of social workers' (p.40). This is of course a sound point to make and the value of purposeful and timely expert assessment has already been noted.

However, a number of studies have identified concerns about the use of experts in assessments in some cases (for example, Dickens 2007; Farmer and Lutman 2009; Farmer and Dance et al. 2010). It has also been noted that experts are often not independent but have been specifically chosen because of their stated view on a subject. One of the main concerns in the research was that the involvement of expert assessors tended to introduce additional delay into care/court proceedings. In a study investigating reasons for delay in court proceedings, Beckett and McKeigue (2003) found evidence of '[o]vervaluing "expert" opinion and undervaluing the conclusions of the professionals most actively involved in a case' (p.40). They found a pattern of repeated or 'repetitive' assessment and what they considered to be an over-reliance on expert assessment, and suggested that this reflected 'an unrealistic hope that assessment would somehow deliver certainty if only it went on long enough and involved enough expert opinion' (p.40). In practice, Beckett and McKeigue concluded, complete certainty was probably an unattainable goal and repeated assessments were likely to lead to delay.

A further problem – and one that was often linked to delay – was the way in which the courts dealt with social work evidence and assessment in contrast with that of the expert witness or assessor. As part of an investigation into how social workers and lawyers work together in child care cases, Dickens (2007) interviewed a small number of social workers and lawyers (n=23 for both groups) about selected cases that they had worked on together. Both groups identified problems with the way social worker's evidence was treated in court. The courts appeared to give little credence to social workers' evidence (a point also noted by Beckett and McKeigue 2003 and by Harwin and Ryan 2007) and routinely ordered further – usually 'expert' – assessments; these were typically commissioned from psychiatrists, paediatricians or psychologists (see also Masson et al. 2008; Selwyn et al. 2006). Dickens noted the impact this had on the costs of the case but also that it built in delay. In addition, a routine recourse to expert assessment had the effect of undermining individual children's social care services practitioners, and social work more generally.

Dickens' study drew attention to the weighting given to different professional opinions and the confidence (or lack of it) in social work assessments, including amongst social workers. Reder and Duncan (1999, p.83) coined the term 'an exaggeration of hierarchy' to describe the phenomenon of social workers backing down from the conclusions of their own assessments if contradicted by those of other 'higher' professionals, for example psychiatrists. Similarly, lack of self-confidence on the part of social workers in their own expertise and that of their legal departments may make them wary of challenging children's guardians (Iwaniec et al. 2004). Yet this can mean that long experience of lack of change by parents in a care proceedings case is cast aside in favour of a recent and one-off guardian or expert assessment which ignores this history (Stevenson 2007). This point is particularly significant as parents' past behaviour is typically a key predictor of their future behaviour.

Farmer and Lutman (2009) in their longitudinal study of neglected children returned to their parents from care, found that many reunifications were unsuccessful. Some of these reunifications were as a result of reports in which guardians or expert assessors had been over-optimistic and too anxious to give parents the benefit of having another chance, even though a deeper reading of the history might have shown that this was not advisable. They point out that this is an example of the 'start again' or 'clean sheet' syndrome being a feature of expert opinion rather than solely of social work practice.

Working with interpreters

As part of a study aimed at providing a 'comprehensive picture' of the lives of South Asian families caring for a severely disabled child in the UK, Hatton and colleagues (2004) found problems with the assessment of family needs. In the overview report on the Supporting Parents research initiative, it was noted that:

> These parents rarely had the fast, comprehensive and regular assessments of needs stressed in current policy. Consequently, service supports were absent, patchy, uncoordinated or unhelpful. Assessments must be in the preferred language of the parents, be relevant to their circumstances, be quickly followed by action, and be regularly updated. 'Colour-blindness' and ethnic and religious stereotyping are detrimental to the identification of individual needs. (Quinton 2004, p.238)

The limitations of some local authority work with non-English-speaking service users were also highlighted by Chand (2005) in a paper that summarised current research on assessment in child protection when English was not the first language of parents. Chand reviewed research mostly conducted in the late 1990s, and noted that, as most studies had involved very few minority ethnic children, the findings needed to be addressed with a degree of caution. However, he found that the research identified: lack of available female interpreters; insufficient time allocated to meetings; interpreters speaking on behalf of service users or conducting the assessment themselves; issues of confidentiality and cultural acceptability; questions about the actual interpretation of words and phrases about sexual abuse; and poor practice in using children (of the family) as interpreters. His conclusions suggested that some local authorities were not well equipped to deal with non-English speaking clients and that this affected action at the point of referral and in relation to subsequent intervention, to the detriment of minority ethnic families.

Chand also commented on the possibility of some families manipulating or obstructing the interview process by using interpretation for their own gains, drawing on the example of Victoria Climbié (see also Cleaver and Freeman 1995). In this case, Victoria's aunt refused to speak English in the first interview with Ealing services – all communication had to be in French and she 'would only talk to, and allow information to be written down by, the French speaking interpreter' (Laming 2003, p.61). It thus appeared that the assessment had been completed by the interpreter rather than the social worker. By the time the aunt was interviewed in Haringey, it was noted that she was speaking very good English, but her grasp of English would fail whenever asked a specific child protection question. As Chand reported, the inquiry recommended that an interpreter should be involved in all child protection enquiries where English is not the family's first language. So it is important that local authorities ensure that access to skilled interpreting services is available.

Working with interpreters takes time and skill and it would appear that this is an area where social workers would benefit from specific training to ensure effective and safe work. Both social workers and interpreters need to be alert to the additional complexity of assessment interviews when a parent or carer may be trying to cover up issues or subvert the process.

Family centres

Family centre workers may find themselves with a role in a variety of assessments. Tunstill and colleagues' (2007) study of 40 family centres identified some very positive relationships with other agencies. Each of the centres provided information about three key agencies that they worked with and these agencies were then contacted by the researchers and asked to comment on the helpfulness of this link to their own agency and/or the families they worked with. Seventy-nine per cent of the agencies thus approached noted positive outcomes from their link with the family centre, and none identified negative outcomes. Tunstill *et al.* found that '[i]n terms of specific services, these agencies reported positive outcomes, *including high quality, improved assessments*' (Tunstill *et al.* 2007, p.51; emphasis added).

However, another study (Clifford and Burke 2004) found that social workers thought that family centre staff had some difficulties in assessing parenting skills and capacity. The authors noted that 'in several interviews social workers commented that family centre workers were sometimes assessing parenting capacity too optimistically because of too close a relationship with the carer, and too little knowledge of family history' (Clifford and Burke 2004, p.314). In addition, Beckett and McKeigue (2003) noted that assessments might be undertaken by staff who were unqualified or less well qualified than the child's social worker. They questioned the value of some family centre parenting skills assessments and suggested that these did not necessarily address the right issues or add a great deal to what was already known.

It would therefore seem important to ensure that such assessments are undertaken by appropriately qualified staff and in situations where they are likely to add substantially to the understanding of the family's needs and circumstances. Otherwise, families might find re-assessment or duplication of assessment intrusive and stressful, and it may also contribute to a delay in decision making.

Housing

Housing is not an area that typically features in discussions of children in need, despite its inclusion among the family and environmental factors identified in the Assessment Framework, and involvement of housing workers in assessment and planning may not be seen as a priority. However, in cases where children were living with domestic violence or parental substance misuse, Cleaver and colleagues (2007) noted that almost a quarter of the families they interviewed (4 out of 17) identified housing concerns as 'a major problem'. Overcrowding can also be an issue for kinship carers and for some minority ethnic families (Farmer and Moyers 2008; Selwyn et al. 2010).

However, it is important in every assessment to ask questions about, and to see, the child's living arrangements within the home. In many studies, there are examples of cases where the reality of the child's living arrangements was not known until the child became looked after, for example older children sharing the parent's bed or sleeping on the couch or chair. It is not possible to generalise, but this does suggest that housing staff should routinely be included as part of undertaking a comprehensive assessment of family's needs and circumstances as housing support workers may well have useful information to contribute and could be part of the plan to improve outcomes for the child and family.

Summary

Overall, the research supports the importance of identifying different areas of professional expertise and skill and accessing these, as needed, to support and inform the assessment process. But alongside that there is also a need to be clear where *social work* expertise lies – for example, in terms of skills and knowledge about relationships, knowledge of the child and family – and to use and value that. This position is summarised by Clifford and Burke:

> It is universally accepted that professions should work together for the benefit of the child, especially in view of the long and well-known history of failures of communication in child care. The danger is that if social workers are not recognised as having some 'expertise' in making social assessments, then they will be in no position to contribute on an equal basis, and service users will be facing the diagnosis of medical and quasi-medical experts without the advocacy or support of a socially oriented professional. The social aspects of children's and families' lives need to be strongly represented if an adequate assessment of their needs is to be constructed. (Clifford and Burke 2004, p.317)

Professional differences of perspective, priority or opinion need not be problematic, in and of themselves, but where there is insufficient common ground and/or substantive differences cannot be resolved within the multi-agency group, the effects on the child or family are unlikely to be helpful.

Promoting 'joined up' working: Making integrated assessment work

Use of the Common Assessment Framework

The Common Assessment Framework is an 'integrated approach to assessment which has been designed, as its title suggests, with a view to harnessing the contribution of everybody in the children's service network' (Tunstill and Allnock 2007, p.35). As such, it is potentially a powerful mechanism for promoting holistic and well-informed assessment of children. A number of studies have looked (directly or indirectly) at the early workings of the Common Assessment Framework

(CAF) and the Lead Professional (LP) role that was introduced alongside it (see, for example, Brandon *et al.* 2006; Gilligan and Manby 2008; Pithouse 2006; Pithouse *et al.* 2009; Tunstill and Allnock 2007).

Brandon and colleagues (2006) carried out an evaluation of the implementation of the CAF in the 12 English local authorities that piloted the new processes and assessed their impact on different sectors of the workforce: education, health, children's social care and the voluntary sector. The agencies involved had all volunteered to be part of the pilot and the researchers noted that there was a high level of enthusiasm and commitment at both practitioner and management levels. However, there were also challenges associated with this new way of working. These included:

- an acknowledgement that assessment of this sort called for different skills and new ways of thinking and working for some practitioners
- the CAF process resulted in increased workload
- it was seen and used by some practitioners 'as a referral mechanism, rather than as an assessment which is linked to a referral'.

Brandon and her colleagues also found evidence of changes in practice in relation to the use of other Assessment Frameworks. Prior to the introduction of CAF, many other types of assessment were used. So one of the research questions was the extent to which CAF was seen as a replacement, alternative or additional structure for assessing children. The researchers found some evidence that the CAF was starting to replace other assessment formats and was particularly valuable where the other professional groups did not already have an assessment model in place, for example working with health visitors. Some agencies were also formally linking the CAF to children in need assessments under section 17 of the Children Act 1989. However, the links were not extensive and they suggested that there was a need for a better 'join up' to statutory assessments by children's social care services. In relation to this latter point, Boddy, Potts and Statham noted, from their study of models of good practice in 'joined up' assessment:

> Relatively little attention has been paid to how to coordinate (and perhaps ultimately combine) 'specialist' assessments, for example of children's social care needs (currently undertaken using 'core assessments' under the Assessment Framework or Integrated Children's System); their special educational needs (SEN); and their

health needs arising from clinical diagnoses. (Boddy, Potts and Statham 2006, p.4)

Professional ambivalence and competing priorities were noted about using the CAF in Brandon and colleagues' (2006) study. Some health and education practitioners raised concerns that they were being expected to take on work that should be done by social workers, while others thought that they were taking on 'social services type work' appropriately. There was a view that this might lower thresholds for intervention (see Chapter 2).

The complexities, challenges and benefits of the CAF process were also explored by Tunstill and Allnock (2007) from the perspective of Sure Start staff in eight programmes. They noted that by the time they conducted the study of Sure Start Local Programmes (SSLPs) in 2005:

> a consensus was beginning to emerge across Sure Start Local Programmes and social services/children's services departments as to how best to meet the most complex needs of children, including their need for child protection services. Inter-professional and inter-agency collaboration, in the context of referrals for child protection, con be maximised where the following characteristics were discernible:
> - shared understanding and acceptance of thresholds
> - confidence in information sharing both with parents and other professionals
> - systematic recording systems.
>
> (Tunstill and Allnock 2007, p.36)

This finding chimes with other studies of inter-professional working. In *Hidden Harm* (2003) the Advisory Council for the Misuse of Drugs recommended that the CAF should be put in place to address the needs of children and young people of substance-misusing parents. However, Corlyon and Clay's study (2008) of interventions for children and young people whose parents misuse drugs found that only 6 of the 66 services they surveyed were using CAF, 'amid concerns about its usefulness and uptake' (p.10). Instead, many different approaches to assessment were in use across the different specialist services they studied, with many services using assessment tools they had developed themselves.

In a wide-ranging exploration of different models of support for young people 'on the edge of care' and their families, Boddy and colleagues (2009) examined a range of approaches in use in four European countries, including England. They drew attention to an interesting approach they found in one local authority where the CAF was 'key to the process of getting help'. They noted that this authority was innovative in its approach to supporting families and was using a 'community cluster' model that emphasised universal services and delivered through locality-based integrated multidisciplinary teams, using a Team Around the Child (TAC) approach.

Box 7.1 The 'community cluster' approach

[T]he unitary authority had five multidisciplinary community cluster teams, which included Education Welfare Officers, Behaviour Support Teachers and Workers, Family Support Workers, Senior Mental Health Practitioners, and Youth Inclusion Support Officers. As an example, the cluster manager interviewed led a team of 14 practitioners in her cluster, which served families of 6000 young people aged 0–19. Working alongside this core cluster team were other professional agencies in the state and voluntary sectors. Some specialist services remained outside the cluster framework, including social work, CAMHS, and the Youth Offending Service, which operated as borough-wide specialist services. According to one senior manager, the decision to keep these as borough-wide services reflected a recognition that not everything could, or should, be based in the clusters: 'We still need specialist services doing specialist things'.

In this local authority, the CAF was key to the process of getting help. Following identification of needs through completion of a CAF, the community cluster would put together a Team Around the Child (TAC). Cases that raised significant concerns could be referred directly to children's social services (initial assessment and outreach team), and the local authority also had a telephone 'helpdesk' service within children's social services. The helpdesk offered consultation and advice, and responded to referrals from professionals as well as contact from parents or young people... [O]ne manager observed that by the point of referral most families already had a CAF completed and a multi-agency TAC group working with them...

In line with this emphasis on 'holding' families within the clusters, close working links were maintained with the clusters even when referrals were accepted by social services. For example, following a case conference, a case management team would be established that linked in with the Integrated Service Manager in the family's local community cluster. This team would work with the family, according to the TAC model, until the child could be taken off the child protection register. A manager commented that this approach ensured continuity in provision for children and families, observing that even after a child is placed 'the people working around the family are always the same people.'

Several managers observed that both the TAC group within the community cluster and the social worker would continue to work with children after they were placed in care, and with their families...

Source: Boddy *et al.* 2009, pp.45–46

Managers stated that CAF had improved early identification of need, but that it had created a corresponding need to develop training for workers in universal services around early intervention and the management of risk of harm. This case study offers one example of how the CAF can be integrated into an effective multi-agency approach to referral, assessment and service provision. In this locality, the different agencies seem to have found a good working balance between the role and function of the integrated, multidisciplinary 'cluster' teams and the wider 'external' specialist services operating borough-wide (social work, CAMHS and Youth Offending).

Effective inter-professional working

The importance of coordinated multi-agency assessment for families with complex, entrenched and multiple difficulties is underlined by Farmer and colleagues' analysis of assessments conducted as part of the process of deciding whether or not a looked after child should be returned home:

> Researcher ratings of the value of these assessments found that, whilst half of the assessments (51%) had been sufficiently analytical and adequately assessed *all* of the risks to the child such that they had been a useful basis on which to make the return decision, the other half had only been partially useful (47%) or not really useful (2%). Only a third (33%) of the assessments conducted by Social Services alone (and only two fifths by another agency alone) were thought to have been fully analytical and useful compared with almost

three-quarters (72%) of those completed by both Social Services and other agencies. (Farmer *et al.* 2011, p.60)

The researchers go on to comment that this finding is not about the competence of either social workers or other professionals, but highlights the importance of multi-agency assessment for families with multiple or complex problems. Overall, they found that children were more likely to be returned home safely where multi-agency assessments had been conducted.

Ward and Peel (2002) discuss a project, undertaken before the CAF process was in place, to help develop inter-agency working practices in relation to assessment and identification of need. They identify five elements that were essential for successful inter-agency working: 'an identified purpose, consensus, choice, reciprocity and trust' (p.223). More recently, while not focusing on assessment specifically, Worrall-Davies and Cottrell (2009) have considered the evidence about what constitutes best practice in inter-professional working and drawn out findings that provide guidance on effective practice. They refer to Anning and colleagues' (2006) review of the literature and their report on the findings of a large qualitative study into multi-professional working in children's services and offer a useful summary of the factors that appear from the research evidence to affect effective inter-professional working. These include:

- Commitment to joint working at all levels of the organisations.
- Strategic and operational joint planning and commissioning.
- Delineation of roles and responsibilities for all staff and clarity of line management arrangements.
- Good working relationships at grassroots level.
- Mutual trust and respect between partner agencies and staff.
- Recognition of the constraints others are under.
- Good systems of communication.
- Clear paths for information sharing, including databases.
- Support, supervision and joint training for staff in new ways of working.
- Commitment to evaluation, audit and change.

(Worrall-Davies and Cottrell 2009, p.340)

This analysis reinforces findings from Glisson and Hemmelgarn's study (1998), discussed earlier in this chapter, which highlighted that *intra*-organisational factors were of more significance than major structural changes in promoting improvements in service delivery and outcomes for children. It draws attention to the importance of relationships and of trust between partners in building effective inter-professional working, a point that is endorsed by Barlow and Scott (2010) in their substantial review *Safeguarding in the 21st Century*.

Conclusion

Policy, legislation and guidance all identify the need for greater inter-agency cooperation and support for working together. However, this is a complex and challenging area of practice, and research evidence on effectiveness, in general, is limited. There is evidence that different professional groups have a significant role to play in the process of undertaking holistic assessments of children in need. Successful inter-professional working is challenging but evidence suggests that one of the key elements that support it is the establishment of effective relationships between the practitioners and agencies involved. Research also highlights the potential contribution of the Common Assessment Framework.

Summary

- Different professional groups have a substantial contribution to make to the assessment of children in need and their families. There were examples in the research of the effective involvement of health, education, psychological and other specialist services. Examples of good multi-agency practice used the Common Assessment Framework particularly effectively.

- Research evidence suggests that there are a number of key barriers to inter-professional working including: conflict and competition between individuals and organisations; lack of role clarity especially in relation to accountability; and lack of a 'common language'. Differences in thresholds for concern, perceptions of 'risk' in a range of contexts relating to different types of risks, and intervention continue to exist between services.

- Although statutory guidance on information sharing has been published (HM Government 2008), the sharing of information between agencies and the collaboration of adults' and children's services continue to be identified by research as particularly problematic. Numerous inquiry reports and serious case reviews have noted that failures to share information can have a profoundly damaging impact on the accurate assessment of a vulnerable child.

- Complex multi-dimensional problems are likely to require assessments that draw on different professional expertise. Appropriate expert assessment can make a key contribution to the quality of assessment. However, increased reliance on expert witnesses in courts has been a factor in increasing delay and reducing the perceived value of social work assessments. The contribution of social workers' knowledge of social relationships, family history and parents' behaviour over time could then be lost – a potentially serious omission, as past parental behaviour is a key predictor of likely future conduct.

- Factors that support the development of inter-agency working are: commitment to joint working across different levels of the organisation; jointly agreed aims; clarity about roles and responsibilities; mutual trust; and good systems of communication. Restructuring and reorganisations were not associated with better outcomes for children.

- Most significantly, the quality of the relationships within and between professional groups was important in promoting effective multi-agency or inter-professional practice. Good working relationships need time and trust, as well as a supportive organisational framework, in order to develop.

Note

1 There are a number of terms in use, each with its own nuances. We do not have space here to go into detail about the different emphases and shades of meaning and have used terms such as 'multi-agency' and 'inter-professional' interchangeably to reflect the range of meanings and implied levels of inter-connectedness without endorsing any one particular approach.

Chapter 8

STRUCTURAL, PROCEDURAL AND ORGANISATIONAL FACTORS

Finding the best approach to the assessment of children and families has proved to be a challenge for countries worldwide. Failings in assessment are not unique to the UK and have been reported in Australia, Canada, New Zealand (White 2005) and the US (Morton and Holder 2000). Commonly identified problems have been: services provided without assessment; using only the parent as a source of information; failure to cite previous reports; lack of a chronology; stating the purposes of the assessment in general rather than specific terms; emphasising parental weaknesses over strengths; and neglecting to describe the parent's care-giving qualities or the child's relationship with the parent. In response to failings, different frameworks and procedures have been introduced in order to promote more systematic and standardised practice. In this chapter we focus on research findings that relate to structures, processes and organisational factors relating to assessment in England.

Using structured electronic formats for recording

A variety of information management systems and conceptual frameworks are in use in the different agencies that work with children and families. Tunstill and Allnock, for example, identified a diverse range of frameworks and information systems in operation in the different agencies that participated in their study of Sure Start Local Programmes:

> This diversity applied to a range of characteristics, e.g. electronic ...versus non-electronic systems; differing professional systems e.g. health and social services; differing purposes of the information held; and variation in quantity and detail of the information held. In addition, staff groups had very different levels of access to hardware. For example, 'hot desking' practices constrained the opportunities to access electronic systems for some workers. (Tunstill and Allnock 2007, pp.24–25)

Good assessment requires the ability to process and synthesise information and to record clearly and accurately what has been learned. The Integrated Children's System (ICS), building on the conceptual framework underpinning the Assessment Framework, published a series of structured electronic templates or 'exemplars' for local authorities to draw on when developing their IT systems. A study of the early implementation of the ICS (Cleaver *et al.* 2008) looked in some detail at the effect of this new system on recording practice in relation to children with complex needs, those in need of protection and children looked after. Overall, the findings from this study suggested that the introduction of ICS improved the quality and the amount of information social workers recorded. However, evidence from other studies has contradicted these positive findings.

The exemplars used for recording have been criticised for being too prescriptive, suppressing creativity and originality of thinking and dispersing the information on the family resulting in a 'loss of narrative' (Bell *et al.* 2007, p.59). The loss of narrative was also highlighted as a concern by the social workers interviewed by Holmes and colleagues (2009). The social workers thought that the exemplars that had been developed by their authority made 'false distinctions' between issues affecting families, which they saw as being interconnected. The researchers stated that:

> one team reported that 'economic circumstances', 'housing' and 'employment' are recorded as separate categories on the Initial Assessment template used in their authority. However, in assessing the needs of families, they analyse the cumulative effects of each of these factors on a family's well being. Therefore, in recording these issues separately, the template does not reflect an accurate picture of a family's needs. (Holmes *et al.* 2009, p.13)

As noted in Chapter 4, a 'one size fits all' format may not suit the varied needs and situations encountered in work with children in need. Although Cleaver *et al.*'s study (2004) of the implementation of the Assessment Framework found that parents of disabled children were as positive or more so about the assessment process as parents in other situations, concerns have been expressed more recently about the use of ICS for the assessment of children with a disability. For example, Bell and colleagues (2007) found that some social workers in disabled children's teams perceived a child protection bias in ICS that was not necessarily helpful in their context. Furthermore, because of the difficulty in including 'non-standard' material, such as visual material, electronic recording systems may disadvantage disabled children by making it harder to capture their contribution to the assessment process through their chosen method of communication. Mitchell and Sloper (2008) found that the system could not easily include children's pictures or drawings and this made it harder for social workers to represent their views properly.

Two difficulties identified in assessments long before ICS was developed have continued to be present in the new system. The first of these is the tendency for information once recorded to be repeated without any checks on accuracy. For example, Selwyn and colleagues (2006) found examples of this in case files dating back to the late 1980s and early 1990s. Children's dates of birth, ethnicity and parents' details were sometimes incorrectly recorded and stayed so throughout the file. The ability to copy and paste in electronic documents has continued this tendency to reproduce errors and misinformation (Farmer and Dance *et al.* 2010).

The other difficulty previously noted (for example, Selwyn *et al.* 2006) was the tendency to write very little about the child's development and/or to describe this in general terms rather than being specific to the child. Holland (2010) found that this had continued, encouraged by workload pressures for workers to simply copy extracts from one assessment to another, leading to a 'standardised view of any child's needs' rather than an individualised response. She further observed that in some assessments practitioners had used wording from guidance documents to describe aspects of the child's development or situation, and thus the report described a 'generic' child rather than the particular child concerned, with clear implications for the value of the assessment of their needs. This is surprising given that the ICS (and the earlier looked after children system) encourages social workers to describe the seven dimensions of children's development.

More recently there have been changes to ICS IT systems following on from recommendations from the Social Work Taskforce (2009). Changes include making the system simpler, more responsive and flexible to meet local needs, and improving the assistance provided to develop IT systems (DCSF 2009c). The use of ICS, and of ICT systems more generally, has also been considered by the Munro review (Munro 2010, 2011).

While electronic records potentially have a number of advantages over paper-based systems, one unanticipated consequence has been a marked change in both how and where social workers spend their time. Electronic information management and recording systems, by definition, require access to a computer and time spent in front of the computer is time not being spent with children and families or with other professionals. Completing paper records properly also took time, of course, but a number of studies (Bell *et al.* 2007; Mitchell and Sloper 2008; Tunstill and Allnock 2007; White 2009) have reported that inputting the data required for the different exemplars is time-consuming and can substantially reduce the time available for face-to-face contact with children and families. It has been stated that this has resulted in a loss of social workers, due to workers' dissatisfaction with the low amount of direct client contact (Munro 2005).

It was expected that a benefit of the ICS would be a saving in administrative time, as word documents could be easily copied. Holmes and colleagues (2009) reported that this indeed could be the case. One Intake and Assessment team in their study noted that if the worker inputted all of the required information, then if a new worker took over, or the case was subsequently re-referred, a considerable amount of time could be saved on data gathering as much of the necessary information would be available in the electronic recording system.

The significant amount of time spent recording information is not just a feature of the research evaluating the ICS, but has also been found in research that pre-dates the implementation of ICS and other types of assessments such as Child Permanency reports (Beecham and Sinclair 2007; Farmer and Dance *et al.* 2010; Selwyn *et al.* 2006) so it perhaps also reflects the time that needs to be spent reflecting and analysing information. Producing high-quality assessments is time-consuming.

It is possible that the amount of time spent recording and collating information also in part reflects the growth in knowledge of the factors that influence development and children's outcomes. Over the last 30 years there has been an explosion in the knowledge base and inevitably this must have an impact on the amount of information collected. Social workers are also mindful that service users can have access to their records or adopters access to children's files and that some agencies have been sued for failing to pass on information or act in response to information and that children's human rights have been breached.[2] Therefore 'paper trails' of actions are created.

IT systems

Practical issues have also arisen with the introduction of computerised systems (Bell *et al.* 2007). Many of the IT systems have not been fit for purpose and not functioned properly. For example, in some agencies the ICS software was so unstable that social workers' recording was lost, or did not allow copy and pasting between documents, or workers found that corrections or improvements could not be made to documents, as the system 'locked' the record once it has been completed (Broadhurst, Wastell *et al.* 2010). Many local authorities also did not have dedicated IT support teams for social workers, computer training was not available and social workers' administrative support had not changed to reflect the new systems. Systems also often did not reflect working practices and were not flexible enough to manage situations such as hot desking, direct data entry during a home visit and access by other professionals such as the Children's Guardian. While teething troubles were no doubt inevitable when rolling out a national scheme of this kind, it is not clear whether, or to what extent, the technological challenges of ICS (Mitchell and Sloper 2008; Peckover, Hall and White 2009) have been fully addressed.

Record keeping

Concern about recording in social work is not new – indeed, poor recording has been identified as a recurrent research finding and a feature of cases that have resulted in child deaths, reaching back over decades. We have discussed some issues associated with content of assessments in earlier chapters, and have also considered aspects of recording in Chapter 5. In this section we look at research findings that shed light on the way frameworks, systems and structures can affect recording.

The Assessment Framework signalled a shift in focus from family to child-based assessment. This process had begun decades before when the single family file was replaced by individual case files for each child within a family. However, concerns about the practice of assessing just the family or a whole sibling group rather than the needs of the individual children within the family/group continued. The introduction of the Assessment Framework required that each child's needs were individually assessed, as well as the parent's capacity to care for each child and the impact of family and environmental factors on each child's development.

It has elicited a mixed response from practitioners. Individual recording has raised concerns about unnecessary duplication of information. However, managers and nearly half the practitioners surveyed by Cleaver and colleagues thought that the Assessment Framework resulted in a better-quality assessment and a clearer focus on the needs of the individual child (Cleaver et al. 2004, p.121).

Two factors appeared to be associated with the social workers' perceptions of the effect of the Assessment Framework on the quality of their assessments:

1. the length of time social workers had been qualified, with newly qualified workers more likely to associate the Assessment Framework with improved quality of assessments

2. the amount and kind of training they had received in using the Assessment Framework.

There have been no consistent findings from research studies on the proportion of assessments that might be deemed of good or high quality. Findings have indicated that good-/high-quality assessments make up 33–80 per cent of assessments (Bell et al. 2007; Cleaver et al. 2004; Farmer and Dance et al. 2010; Selwyn et al. 2010). It is probable that some of the differences between the findings in these different studies can be explained by variation in local authority practice and the way researchers rated quality, and, in addition, the studies were assessing different assessment formats. However, it seems likely that Selwyn and colleagues' (2008, p.7) observation – made in relation to adoption cases – has more general application: 'the lack of good assessments of the children makes it likely that support for children's problems will be reactive rather than proactive'.

Missing assessments

Two issues are addressed here under the heading of 'missing assessments': situations where assessments may have been carried out but the reports were not on file and others where assessments appeared not to have been undertaken at all. Absence of assessments on file has been noted in many studies. Macdonald and Williamson, in their evaluation of child and family support services (2002), considered whether missing assessments were likely to be a 'paper omission' – that is, simply a failure to file the appropriate record – or to be indicative of a failure in practice. They concluded:

> Our analysis of the closed files revealed a dearth of recognisable attempts at undertaking an assessment. Given that assessment is an analytic and reflective task, it is unlikely that the absence of assessments on files can be taken only to indicate an absence of a formal record. Indeed, it is difficult to conceive of one without the other. The case record is itself as much an assessment tool as a record of the process and its conclusions – or should be. (Macdonald and Williamson 2002, p.38)

Cleaver and her colleagues (2007 and 2004) suggested that, in the absence of key assessments, it was not clear whether statutory requirements or guidance had been followed. In their study of the needs and outcomes of children living with a parent with learning disabilities, Cleaver and Nicholson (2007) found a level of inconsistency between decisions recorded as part of the initial assessment and documentation found elsewhere on the case files. The kinds of discrepancies found included:

- failure to carry out a core assessment when the decision to do so was recorded as part of the initial assessment

- recorded strategy meeting decisions to move to section 47 inquiry but no core assessment on the file.

The researchers suggested a number of possible reasons why recommendations were not followed. For example, in some cases, the family was already well known to adult care services and so the children's social care worker moved straight to a core assessment on receipt of a referral from adult care; in other situations, where a file decision was recorded to undertake core assessments on all members of a large sibling group, the social worker had only carried out the core assessment on a selected child or children.

However, the researchers concluded that a robust management response was necessary to ensure that practice was in line with guidance. They advised the introduction of a system for routine internal audit of case files, with checks being carried out by managers who were not themselves responsible for the particular cases. This proposal perhaps fits with the idea mooted by the Social Work Task Force for regular organisational 'health checks' and is already practised in some local authorities.

In other studies (Farmer and Lutman 2009; Farmer *et al.* 2011; Selwyn *et al.* 2010) researchers considered that it was not possible to ascertain from the case files which assessments had been carried out and identified many cases where no assessments had taken place. In Farmer and colleagues' (2011) study of reunification a third of the sample of 180 children did not have an assessment either before or during the return home. The researchers noted that the social workers' explanation for the absence of formal assessment before reunification was that 'this was generally because the family was already known to children's services, so an assessment was not considered necessary'. Such a response was not always warranted and that assessment prior to the return would have provided additional up-to-date and relevant information. This may have prevented the large number of failed reunifications.

Missing information

The problem of 'where to put things' has already been identified in relation to the kinds of material social workers with disabled children wanted to include in their records, but Bell and colleagues' findings (2007) suggested that this was a more general concern. And the practitioners' problem here was balanced by a difficulty identified in a number of research studies of 'how to find things'. In some cases, researchers found that paper files were not easy to navigate – for example, it was not clear where assessments began and ended, as the assessment 'tended to be indistinguishable from running records' (Preston-Shoot 2003, p.46); in another study, the researchers noted that key information was 'scattered' across the case files they searched (Iwaniec *et al.* 2004).

If it was not clear to the researcher what had taken place, it is likely that it would be equally unclear to a new practitioner coming to the case. It would also be much harder for a service user to make use of the information, for example an adopted adult seeking information on their history to understand why decisions had been taken, such as why they had been separated from their siblings.

The amount of information and number of paper files could also act as a disincentive to the worker reading the *whole file* and new workers often relied on the transfer summary, particularly when no chronology was in place. This was often insufficient to plan. Selwyn and colleagues (2006) give an example of such a case when the Leaving Care team were unaware, as they placed a young person in a flat, that he had epilepsy that was often triggered by stress. Indeed, that agency had a policy of *not* reading the young people's files because they believed in a 'fresh start' once young people were ageing out of care. The research evidence would suggest that this was a very misguided approach.

Problems with file keeping are clearly not unique to social work but are significant in terms of their possible consequences for children's welfare and protection. Where information about the child and family is unclear and reports are incomplete or missing, the scope for misunderstanding the child's needs or the nature (and possible severity) of a situation seems likely to increase. Gaps and missing information were a recurrent feature in many studies and seemed to occur regardless of which format or structure was used.

A number of studies noted that assessments rarely contained a full social history (see, for example, Macdonald and Williamson 2002) and, as we have seen, the absence of a chronology on file was also noted (Farmer and Lutman 2009; Glaser, Prior and Lynch 2001; Selwyn *et al.* 2006). These are significant omissions as, without 'a clear and concise chronological record of reported concerns and professional responses to them' (Glaser *et al.* 2001, p.46), it is hard to track the progress of a case. This was found to be a particular problem with neglect cases; Farmer and Lutman (2009), for example, found that social workers had not always read and absorbed the background information on the file, where it existed, and therefore tended to 'focus only on the present, out of context' (p.363). The critical importance of the family history and/ or chronology in supporting a properly contextualised understanding of the case was also underlined by Brandon, Bailey *et al.*'s second review of serious case reviews (2009). As we have seen, the researchers identified what they called 'start again syndrome' as a recurrent – and dangerous – feature of practice in chronic neglect cases.

Missing information on children's needs and characteristics potentially affect the stability of all types of placements (see, for example, Farmer and Dance *et al.* 2010; Selwyn *et al.* 2006; Sinclair 2005).

While in some cases, it appeared from the files that necessary information had simply not been collected, or had not been read, in other studies (Daniel and Baldwin 2001; Thomas and Holland 2010) the issue seemed to be that information *was known* but remained in the social worker's head. Clearly, where it was not recorded in the file, this information could only be of limited use to anyone else.

Management of social work recording

Preston-Shoot has provided a concise and useful summary of the kinds of criticisms that have been raised in relation to the supervision of social work recording. His findings appear to reflect some of the longstanding criticisms of social work recording:

> It appeared to be a haphazard activity, largely unmonitored, such that it proved difficult to discern the nature of social work involvement, concerns or assessment. The processes by which decisions had been arrived at were obscured and the outcomes of social work practice and supervision often unclear. (Preston-Shoot 2003, p.32)

His response to these findings, though, raised some interesting questions about the nature of the problem and is therefore quoted at some length:

> It could be hypothesised, of course, that the evidence on recording offers further evidence of deficient knowledge-bases and skills in assessment, which reforms of social work education are designed to address. Alternatively, and arguably supported by the varied picture reported here, social workers know that recording is an important part of working in partnership with 'clients' and of informing practice. They know that records should clarify how assessments were undertaken, needs and goals determined, and case plans constructed. A failure, then, to understand what happens to practitioners in practice might simply mean that further training and managerial oversight would lead only to an even greater recognition of the gap between the ideal and the actuality of practice. (Preston-Shoot 2003, pp.47–48)

He concluded that attention must be paid to the experience of social workers in order to understand how and why practice had gone awry. He referred to evidence gathered by both the Audit Commission (2002) and Lord Laming (Laming 2003) which suggested that at least part of the problem lay in the fact that practitioners were 'overwhelmed by bureaucracy, targets and unmanageable workloads' and were continuing to operate in a largely 'unsupportive context' (Preston-Shoot 2003, p.48). Concerns about social work caseloads and work pressures are not new and are a continuing feature of practice, as noted in Lord Laming's later report (Laming 2009).

Performance indicators and workload demands

The impact of different assessment frameworks on workloads has been documented in a number of studies, many of which have highlighted the amount of time needed to complete each form of assessment (see, for example, Bell *et al.* 2007; Brandon *et al.* 2006; Broadhurst, Wastell *et al.* 2010; Cleaver and Walker 2004; Farmer and Dance *et al.* 2010; Holland 2010). While Ward, Holmes and Soper's findings (2008) suggested that the time (and cost) associated with completing a core assessment had decreased since Cleaver *et al.*'s earlier investigation (2004), elsewhere the time taken to complete other forms of assessment does not appear to have changed much over time – for example, Farmer and colleagues' (2010) findings on the number of hours taken to complete a child permanency report were virtually identical to an earlier study of the old Form E forms. And, as previously noted, it is clear that assessment is time-consuming. But some recent studies (Bell *et al.* 2007; White 2009) have suggested that the *amount* of work required, coupled with the need to complete certain types of assessment within a prescribed timescale, has resulted in very particular pressures on practitioners and have adversely affected practice. For example, Broadhurst, Wastell and colleagues (2010, p.353) noted that 'the immutable timescales set for the completion of the initial assessment inevitably pushed workers to make quick categorisations based on, at best, one home visit' – which were unlikely to be of the same quality as those which assemble information from many sources. Further, the fact that evidence of meeting the timescales is one of the performance indicators against which local authorities are themselves judged adds another critical element to the picture.

The various papers from White and colleagues' (see, for example, White *et al.* 2009) study of initial assessment processes have provided extensive commentary on the difficulties experienced by practitioners but have also highlighted how social workers find ways around the system that open up the possibility of a variety of 'latent errors'. They found that practitioners took various short cuts through the initial assessment documentation and in some cases simply missed out sections. They suggested that this was a response to a system that required: 'copious information that is difficult to garner from one home visit and from other professionals; it thus invites workers to discard the majority of its sections as irrelevant' (Broadhurst, Wastell *et al.* 2010, p.363).

The authors described a practice of 'front and back-ing' or 'back-to-back-ing' that had apparently spontaneously developed across all their research sites, where middle sections of the (initial assessment) document were omitted altogether. This practice raises concerns that errors in judgement based on inaccurate or incomplete information will be made and that lack of time will have an impact on engaging with parents. This is important as an earlier study of the Assessment Framework (Aldgate and Statham 2001) suggested that parents perceived social work interviews as less threatening using the Assessment Framework, and that there was therefore a greater likelihood of parents engaging with services. Cutting corners also raises concerns that particular types of families will be more disadvantaged. For instance, in studies examining working effectively with parents with learning disabilities (for example, Booth and Booth 2005; Cleaver and Nicholson 2007) it was found that additional time was needed to ensure that a fair assessment was conducted.

Delay in assessments and intervention

While the White and Bell studies emphasised the downsides of rigid timeframes, delayed assessments (and therefore interventions) were a feature in many other studies. Cleaver and colleagues (2007) reported that less than half (46%) of the initial assessments had been completed within seven working days, as was then required. They noted that this was lower than in previous research (Cleaver *et al.* 2004) where two-thirds were completed on time, and lower than the 57 per cent identified in national Government statistics for that year. They suggested that one of the reasons for this was that there was a reluctance to carry out core assessments on complex cases. This resulted in social workers trying to gather all the required information, involve other relevant services and make considered judgements all within the seven working days of an initial assessment. Therefore, the timescale for carrying out initial assessments overran and Government targets were not met. Moreover, the high rate of re-referrals and the views of parents suggest that a desire to get assessments completed quickly (by carrying out an extended initial assessment rather than moving to a core assessment) may mean social workers do not gain a comprehensive understanding of the child and family's circumstances. Roach and Sanders (2008) found a similarly high level of delay (80%, n=16) in completion of core assessments in the cases they sampled.

Delay was also a feature in relation to kinship care assessments (Farmer and Moyers 2008) and more widely within the adoption process (Farmer and Dance *et al.* 2010; Selwyn *et al.* 2006; Selwyn *et al.* 2010), in neglect cases (Farmer and Lutman 2009) and in a range of situations where court proceedings were involved (Harwin and Ryan 2007; Masson *et al.* 2008; Roach and Sanders 2008; Sinclair and Bullock 2002; Ward *et al.* 2003). The detrimental effect on vulnerable children of delay has been documented (for example, see Ward *et al.* 2003) so the widespread nature of the problem is a matter of concern. However, a cautionary note is added by Roach and Sanders:

> It must be emphasised that even in the best laid plans delays will occur; the complexity of family life means that a family's situation can change suddenly, rendering plans and their associated tasks obsolete. However, that does not mean that systems and procedures should not be in place and, more importantly, utilised to mitigate such problems. (Roach and Sanders 2008, p.40)

Organisational issues

It is perhaps reasonable to suppose that effective and high-quality assessment will be more likely in a well-organised and adequately resourced agency. But organisational and system change have been a key and persistent feature of the period covered by this review, with a raft of new policy and practice initiatives to accommodate, alongside increasing pressure on resources. In this last section we consider some of the effects of organisational change on practice.

Extent and impact of change

Cleaver and Walker (2004) noted that at the time the Assessment Framework was being implemented many councils were dealing with a high level of organisational change and that this was also a period of particular pressure in relation to staff recruitment and retention. The researchers suggested that these factors could have had implications for the ease with which new systems and frameworks could be introduced. They identified the organisational features that were necessary to support new systems. These included:

- strong senior management and leadership
- a clear plan for implementation of the new arrangements that involved practitioners and managers at all levels within the organisation
- a flexible approach to the training needs of both practitioners and managers.

Recruitment and retention of staff in children's social care services has been a longstanding concern and the impact of staff turnover on children can be considerable. In terms of the effect on assessment, frequent changes of worker can result in continuity of knowledge about the child and their needs and the broader family situation being lost, and encourage a tendency (as noted by Brandon and colleagues 2008; Selwyn *et al.* 2006) to 'start again' from scratch each time. A lack of in-depth knowledge of the child could also have particular ramifications in terms of the time taken to complete the Child Permanence Report (Dance *et al.* 2010) with knock-on effects on family finding (Farmer and Dance *et al.* 2010; Selwyn *et al.* 2010).

A slightly different concern was noted by Tunstill and colleagues (2007, p.131) in relation to the way turnover of field social workers affected work with family centres, with reports of mainstream social workers undervaluing, underusing or wrongly using family centre services, through a lack of understanding of the centres' work. This was seen by centre staff as a further by-product of a rapid turnover of staff in social work teams, and of inexperienced social workers, who were under stress and not totally confident as to how to work with families.

However, there are times when a change of worker is beneficial. For example, earlier studies suggest that in some safeguarding cases when negative associations have built up with the worker involved at the investigation stage, it may be helpful to introduce a new worker at a subsequent stage (Cleaver and Freeman 1995; Farmer and Owen 1995). Moreover, Farmer and colleagues (2010) found that 'early transfer' of adoptive children from the child's social worker to the adoption team when the adoption recommendation was agreed was associated with better matches between children and adoptive parents. This finding runs counter to the anxiety that early transfer of cases results in new workers not knowing children well enough.

Organisational culture: Managerialism and the rise of 'audit culture'

Standardised systems feed in to a performance management culture of indicators, timescales and targets. One of the features of an electronic information management and recording system is that it provides a clear 'audit trail' of everyday practice and, as Cleaver and colleagues (2007) noted, the use of such a system 'should alert practitioners and line managers when agreed processes are not being followed'. But, as we have identified, concern has been expressed by a number of researchers that there is a danger that the needs of the system have taken precedence over the needs of children. The suggestion remains that some rebalancing may be necessary to ensure that practice is properly accountable but within systems that support rather than drive it. None of the studies reviewed provided any evidence that children's social care services were using the information on the needs of individual children held in their systems to ensure services were commissioned and targeted to meet the needs of their own populations of children.

Conclusion

Having systems and structures in place to manage the information required for assessing children's needs and monitoring their developmental progress is fundamental to safe and effective practice, inter-agency working and better outcomes for children. But working within formal systems can be challenging at a number of levels, with particular difficulties associated with the move to highly structured electronic information recording and management systems. So while it is necessary to ensure that practice is properly accountable, this needs to be done within systems that support rather than drive it.

Studies continue to note that new structures and frameworks have not improved the longstanding concerns of missing assessments, gaps and inaccuracies in information recorded, and a tendency to lose the individuality of the child. At the same time, though, it is important to acknowledge that broader organisational and systemic issues – for example, time constraints and workload pressures associated, in part, with a system of strict performance management – have a significant impact on assessment and recording practices. Having considered a range of systemic, structural and organisational factors that impact on assessment, the next chapter moves on to consider the links between assessments and outcomes for children and families.

Summary

- Difficulties in relation to recording have a longstanding history.

- Frameworks such as the Assessment Framework and the Common Assessment Framework (CAF) and information management systems such as the Integrated Children's System (ICS) have given more structure to the way information is recorded during assessment. But much of the software for electronic recording has been unstable and is not fully fit for practitioner needs.

- Some studies have suggested that pre-set report structures make it difficult to manage the inclusion of 'non-standard' content (such as visual material) which may be needed to ensure that the views of particular children – for example, those with disabilities – are properly represented. They can also make it harder to get a sense of the 'whole child' and militate against the processes of synthesis and analysis that are essential for effective holistic assessment. However, recent moves to allow more flexibility to local authorities in the use of the exemplars may go some way towards addressing these concerns.

- Assessment takes time and thought, and the recording requirements of standardised assessment formats were sometimes felt to be cumbersome and overly time-consuming and to take practitioners away from direct work with children and families.

- Gaps and missing or inaccurate information appeared to be a matter of concern across a range of assessment formats. A significant number of cases lacked a full social history and/or chronology, making it harder to develop a properly contextualised understanding of the child and family's needs and circumstances and to make effective plans. This has been identified in previous research and is a longstanding problem.

- Process issues (for example, delay and inconsistency) and organisational factors, such as the extent and speed of change and the increase in the use of targets and performance indicators, have an impact on assessment practice. Some studies have suggested that the pressure to meet the very tight timeframes set for initial and core assessments has led to the development of short cuts and 'work arounds' that may provide the latent conditions for error and increase the risk that vulnerable children's needs are not properly identified and addressed.

Note

1 *A and B v Essex County Council* [2003] EWCA Civ 1848 E. and *Others v. The United Kingdom* (33218/96) [2002] ECHR 763 (26 November 2002).

Chapter 9

ASSESSMENTS AND CHILD OUTCOMES

In this chapter we ask how the conduct and quality of assessments are related to outcomes for children. Research studies that specifically tackle these questions are rare, and the methodological problems are significant. We begin by exploring the methodological difficulties and, in particular, the question of what outcomes may be measured.

What are the outcomes of an assessment?

In examining how and whether social work and related assessments may enhance outcomes for children, we had to consider in what form those outcomes should be framed: different interest groups or participants define outcomes in a variety of ways. For example, a parent might report positive results of social work involvement based on a good feeling about his or her relationship with the social worker. A researcher, on the other hand, might wish to apply measures of the emotional wellbeing of the child or of actual changes in parenting. Any such measures may give different results at different points in the assessment and intervention and at different points in a child's development. We illustrate the connections between assessment and outcome measures using Figure 9.1.

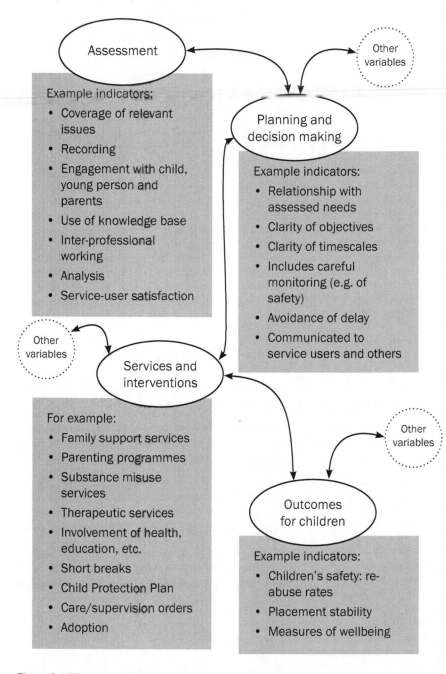

Figure 9.1 Diagrammatic representation of outcomes from assessments

Figure 9.1 illustrates how the quality and effectiveness of an assessment could be determined by examining the assessment itself, by looking at the immediate outputs of the assessment in terms of planning and decision making, or by measuring the outcomes for children arising from subsequent service provision or other intervention. The generally accepted pattern is for assessment to precede decision making, which leads to services and interventions, which in turn are assessed as to whether services/interventions have had the desired effects. The arrows connecting each of these elements are shown as two-headed, indicating that in real-life practice it is generally necessary to revisit earlier elements in the process rather than treating the approach as linear or one-dimensional. In the search for reliable and valid research results, no one measure is problem-free, and the inclusion of 'other variables' serves as a reminder that other factors in addition to the assessment will influence the outcomes for the child. The following sections review the potential and difficulties of empirically assessing quality and outcomes in each of the three areas, before we move on to examining relevant research findings.

1. The quality of assessments

This section relates to the first heading in Figure 9.1, that of *Assessment*. Whether the work involves a core assessment, an assessment related to possible adoption, to reunification or to other contexts (see Chapter 4), researchers might look for indicators of quality in terms of how the assessment itself is carried out. A variety of opinions about what constitutes a quality assessment have grown up over the years. Indeed, the Assessment Framework itself is a comprehensive statement of the areas a good assessment should cover. Similarly, government guidance offers an indication of key practice points when conducting an initial assessment. The relevant statements, which appear in *Working Together* (HM Government 2010a), are also used to inform inspections of practice. They advise, for example, that initial assessment should involve:

- seeing and speaking to the child, including alone when appropriate
- seeing and meeting with parents, the family and wider family members as appropriate
- involving and obtaining relevant information from professionals and others in contact with the child and family

- drawing together and analysing available information (focusing on the strengths and positive factors as well as vulnerabilities and risk factors) from a range of sources (including existing agency records).

(HM Government 2010a, para 5.41)

Additionally, in terms of content, the initial assessment should address the following questions:

- What are the developmental needs of the child? What needs of the child are being met and how? What needs of the child are not being met and why not?

- Are the parents able to respond appropriately to the child's identified needs? Is the child being adequately safeguarded from harm, and are the parents able to promote the child's health and development?

- What impact are family functioning (past and present) and history, and the wider family and environmental factors having on the parent's capacity to respond to their child's needs and the child's developmental progress?

- Is action required to safeguard and promote the welfare of the child? Within what timescales should this action be taken?

(HM Government 2010a, para 5.40)

A small number of studies in our review also attempted to identify the components of a quality assessment prior to examining files or collecting other data from social work staff. Preston-Shoot (2003) assessed cases in his sample against criteria developed by the Social Services Inspectorate in the 1990s: criteria that largely related to the different aspects of family functioning that were addressed, and the relevance of the overall assessment and plan. Macdonald (2001), similarly, reported on a schedule developed for a detailed analysis of 18 comprehensive assessments undertaken in four family centres.

Bell and colleagues (2007), in their study of the Integrated Children's System (ICS), developed a framework for analysing the content of ICS records. The framework included: whether service users' views were expressed; whether a coherent narrative giving an holistic picture of the child was present; and evidence of analysis by the social workers that supported the recommendations. Wade *et al.* (2005), in their study of unaccompanied asylum-seeking young people, took a similar approach that examined the extent to which needs had been assessed, and the coherence of the service response in relation to this assessment.

Other studies used rating scales. For example, Farmer and colleagues' study of reunification (2011) used researcher ratings of the quality of assessments, according to whether, for example, the assessments had been 'sufficiently analytical' and the extent to which they 'adequately assessed all of the risks to the child' (p.114). Selwyn and colleagues (2010) also used researcher ratings of assessments on a four-point scale, where the poorest had 'large chunks of information missing and only descriptive writing' and the best included 'good information and analysis' (p.70).

Understanding the quality of an assessment thus involves information about the way the assessment itself was conducted. To explore more fully the impact of an assessment, it is necessary to consider what happens after the assessment has taken place.

2. Planning and decision making as the outputs of an assessment

In some instances outcomes were described in terms of the processes and decisions that followed on from an assessment (see *Planning and decision making* in Figure 9.1). Such decisions might have involved a straightforward, often immediate response, such as whether a child who had had an initial assessment also received a core assessment or whether no further action was taken (see also Chapters 2 and 8). These actions are often described as outputs rather than outcomes. Many studies considered the outputs of assessments at a more detailed level. For example, whether services should be offered to enable a child to remain with the birth family, what types of interventions were appropriate, whether substitute care arrangements should be sought, and so on.

One of the problems, of course, with examining outputs is that, without an assessment of some kind, plans are unlikely to be established and services are unlikely to be offered. Consequently, a statistical link between assessment and service provision is more or less inevitable. Evaluations of the impact of assessments on this basis, unless accompanied by a reasonable amount of detail, need to be viewed with some caution.

3. Outcomes as medium- or long-term consequences for the child

Some studies offered information about the medium- or long-term progress of children (see *Outcomes for children* in Figure 9.1), progress that might have been connected with the decision making that resulted from an earlier assessment. In this overview the longest follow-up period was eight years. Ways in which the children's progress (or otherwise) was measured included: assessing the developmental status of the child; comparing children's development at different time points; the stability and/or quality of the placement; and the safety of the child in terms of recurrence of abuse.

In the analysis below we have amalgamated findings from each of the above approaches. Before turning to the findings, however, we consider the wider problems associated with research into outcomes in relation to assessments.

Assessments, outcomes and research

General questions about outcome-focused research have been addressed fully in other contexts (for example, Logan and Royse 2001; Ruffolo, Thoburn and Allen-Meares 2009) and need not be repeated. Nevertheless, particular problems arose in relation to the present review. It is superficially appealing to evaluate the success or otherwise of an assessment by examining the progress made by the child at a later date. For example, if a child's behavioural problems led to the need for a social work assessment, it ought to be possible to take another look at that child two or three years later to see whether the difficulties in question have improved. The improvement, if any, might then be attributed to the efficacy of the treatment as determined by the original assessment. This is, indeed, an approach that many studies have taken, but there is a difficulty in drawing valid conclusions, depending on how far studies have been able to take account of other factors that might also have affected the outcome. Such factors will include genetic vulnerability, treatment approaches, general life circumstances and individual characteristics such as the age of the child and severity of problems at the beginning of the intervention. Time since the assessment also has an impact on associations that might be made. The effect of an assessment a number of years after it was undertaken may have become statistically insignificant (Farmer and Lutman 2009) and may be less relevant in practice than it would have been when first undertaken.

Not only may the passage of time bring about a diminution in discernible effects of an assessment, but there is also the issue of varying results depending on the age of the children at follow-up. For example, outcomes for children in contact with the child welfare system are often measured during the teenage years. There are very few studies that have considered outcomes when children reach adulthood. Consequently measures are taken at a time when young people may be having a turbulent adolescence. Another few years on, results might look very different. Most of the studies in this review, of course, were not studies of assessment and the outcomes of assessment were not their focus. A few studies examined the statistical associations between assessments and outcomes through the use of binary or multivariate analyses. In some cases variables were combined to produce an indication of whether there was a correlation between the presence or absence of an assessment, and 'success' was defined as the presence or absence of the specified outcome (such as no abuse/re-abuse). Other studies used binary logistic regressions to examine the contribution assessments made to predicting an outcome. Two studies used Cox regression techniques to analyse the impact of delayed decision making on children's placement outcomes (Selwyn et al. 2010), and one used CHAID (Chi-squared Automatic Interaction Detector, a type of decision tree technique) to examine the impact of assessments (Farmer and Lutman 2009).

Perhaps as a consequence of these complexities, much of the research relating assessment to outcomes was limited to general points such as the effect of the presence or absence of assessment. Areas where greater depth to the research would be desirable were underdeveloped. For example, Quinton's (2009) review of matching arrangements identified considerable interest in practice regarding a child's capacity to form new attachments when placed in adoptive care. He reported that no prospective studies had been undertaken to consider whether any assessment of attachments can predict the nature of attachment relationships in the new family.[1] The present review is therefore constrained by limitations of this kind. Indeed, with regard to some of the research findings, we have had to present data on outcomes where it can only be inferred that the assessment may have had an effect. In these instances, we have attempted to show the pathway by which that effect may have operated, referring where appropriate to the diagram present at the start of this chapter. There is a danger that inferences of this kind may lead to exaggerated conclusions as a result of hindsight bias.

In addressing research that presented findings on outcomes and outputs, we begin by examining children's and parents' perspectives on services, since they might be expected to have some relationship with the quality of an assessment. Then we review outcome findings in relation to the key indicators, namely child safety, placement stability and children's wellbeing.

Children's and parents' perspectives on assessments and subsequent interventions

In this section we present more general findings on workers' attempts to engage with parents, children and young people. As a means of evaluating the outcomes of assessments for children, user engagement is not particularly robust, since service users' views on how engaged they were, however positive or negative, may not necessarily reflect actual outcomes/changes for children. In terms of the research reviewed, there was more information on parents' perspectives than on children's (see Chapter 6).

Nevertheless, as we saw in Chapter 6, the engagement of parents in work to improve the welfare of their children is important, parental engagement is linked to decisions about children's futures and parental commitment can contribute to the success of a plan of intervention.

Parental engagement

One of the key contextual factors, in the UK, relevant to the research undertaken within our timeframe, was a cluster of research findings from the 1990s. These studies examined, amongst other things, parents' perspectives of the child protection process. In particular, they highlighted the damage, such as marital breakdown, economic hardship or homelessness, that can follow a child protection investigation, and the distress that may occur within families encountering such interventions (Brandon et al. 1999; Department of Health 1995).

In the research selected for the present review, there was some evidence that the more recent picture might be a little more positive. Brandon et al. (1999) found that 20 per cent of parents were thought to have participated or been partners at the stage of investigation into allegations of harm to the children. A further 40 per cent were considered to have been fully or partially informed (i.e. being informed was a lesser measure of the degree of participation). They contrasted these findings with an earlier study (Thoburn et al. 1995), where only 11 per cent were thought to have participated or been partners at the investigation stage. Taking the lesser measure, however, Thoburn et al. (1995) found that 82 per cent had been fully or partially informed or consulted.

Aldgate and Bradley (1999), in a study of short-term fostering, identified a very high proportion of parents who felt they had been consulted as part of the assessment and planning process, and concluded that partnership working had been very successful in their sample. However, with regard to children in the same study:

When it came to having the opportunity to talk about how they felt and having an input into the decision-making, just over half the children (22) thought that this had happened, eight said it definitely had never happened while the remaining 11 (27%) were uncertain. (Aldgate and Bradley 1999, pp.179–180)

A key conclusion of Cleaver *et al.*'s (2004) study of the Assessment Framework was that its implementation had led to improved parental involvement in assessments. Despite some mixed opinions from social workers and managers, the views of parents were clear in this regard. The majority of parents (75%) in their sample reported positive experiences, and felt consulted and involved at all stages. Cleaver and colleagues presented these findings as an indication that involvement and partnership working had improved since the studies of the 1990s. Further support for the proposition that the participation of parents in assessments improved between the 1990s and the decade to 2010 comes from Millar and Corby (2006). Their study found that the *Framework for the Assessment of Children in Need* had created conditions that promoted the involvement of parents; about half the parents in their sample felt they had made a positive contribution to the assessment.

Parental satisfaction

Parental satisfaction with the assessment and the resulting plan can be considered as one kind of outcome, albeit an outcome that occurs at an early stage in the process (see Figure 9.1). Cleaver *et al.* (2007) suggested that parental satisfaction was associated with the parents being able to acknowledge problems and engage with services, and being kept fully informed about the assessment, planning process and subsequent developments. Satisfaction with the outcome of the assessment was also linked, not surprisingly, with the degree to which parents thought they had received the services they required. And Cleaver *et al.* (2004), when they explored the degree of parental satisfaction with child in need plans in their study of the Assessment Framework, found that it was related to the degree of parental involvement in the assessment and planning processes.

The importance of appropriate service provision and the link with parental satisfaction has been found elsewhere. For example, Platt (2007), in a qualitative study of initial assessments, noted the greater satisfaction of parents who agreed with the social worker about the services provided or planned. Tunstill and Aldgate (2000), in their study of responses to children in need, reported that more than half of the parents felt that they had participated actively in decision making and this appeared to be linked to parental satisfaction with the provision of practical services. From each of these studies, there remains a general question as to whether parents are satisfied with the services because they felt involved and consulted. They might, alternatively, feel involved and consulted because they have been provided with services that met their needs.

Corby *et al.*'s (2002) study may help understand this interaction. They found that parents in their sample reported positive outcomes for themselves from both initial and core assessments. The way this effect worked was, for example, enabling them to deal with difficulties that needed to be addressed. There was also an important element of good relationship management by the social worker (see also Chapter 6). Where positive outcomes did not occur, there appeared to be greater disagreement between professionals and parents. Millar and Corby (2006), similarly, found that using the Assessment Framework could lead to outcomes that service users found helpful, and that the attitude of workers to the Framework itself affected this outcome. Corby and colleagues' findings (2002), furthermore, showed that initial assessments were appreciated by parents, and the reason for their positive response was the way in which the assessment process and the purpose of the questions were easily understood. With regard to core assessments, they found that two-thirds of families were generally positive.

Children's participation in and views of assessment

Cleaver and colleagues' (2004) results were less positive in relation to social work engagement with children and young people in assessments. Unfortunately, their sample size, of only eight children and young people, was too small to generalise from but, broadly speaking, the young people were less satisfied, with the assessments and with the relationship with their social worker than were their parents. Few studies gave information about children's views of assessment or of services (see Chapter 6). A small number of studies of children's views of services might suggest that assessment had made some contribution. Berridge *et al.* (2008), for example, in a study of the education of looked after children who had emotional and behavioural difficulties, found a positive picture. The young people interviewed felt that they received good care and good educational support, and most had made some progress behaviourally and educationally. We might speculate that earlier assessment/s had contributed to decisions about the assistance they received, and thus might have affected these outcomes.

However, Stein and colleagues' (2007) review of research related to neglected adolescents drew on US research that suggested young people's own assessments of their situation were linked more strongly to outcomes than professional assessments. The original study (McGee *et al.* 1995) compared the predictive validity of different approaches to the measurement of maltreatment. They found that young people's assessments of the severity of their own maltreatment were more predictive of behaviour problems than both social workers' and researchers estimates of severity. These findings reinforce the importance of working with the child or young person and hearing their viewpoint.

Assessment and safeguarding

In this section we consider assessments in the context of safeguarding children. One key outcome in safeguarding is rates of re-abuse, although we refer to other measures where appropriate. Outcomes considered may, thus, be outputs at the level of *Planning and decision making* (see Figure 9.1) or later *Child outcomes* that follow from the provision of services.

A considerable literature over recent decades has drawn attention to ways in which assessment should be carried out in the context of safeguarding children and responding to concerns about child maltreatment. Many of the relevant aspects of assessment have already been addressed in this report, and the importance of conducting an assessment of the needs of a child who is believed to be suffering or likely to suffer significant harm is often treated as self-evident. Assessment is assumed to lead to a detailed understanding of the child's difficulties and experiences, a plan of action to address key adversities and the provision of services to deliver the intended changes or outcomes. Experienced practitioners will be well aware that this picture is somewhat oversimplified. Nonetheless, we examine some research studies here that indicate the importance of assessment through making relevant links with outcomes.

Perhaps best known, for example, are the findings of reviews and inquiries into child deaths and serious cases. Original reports (for example, Laming 2003), as well as overviews of serious case reviews (for example, Rose and Barnes 2008), have concluded that shortcomings in assessments (especially initial and core assessments), in many cases, are likely to have contributed to the children's deaths. These conclusions may, however, be limited to the most serious cases. Consequently the following paragraphs give greater attention to evidence from studies examining broader populations of children.

Research that made a direct connection between safeguarding children, outcomes and assessment in the studies reviewed was rare. In studies of reunification in practice, Farmer et al. (2011) and Wade, Biehal et al. (2010) each found that assessment and a proactive approach to planning were associated with better reunification outcomes for looked after children. In addition, other findings about reunification are relevant to assessment. Farmer et al. (2011) found that 64 per cent of the children in their study had one or more failed returns home (including 35% of children with two or more), during a two-year follow-up period; Biehal (2006) estimated that between a third and half of children who returned home experienced return breakdowns, whilst Sinclair, Baker et al. (2005) found that almost half (48%) of their sample of children re-entered care within less than 22 months. Not only has a high rate of return disruption been found, but in addition, Farmer et al. (2011) found that 36 per cent of the continuing returns home in their study were of poor quality for the child and that 16 per cent of the children remained at home despite ongoing abuse or neglect.

Taking these issues further, Beecham and Sinclair (2007), in their research overview *Costs and Outcomes in Children's Social Care*, reported that support after a return home was often discontinued without any assessment of whether the families' problems had diminished. This led to breakdowns of the home placements, whilst at the same time the prospects of adoption had been delayed or prevented. Children who are returned home have poorer psycho-social outcomes and experience higher levels of maltreatment compared to children who remain in substitute care (see, for example, Biehal 2006; Farmer 2009; Sinclair 2005; Sinclair, Baker et al. 2005; Wade, Biehal et al. 2010). It is therefore important to avoid poorly assessed and unsupported reunifications, since they expose children to the risks of further abuse and instability, and children returning to care rarely return to their previous foster carers (only 17% did so in Farmer et al.'s 2011 study).

Strong evidence of the importance of assessment was cited by Fauth and colleagues (2010), who drew on an American study (Fuller, Wells and Cotton 2001) examining the implementation of a risk assessment and management protocol in a community-based social work context. They found that children for whom a detailed assessment had not been completed were four times more likely to experience a recurrence of maltreatment within 12 months of referral than those who had such an assessment. The reasons for non-completion of assessments were unclear.

Similarly, in relation to neglect, Farmer and Lutman (2009) found that, except in cases where there were care proceedings, assessments (mainly core and initial assessments) were infrequent in their sample, workers often lacked knowledge of the history of the case, and 40 per cent of the cases were closed at some stage when difficulties were still in evidence. In many cases there was involvement of children's social care services over many years, but without effective action to protect the children. There were also significant gaps in services for parents with problems of drug and alcohol misuse. The study showed that a variety of factors were associated with better outcomes for the children in the sample (in terms of their stability and wellbeing at the five-year follow-up). Whilst some of the factors associated with outcomes concerned children's characteristics (for example, age and behaviour problems), many of them related to how their cases were managed. Where return home took place, children's outcomes were best if they were *under the age of six* at the time of reunification with their birth parents and there had been appropriate service provision. The researchers concluded that there was a need for more proactive practice with children of school age and older, and for earlier and more effective intervention when safeguarding concerns were evident. There were clear local authority differences in relation to children's outcomes, reinforcing the message that how cases are managed does make a difference. The researchers were unable to show that *assessment* itself was a significant determinant of outcomes, although this may well have been due to the methodological problem of demonstrating such a correlation after a lengthy follow-up period (five years). Nevertheless, good case management is likely to be linked to good ongoing assessment.

Thoburn *et al.*'s (2000) study of emotional abuse and neglect also failed to establish a statistical association between better or worse outcomes (measured after 12 months) and the presence on file of an assessment or family support plan. However, they pointed out that those cases most likely to improve were the more straightforward ones, and at the time of their research were more likely to receive a quick, unrecorded assessment. They suggested there was evidence of social workers using practice wisdom in making decisions about allocating cases, an approach that was effective in the majority of cases, although a small proportion of cases closed quickly (14%) had worse outcomes. In relation to this minority where outcomes were worse, Thoburn and colleagues speculated that a more careful assessment might have made a difference. On the other hand, Forrester's study (2008), in the somewhat different context of re-referral patterns following initial assessment, suggested that there was very little evidence of social workers closing cases with significant concerns inappropriately. Based on data collected in the late 1990s and early 2000s, he concluded that practice at that time 'was comparatively good at avoiding closing referrals that appeared to place children at high risk of a negative outcome. There is every possibility that the new systems are equally good or better: however, this needs to be empirically tested' (2008, p.297). Thoburn and her colleagues (2000), in suggesting that more careful assessments might have avoided some of the poor outcomes of cases closed too quickly, acknowledged the expense of undertaking assessments for 100 per cent of such families when the target group (those cases closed quickly who had worse outcomes) was merely 14 per cent.

The question of costs can be looked at another way. Aldgate and Statham (2001), in their overview of earlier research into practice following the implementation of the Children Act 1989, noted that families may sometimes be offered inappropriate services, based more on available resources than on assessment of need. In this situation, effective assessment, arguably, is relatively cost-effective if it avoids wasting resources on services that do not meet the needs to be addressed. We return to the cost issue in a later section on stability and permanence.

A review by Daniel (2004) of child protection arrangements in Scotland gave some indication of the aspects of assessment that have the potential to improve practice. Cases in her sample were given ratings that combined the extent to which guidance was complied with and the outcomes for the child. These outcomes followed from a range of interventions, of which assessment was part, and the conclusions made significant references to the importance of assessment.

Features that were associated with lower overall ratings were:

- enquiries that were not sufficiently extensive
- poor assessments, in particular the lack of recognition of patterns
- insufficient use of intra-agency information
- insufficient use of interagency information
- lack of focus on the child
- lack of attention to the role of at least one key adult
- lack of assessment of the parent's ability to use the support and to change.

Some of the key features associated with a high overall rating were:

- a child-sensitive and appropriate response to 'minor' incidents
- effective preventive intervention, for example provision of support within school
- detailed advance planning for potential risk, for example the use of pre-birth case conferences
- good inter-agency collaboration
- good record keeping by all agencies
- sustained commitment to working with parents
- the determined efforts of one practitioner to improve the life of a child
- the social work practice being of a high quality.

Greater detail of these specific aspects of assessment appears elsewhere in this report. In terms of safeguarding, then, our review found evidence of the importance of assessment in a number of contexts. The need for assessment came up repeatedly in serious case reviews. Studies of reunification and risk assessment and management showed a clear link between good assessment and better outcomes for children. Insufficient attention to assessment was of concern in key areas such as neglect, emotional abuse and reunification. Similar evidence of the importance of assessment could be inferred from other research, particularly where process outcomes were addressed.

But good assessment is not the only factor that may affect outcomes. Various authors cited other variables affecting their results, including the more severe the problem, the worse the outcome, irrespective of the involvement of services (Carpenter et al. 2003; Macdonald and Williamson 2002; Thoburn et al. 2000); the availability of resources (Brandon and Thoburn 2008); the different needs of parents with learning disabilities (Cleaver and Nicholson 2007); parental unwillingness to engage (Brandon and Thoburn 2008); and the strength of different local authority's planning processes for individual children (Wade, Biehal et al. 2010).

Summary

With regard to the safety of children in a community context, whether continuing to live with parents or returned under a reunification plan, the evidence suggests that good assessment is likely to lead to improved outcomes.

Stability and permanence

We turn now to outcomes relevant to the achievement of stability and permanence in children's placements outside their families of origin. A key indicator of the probable success (or otherwise) of placements, used by researchers over several decades, has been the rate of placement disruption. Where placements break down, children may then move through a succession of placements, leading to potentially damaging instability in their lives. The discussion in this section draws on outcome findings related both to placement disruption and to the psycho-social effects of instability. It addresses key points found in our review, namely maintaining placement stability, variations in practice, the problem of delay and ways of addressing psycho-social problems of children and young people.

Assessment and placement stability

Instability is a major factor affecting a child's development, a point that has been recognised across a range of research (see, for example, Tarren-Sweeney 2010). In an important study from the United States, Rubin (2007) showed that the experience of placement breakdown can exacerbate or cause emotional and behavioural problems for looked after children. Harwin *et al.* (2003) showed that welfare progress was worse the greater the number of moves the child or young person had experienced. Poor educational attainment has also been related to unstable care experiences (see, for example, Berridge 2000; Stein 2006). Ongoing effects of poor educational attainment are that levels of disadvantage for children increase, with major consequences for young people's future prospects and chances of (stable) employment. It is obviously important that, where feasible, assessment practice should contribute to the establishment of stable placements, and to the prevention of placement breakdown (see also Chapter 4). These outcomes, however, occur at the end of the chain shown in Figure 9.1, so the connection with assessments is difficult to demonstrate.

Farmer and Dance *et al.* (2010) traced disruptions in some adoptive placements back to inadequate assessments of the children, although the numbers of disruptions were small (seven disruptions in total, only some of which were related back to assessments). More importantly, they showed that poor-quality matches between children and adoptive parents (which are based on assessments of the children and the prospective adopters) were related to poorer outcomes in these adoptive placements.

Selwyn and her colleagues (2006), in their study of non-infant adoptions, examined the experiences of a small group of children who by follow-up had experienced multiple disruptions and were often in specialist residential care. They found that inadequate assessments played a major role in failing to identify specific conditions, and that even at an early stage their behaviour had been unusual or extreme and would have merited a thorough investigation (Beecham and Sinclair 2007).

In the practice context, assessment should address the factors that may affect placement stability. Although we explored these issues more fully in Chapter 4, key factors were identified by Quinton (2009, p.42) as 'behavioural problems, over-activity and restlessness, and difficulties in making relationships'. Sinclair et al.'s (2007) findings were similar, identifying more challenging behaviour as a key issue, doing less well at school, and the child or young person not wanting to be in care – all of which affect outcomes. Clearly, again, there is an inferred relationship between assessment and outcomes, and effective assessment of these factors should have the potential to improve things for the children involved, if appropriate action follows.

In addition to child-related factors, a key finding from several studies was that the provision of good-quality information to foster carers or prospective adopters contributed to improved outcomes for the children. Where foster carers or adoptive parents found that children had more problems than they had anticipated, this lack of information increased the chances of placement breakdown (Farmer et al. 2004, 2010). Relevant details included school attendance and educational progress, children's health and the current placement plan and, in the case of adoption, children's difficulties in making relationships or 'attaching' to carers. The quality of information provision can be linked to the quality of assessment, but may also be determined by other factors such as worker openness, and skills in collaboration with carers and other professionals (Dance et al. 2010; Farmer et al. 2004; Farmer and Dance et al. 2010; Randall 2009; Triseliotis et al. 2000). Clearly, the sharing of information following an assessment is a significant part of the overall process for relevant children.

Variations in practice

Our review identified some major variations both between and within local authorities in the conclusions of the assessments and the resulting consequences (Farmer et al. 2011; Farmer and Lutman 2009; Sinclair et al. 2007; Wade, Biehal et al. 2010; Ward et al. 2010). For example, in Sinclair and his colleagues' (2007) study of the English care system, differences in placement outcome, such as whether a child went into residential care, foster care, kin care, was adopted or returned home, were related to the practice of the local authority. Local authority differences were also evident in the use made of adoption (Biehal *et al.* 2010), kinship care (Farmer and Moyers 2008) and special guardianship (Wade, Dixon and Richards 2010), as well as in the long-term management of neglected children (Farmer and Lutman 2009). Sinclair *et al.* (2007) and Wade, Biehal *et al.* (2010) showed that differences in assessment, planning and case management in different local authorities shaped children's overall care pathways. It is likely that care pathways will sometimes have an influence on children's chances of achieving stability, and Farmer and Lutman (2009) showed that proactive case management was related to better child outcomes, a factor that is suggestive of the importance of assessment.

The reasons for these differences were not simply to do with the practice of individual social workers, but were influenced by different local authority policies and procedures. Practice differed not only between authorities but also between teams in the same local authority. The evidence suggested that local authorities may influence relevant practices through decisions about resources (for example, by increasing the number of in-house foster carers), and through a combination of procedures and personnel. Placement panels, for example, may have a major effect on the proportions of children in out-of-home care or adopted. The staffing and resources available to social work teams and the beliefs of the particular social workers were also a major influence (Sinclair *et al.* 2007).

In relation to variations between groups of service users, children whose parents had learning disabilities have aroused particular interest in recent research. Cleaver and Nicholson (2007) found, in contrast to the view that parents with learning disabilities may find their children are removed rather hastily, that social workers' decisions in such cases to place children away from home were not taken precipitately. In no case was a child removed solely because of a parent's learning disability, but other difficulties had been taken into account. Furthermore, once placed, all the children showed progress. When such placements were made as a result of care proceedings, these decisions would have been based on assessment/s, and the fact that workers made efforts not to remove children precipitately might suggest carefully considered work. It should be noted, however, that other authors (for example, Booth and Booth 2005) have taken a different position on this issue, suggesting that parents with learning disabilities involved in care proceedings are often seriously disadvantaged.

A cautionary note is necessary in the context of variations in practice. Harwin and colleagues' (2003) study of the implementation of care orders presented some interesting findings. Their research included an examination of care plans, which could be considered as the final part of a process of assessment and reflective of the quality of assessment in the relevant cases. They found no automatic link between the quality of care plans and whether the planned placement was actually fulfilled, even where there was detailed itemisation of issues and proposals. Their explanation for this is partly that some of the detail in the plans would have no possible bearing on placement fulfilment, and partly that greater detail was evident in the cases that were most problematic but where by definition the plan would also be most difficult to implement. (This type of paradox in uncovering the link between assessment and outcomes was noted earlier.) At the same time Harwin et al. (2003) found that social workers' *informal* predictions of which plans were likely to be implemented most easily were generally accurate. It is reasonable to assume that these predictions were based on either formal or informal assessments. The aspects that social workers found most difficult to predict were the actions of parents, where there was evidence of unjustified levels of either optimism or pessimism. This finding has interesting implications for assessment in general.

The variations in practice noted in this section suggest that factors such as local authority policies and practices and probably also team cultures can influence assessment, planning and case management. This is the context in which any changes in practice need to be considered. This is a question to which we return in Chapter 10.

The impact of delay

As suggested in Figure 9.1, delay at the stage of *Planning and decision making* may impact on service provision and intervention, and may have consequential effects on outcomes. The evidence for this effect is examined more fully in this section. A significant issue that affects placement stability is that of delayed decision making about removal and placement of children. Sinclair (2005), in his research overview on fostering, which included studies of adoption, noted that, in the adoption study by Selwyn and her colleagues (2006), delays in achieving adoption arose in part from continued attempts at preventive work, which were commonly 'not grounded in a full assessment' nor 'sufficiently intensive or prolonged to mitigate the appalling circumstances in which the children lived' (Sinclair 2005, p.32). Such work often continued long after it was clear that it was not succeeding, and for some children (41%) no permanence plans were made within two years of entry to care.

Ward et al. (2006) also showed the frequency with which failed attempts at return delayed placement for adoption amongst very young children. The researchers pointed to a failure by social workers to make a realistic assessment of parental capacity, as well as the role of the court in these attempts and delay in the provision of drug and other adult services. Yet this study found that babies with mothers who had serious problems of substance misuse, domestic violence and mental health rarely returned home successfully. Unfortunately, in many such cases, decisions appeared not to be taken quickly (Sinclair 2005). Ward and her colleagues suggested that, with better information from assessment, unpromising returns might be avoided.

The ways in which such delays affect outcomes such as placement stability are worth explaining. A number of studies have shown the likelihood of children achieving permanence through adoption to be age-related (see for example Harwin et al. 2003; Sinclair, Baker et al. 2005). Selwyn and colleagues (2006) found that the chance of *not* being adopted increased by 1.8 for every extra year of age at entry to care and by 1.6 for each subsequent year before an adoption recommendation was made. Lowe et al. (2002) found that four times as many children over the age of five were placed in foster care rather than adopted. Farmer and Dance et al. (2010) confirmed both this age-related effect and the continuing occurrence of delays caused by repeated attempts at reunification. Thus, service interventions such as adoption become increasingly difficult to achieve where delay at the assessment stage has resulted in adoption being sought when the child is older.

Delay is a particular issue for minority ethnic children. As we have seen, Selwyn et al. (2010), in their study of pathways to permanence, found that the quality of information gathered, in relation to black and Asian children, was poor in comparison to other groups, and that there was more evidence of delay in permanency decisions for them. Farmer and Dance et al. (2010) also found that delay was a serious issue in relation to black and minority ethnic children and both studies showed that, as a result, fewer black and minority ethnic children were placed for adoption and more 'aged out' of the chance of adoption. Again, such delays can have detrimental consequences in reducing the chances of a permanent placement and stability for a child.

Absence of assessments, difficulties in arranging them and repeat assessments, can also contribute to delayed decision making. Selwyn *et al.* (2006), in their study of the costs and outcomes of non-infant adoptions, found that drift, in terms of lack of social work assessment, planning and action, accounted for 53 per cent of delay in decision making. Problems of case allocation and managerial oversight contributed to delay in 15 per cent of cases. Slowness to act was also associated with unfocused social work practice combined with a number of other circumstances. Similarly, Farmer and Dance *et al.* (2010) found that sibling assessment for adoptive placement was an area where some social workers lacked confidence. As a result, there could be delay while children's social workers questioned how to undertake or obtain such an assessment.

Specialist assessments, usually by psychologists, as we have seen, could be very helpful when uncertainty, such as that involved in sibling assessments, was evident. This was also important, because the outcomes of placements were better where there were fewer tensions between siblings placed together (Farmer and Dance *et al.* 2010). Furthermore the same study, in the context of repeated attempts at reunification, indicated the importance of specialist assessments, such as those made by psychologists, in providing a basis for deciding whether long-term permanent care away from parents was needed. And Brophy (2006) reinforced the point about the value of specialist assessments in her review of research on care proceedings. She concluded that there was a need for a range of assessment-related skills beyond simply those of social workers, in cases of highly vulnerable children and parents with complex, multi-dimensional problems.

In summary, then, there is evidence in the studies reviewed to suggest that poor assessment, prior to decisions about adoption, can lead to delays in achieving permanent placements, which may contribute to placement instability – and, indeed, some children never achieve a permanent placement. In some studies the link back to the assessment was clearer than in others. Nevertheless, the findings reinforce the importance of good assessment, which appears to have the potential to help improve outcomes for children, especially when combined with proactive case management. This point takes on greater importance when we examine the role of psycho-social problems in relation to achieving permanence for children, in the next section.

Psycho-social problems

Our review also indicated some links between assessments and looked after children's psycho-social problems. One key issue is that of the increasing difficulties experienced by some children as they get older. Ward and her colleagues (2008) found that children's worsening emotional and behavioural difficulties, often after placement breakdown, increased the risk of further instability with negative impacts on the children but also escalating costs for the local authority. Berridge and colleagues (2008) found that young people with more emotional and behavioural problems required more expensive placements, and Farmer and Lutman (2009) found that the lack of sufficiently early interventions can mean that children's worsening behaviour not only requires increasingly expensive placements but, if left too late, such children may become 'hard to contain' in any placement, particularly once they reach adolescence. Arguments such as this have emphasised the importance of early intervention in the lives of children who may be likely to experience welfare problems, a point that is now widely accepted (Allen and Smith 2008).

The needs of other vulnerable children also emerged from our review. Rushton and Dance (2005) examined a sample of children placed with the intention of permanence, a significant sub-sample (22) of whom had been singled out for rejection by their birth parents. They noted the lack of detailed assessments of this group of children and suggested that this may have been a contributory factor to the significant psycho-social problems many of them experienced in their adoptive placements. It may be that identifying a child as rejected within his or her family is a difficult area to assess and one where there is room for development of particular skills, but the importance of trying to do so is clear.

Building on Ward and her colleagues' (2008) research, Hannon, Wood and Bazalgette (2010) in the Demos report on looked after children, calculated that greater stability and improved mental health for children could reduce the immediate costs to the local authority by reducing social workers' time and the use of expensive agency and residential placements and therapeutic support. They estimated that the average saving would be over £32,000 per child per year when comparing children with long-term stable placements with those with unstable care careers. The difference in costs of earlier intervention, compared with the projected costs associated with the likely trajectories of these children into adulthood was huge. Not only does the lack of appropriate early intervention for looked after children have a deleterious impact on those children, but it is also very costly for local authorities in the long run.

A further area where assessment might contribute to the provision of appropriate services is in relation to older children, including those placed with kin carers. In common with other kinds of placement, Hunt, Waterhouse and Lutman (2009) and Farmer and Moyers (2008) found that age was related to kinship placement stability, in that placements of younger children were more stable (see also Chapter 4). One implication for assessment is to address the need for services to support adolescent kinship placements, since greater problems would be anticipated.

This point is important for other kinds of placement too. Farmer *et al.* (2004) showed that foster placements for adolescents were more likely to be successful when a range of informal, formal and, where necessary, therapeutic supports were in place. They argued that assessment of the need for mental health services or counselling for adolescents is needed before each placement or soon after (see also Chapter 7). In terms of assessment, this reinforces the value of identifying the strength of existing informal support and assessing the need for formal services in addition to the provision of a placement (see also Quinton 2004).

Unfortunately, assessment for and provision of therapeutic services is not always a priority. Selwyn *et al.* (2006), in their study of the costs and outcomes of non-infant adoptions, found that mental health assessments were undertaken on only ten of the children in their sample, and very few received a sustained therapeutic service (see also Hunt and Macleod 1999). They referred to case files containing sheaves of letters, pleading for services without success. Beecham and Sinclair (2007, p.115), in their review of costs and outcomes in children's social care, concluded that: 'Good quality assessments can benefit…children's care careers and the costs are low compared to the potential costs of subsequent support. It therefore seems unwise to reduce the level of resources devoted to assessment as a means of saving money.' The key point is that decisive early intervention is important in achieving good psycho-social outcomes for children. Clearly assessment is necessary to identify the relevant needs and the most appropriate form of support or therapeutic service needed (a point to which we return later in this chapter). In addition, since difficulties often increase with age for looked after children, provision of therapeutic and other services for teenagers is well worth considering, at as early a stage as possible. Again assessment is necessary to identify needs in each case.

In summary, then, in terms of the relationship between assessments and children's placement stability, delays in assessment and decision making can lead to difficulties achieving permanent placements because of the child's increasing age and the need for more costly interventions as problems become more entrenched in later childhood and adolescence. Practice by local authorities in terms of assessment and case management is variable and affects children's pathways in care. Instability in care often leads to further instability, with negative impacts on children and spiralling costs for local authorities.

Children's wellbeing

In this section we consider a number of more general questions about children's wellbeing. Clearly the importance of wellbeing is somewhat self-evident: the purpose of most of the work that forms the subject matter of this report is to improve children's wellbeing. Assessment should identify the best ways of achieving such improvements. The issues in this section are of particular interest in the context of providing community-based services, rather than substitute care. Our review identified relevant findings about assessment of children in need, the inter-disciplinary assessment processes using the Common Assessment Framework, initial assessments, targeting of services, South Asian families with disabled children, and unaccompanied asylum-seeking children.

Part of the rationale for the Common Assessment Framework (CAF) was to share responsibility for responding to children with additional needs across the range of relevant professionals, and to offer services at the level that best meets those needs. One indication of failure to achieve this intention would be if there was an increase in referrals to one particular agency such as children's social care services. Pithouse (2006), in a Welsh study of a pilot of the Common Assessment Framework, found tentative evidence of a decrease in the number of referrals to social work services and of more focused social services responses. This decrease was not accompanied by an increase in child protection referrals, all of which suggests a positive outcome. (In more recent years there has been an increase (nationally) in such referrals – considered to be a consequence of the publicity surrounding the Peter Connelly case.) Part of the arrangements related to use of the CAF is provision for a lead professional to take responsibility in individual cases. Whilst this is subject to more detailed discussion elsewhere (see Chapter 7), lead professionals in Brandon et al.'s (2006) study were seeing the benefits of this system, and there was some limited evidence that it took less time to bring about results with families. Arguably, the introduction of this assessment as an inter-disciplinary process will have contributed to these benefits.

Selwyn and colleagues (2006), in their study of the costs of non-infant adoption, found that many families received a lot of support, but it was not targeted at specific problems. This was because no core assessment had been completed, and they concluded that the service provision had been wasteful of scarce resources. Similar points were made by Barlow and Schrader-Macmillan (2009) in a review of what works in preventing emotional maltreatment. Their conclusion went further in suggesting that the long-term effectiveness of some interventions is dependent on effective targeting and that providing services to those who do not need them can undermine confidence in service recipients. In the context of emotional maltreatment, they suggest that attachment patterns may be used as the basis for this targeting. Some of the interventions they reviewed showed the importance of inputs addressing multiple aspects of families' lives, as well as building upon the positives in them. Clearly, assessment of attachment styles and relevant family functioning are important here.

Cleaver et al. (2004), in their study of the implementation of the Assessment Framework, showed that the referrals most likely to progress from initial to core assessment were cases involving child protection issues, parental alcohol or drug misuse, and referrals from other social services departments. Those least likely to progress to a core assessment involved parental mental illness, financial and housing problems, and referrals from non-professionals. In terms of ethnic groups, black children and children of mixed ethnicity were least likely to proceed to a core assessment. There was evidence in the same study that families where there were multiple problems were more likely to be offered services – a finding that suggests some consistency between assessments and service responses. In only a minority of cases involving initial assessments was there insufficient service provision, although this included 17.5 per cent (10 out of 61) of those cases recorded as having multiple problems. These ten assessments led to no further action.

The findings of a study into the experiences of South Asian families with severely disabled children appear to reinforce Cleaver et al.'s (2004) findings on black and mixed ethnic groups. Hatton et al. (2004) found that comprehensive assessments of need were rare, there was a need to use the preferred language of the parents, and service provision was patchy. Clearly, this is likely to have an effect on the children's wellbeing, given the severity of their disabilities.

Some limitations in assessments were also evident in relation to unaccompanied asylum-seeking children and young people (Wade *et al.* 2005), with placement decisions being made in many cases in response to the urgency of the situation rather than on the basis of clear assessment. Even when areas of difficulty emerged in assessments, a plan of action did not necessarily follow. For example, where information was collected on the isolation and social networks of young people, in 45 per cent of cases no outcome or plan of action was recorded. Many such young people had encountered considerable trauma prior to entering the UK and, in a number of cases, where children or young people felt able to discuss these issues, the assessment led to an offer of counselling or therapeutic help. Often, however, the young person was simply not ready to undertake this work, illustrating the difficulty of moving clearly from an assessment to an intervention.

In relation to substance misuse, Cleaver *et al.* (2007) found that in families where parents misused drugs or alcohol, assessments were more likely to lead to services to help with their difficulties than in cases of domestic violence. Forrester and Harwin (2008) showed that, where parents were misusing drugs, early referrals to social work services, particularly at or around the birth of a child, were associated with good outcomes for the child. Part of the explanation for this finding was that a number of the children concerned were in placements with alternative families at the time of follow-up (two years after referral).

The key message on children's wellbeing concerns the importance of assessing families' circumstances with a view to targeting interventions effectively. This is particularly important in relation to choice of therapeutic services, such as provision for drug-misusing parents and for emotional maltreatment. There was evidence of variable levels of assessment, especially in relation to black and minority ethnic groups and unaccompanied asylum-seeking children. Findings related to substance-misusing parents re-emphasised the importance of early referral for social work services.

Conclusion

In this chapter, we reviewed the methodological difficulties of evaluating assessments and presented an overview of the state of knowledge about outcomes from assessments. Parents' and children's reactions to the experience of assessment and related interventions were, on balance, positive, and findings suggested improvements in relationships between social workers and parents in the UK between the 1990s and the 2000s.

In relation to safeguarding, good assessment appeared likely to lead to better outcomes for children. With regard to children's placement stability, good assessment has the potential to bring about considerable improvements through the prevention of delay and the provision of adequate support and services to foster carers and others. Early intervention was re-emphasised, and assessment can assist in the effective targeting of interventions.

Nevertheless, it should be noted that assessment is not a panacea. A number of other variables can affect outcomes, including the degree of difficulty experienced by the child in question and the availability of resources.

Summary

- There are methodological problems in linking assessments to outcomes, particularly in relation to clarifying the influence of other variables.

- Nevertheless, good assessment is unequivocally important and contributes to good outcomes for children.

- There was evidence of positive views of assessments from parents, particularly where there was good relationship management and they were involved and consulted about assessment and planning.

- Absence of assessment of maltreated children was related to repeat abuse.

- In relation to planning children's placements, assessments need to take into account the factors that may lead to placement breakdown and identify where there is a need for therapeutic or other services.

- Multi-disciplinary assessments may be valuable in a range of contexts, particularly more complex cases, sibling assessments and where there are concerns about repeat attempts at reunification.

- Delays in decision making about removal and placement of children are linked to assessment, planning and case management procedures. Avoidance of delay is well known as a factor that contributes to better outcomes for children, particularly in terms of placement stability.

- There was evidence of shortcomings in the assessments of minority ethnic families and of unaccompanied asylum-seeking children.

- The value of early targeted intervention was re-emphasised.

- There was evidence that assessment and proactive planning improved outcomes for previously looked after children, who were returned to their parents' care.

Note

1   It should be noted that a relevant study is currently under way at the Anna Freud Centre – *The Adoption and Attachment Study: Into Adolescence* (see www. annafreud.org/adoption-followup.htm).

Chapter 10

CONCLUSIONS

In this chapter we review and summarise the key points arising from our exploration of social work research findings on assessment. In brief, we emphasise that good assessment matters and that it should be underpinned by a clear focus on the child and careful attention to analysis. However, it requires time, resources and appropriate supporting tools or materials. Since assessment makes a range of practical and emotional demands on practitioners, good access to reflective supervision is essential. Assessment is a core activity on which subsequent professional activity and interventions build. Without a solid foundation of assessment, the edifice of professional interventions is unsafe.

This review has pointed to a very wide and growing range of knowledge areas that are needed in assessment and to a range of obstacles that need to be surmounted by workers. It is not surprising that social workers lack confidence in their assessment skills, since feedback on how their decisions work out in practice may not be available for many months or years, by which time they may have moved on or no longer be managing the case. In what follows we suggest the need to put assessment skills and knowledge centre stage in practice, in management and in training. This requires a more clinically focused approach and opportunities at different levels to learn and develop assessment practice.

The study

Drawing primarily on social work-focused literature, this study brought together UK research findings published in the last ten years that provide information on the assessment of children in need and their families. The studies reviewed were very diverse and relatively few had assessment as their main focus. This is itself interesting, particularly during a time when there was considerable emphasis on initiatives to guide the practice of assessment, for example through the Assessment Framework and the use of the Integrated Children's System (ICS).

There were limitations on what could be addressed in the review, and we note three specific areas here. First, it was not a part of this review to undertake a detailed exploration of the social work knowledge base, as it applies to the range of assessment contexts. Second, the review did not include an evaluation of the different risk assessment protocols or measures that may be used in a range of assessment contexts.[1] Third, the remit for this study was to focus on UK-based research, and more particularly on findings that applied to the context of social work in England. This excluded systematic scrutiny of the international research base. No doubt valuable insights would to be gained from a study of findings on assessment from a non-UK perspective and this may be a fruitful focus for future work. We included a small number of references to material from other countries, where it had particular relevance to the UK-based research we reviewed.

Understanding assessment in context

Assessment is a complex activity and clearly depends, to some extent, on the knowledge, skills and abilities of individual practitioners. But practitioners are themselves working in a broader milieu, so an important starting point for understanding research findings related to assessment is an appreciation of the context of practice. Inter-personal and inter-professional factors affect assessment processes and outcomes. Organisational culture and practices also have an impact on the ways in which people work, as shown by the considerable local authority differences noted in the research. In addition, practice is also governed by broader external policy directives and guidance, as well as decisions about resources at the national and local levels.

In the following sections we draw together some conclusions from the review and highlight some of the conditions that could enable assessments to be done better. But it is important to recognise that the responsibility for the quality of assessment practice does not lie solely at practitioner level. Improvements are unlikely to take place without support and change within and across systems.

The importance of assessment: Why it matters to do it well

Good assessment matters. It is not always straightforward to show that good outcomes for children necessarily follow from good assessment, but there is certainly evidence to support the link. At the same time, the opposite presumption – that bad or inadequate assessment is likely to be associated with worse outcomes – is easier to demonstrate. There is evidence, for example, that the absence of assessment of maltreated children is related to repeat abuse, and shortcomings in assessment have been a consistent feature in many cases of severe injury or child death. Delays in assessment and decision making in relation to the removal and placement of children can lead to difficulties in achieving permanent placements, and successful placements get harder with the child's increasing age; indeed, because of such delays some children never achieve a permanent placement. Poor assessments may expose children to risks of further maltreatment and placement breakdown. Instability in care often leads to a downward spiral: worsening emotional and behavioural difficulties, further instability, poor educational results, unemployment and a lifetime of poverty. So, overall, poor assessments can have potentially far-reaching consequences.

Arguably, good assessment is a necessary (although not always a sufficient) condition for positive outcomes for children. For example, assessment is related to improved chances of reunification success. Moreover, good assessment has the potential to contribute to placement stability for children, for example by preventing delay and helping to ensure the provision of appropriate and adequate support for foster carers, kin carers and adoptive parents. Good assessment also has a role to play in early intervention strategies, contributing to the effective targeting of interventions.

Nevertheless assessment, whilst clearly important, is not the only thing that affects outcomes for children. A number of other factors are involved, such as genetic vulnerabilities, parental behaviour and motivation, the availability of resources (including having the right kinds of interventions available and skilfully undertaken, to address identified needs, issues and difficulties) and so on. It is also evident that assessments can be wrong. The reasons for such failings are not simply to do with the judgements of individual practitioners, but must be understood at the structural as well as the individual level.

Using the Assessment Framework

The Assessment Framework requires that each child's needs are individually assessed, as well as the parent's capacity to care for each child and the impact of family and environmental factors on each child's development and on the parents' capacity to meet the particular child's needs. In this section we highlight some messages from the research that addressed the three domains (children's developmental needs, parenting capacity and family and environmental factors) which comprise the 'assessment triangle'.

The research we reviewed did not seriously question the overall value of the holistic model offered by the Assessment Framework. It is, however, a *generic* framework, and every case will have its own particular issues and circumstances that demand attention, so specific areas of knowledge and, in some situations, relevant tools will be needed. The Assessment Framework offers a useful 'scaffold' for practice and is not intended for use as an instruction manual: its use needs to be supported by appropriate practice and research-based knowledge. Studies have, however, identified a lack of reference to research or explicit use of theory in social workers' assessment reports.

The assessment of disabled children raises a number of complexities and challenges; for example, the child development model underpinning the Assessment Framework can be seen by some social workers as not appropriate for disabled children. And some studies have suggested that the assessment of disabled children may require some tailoring of the recording templates, to reflect their particular strengths, abilities and needs and to capture their contribution to the assessment process through their chosen method of communication. The Assessment Framework guidance makes it clear that this should happen for disabled children, but concerns remain as to the usefulness of some electronic formats for recording these young people's views. However, the position was not uniformly negative; for example, one study of the implementation of the Assessment Framework found that the parents of disabled children did not appear to share the social workers' concerns and were positive about the assessment process.

Knowledge of child development is vital for good assessment but the presentation of information regarding children's developmental needs in assessment records was variable, with some reports characterised as presenting the 'standardised child', rather than reflecting the particular child's individuality. Problems with assessing attachment were identified in some studies: for example, clingy behaviour was misinterpreted as evidence of strong attachment, and some assessments were based on observation of an insufficient number of different situations to be reliable. In addition, a tendency to over-emphasise resilience in children was noted. Resilience is a difficult notion to conceptualise and to apply, but one exploratory study suggested positive effects from training staff directly in this area. Overall, the research highlighted a need for further professional education in relation to children's identity, resilience, self-esteem, attachment, and the identification of specific behavioural problems that contribute to poor placement outcomes.

Key research findings relating to the assessment of parenting capacity include the importance of understanding the basic requirements of parenting and of considering parents' ability to change. On occasion, social workers have over-estimated the ability of some parents to understand professional concerns and make the necessary changes. In such cases, psychological assessment can be valuable to assess parental capacity, including sometimes their IQ. It has also been suggested that one way of assessing capacity to change is by giving parents 'managed' opportunities to change. In these cases, it is important to be clear what needs to change, how change will be measured or assessed, and over what timescale, how parents are to be supported and the consequences if no, or insufficient, changes are made. Studies involving children who are reunited with their parents after a period of being looked after indicate that outcomes are better if, before the return home, there is a clear plan of action, a written agreement with the parents and ongoing monitoring. In one study involving babies and very young children who had suffered or were likely to suffer significant harm, parents who overcame their difficulties generally did so within the first six months of the child's life – often referring to a 'defining moment' when they realised that they needed to make significant changes in order to be able to parent their child. Elsewhere, motivational interviewing techniques have been found to be useful in addressing readiness to change in situations of alcohol or drug misuse.

Assessment of parents generally relies on verbal communication, and there is evidence that if parents are inarticulate, passive, have learning disabilities or communication impairments, or there are cultural misunderstandings, cooperation and engagement might be misinterpreted, and they and their children risk being disadvantaged. Improving the assessment of parenting capacity therefore requires a combination of approaches to the collection of information. In addition to conducting interviews (including taking a full family history), the range of approaches may include observations, assessing changes in parenting practices, use of validated tools and consideration of previous reports regarding the child and family. It is important that assessment is done on a 'child by child' basis as a parent may be able to care for one child but not another within the family.

A particular aspect of parenting that is covered in the research is the role of fathers. Recurrent shortcomings have been identified amongst many groups of professionals in taking account of men in the households with which they were working. There is an extensive literature on fathering, and within that a considerable range of research findings indicating how social workers and other professionals can fall into the trap of ignoring fathers, of dismissing their contribution or of loading responsibility onto mothers to protect children from any dangers coming from the father (for example, Scourfield 2003). Professional vigilance is necessary to ensure that information about fathers is available whenever possible, especially as fathers may exert a considerable influence even when they are not living with their children.

Studies also highlight the need to take account of the impact of factors related to family functioning and family history – for example, domestic violence, parental mental illness, substance misuse and learning disability – on parents' capacity to meet their children's needs (see below for further discussion of family and environmental factors in assessment); they also note the difficulties encountered by social workers in assessing the capacity of parents who misuse alcohol and drugs (Farmer et al. 2011; Harwin and Forrester 2002).

The third domain of the Assessment Framework focuses on family and environmental factors. Assessment of family functioning is important, as it has been suggested that the best predictors of multi-type maltreatment are poor family cohesion (family members feeling disconnected from one another), low family adaptability (rigid roles and inflexibility in relationships and communication) and the poor quality of the adult relationship. Assessing family functioning can also provide a basis for a strengths-based approach that accepts that all adults and children possess strengths that can be tapped to improve the quality of their lives. Such an approach is associated with recruiting parents into positive parenting programmes. While this does not appear to be an area that has been prominent in assessment, one study reported improvements in the extent to which family strengths were recorded, following the piloting of the Common Assessment Framework in Wales.

Studies have suggested that the impact of environmental factors on children's welfare is not fully appreciated by many practitioners and is given less attention in assessment. For example, one study of minority ethnic children who were looked after found that little attention had been paid to family issues such as how and why parents had become dislocated from their country of origin and the impact this had had on them. More generally, referrals relating to financial or housing problems were found to be less likely to lead to an initial assessment. However, a relatively high level of recording was found in core assessment reports of family and environmental factors that were likely to impact *negatively* on the child. Although these findings appear contradictory, they relate to different parts of the process (i.e. response to referrals, and recording of core assessments respectively).

Assessment requires careful analysis of the inter-relationship between multiple positive and negative factors in a child's life, the risk factors that are likely to impact on the child's health and development and also any protective factors already in the child or family's situation or that could be developed to support the child. It is important therefore that the different domains of the three domains of the 'assessment triangle' are not seen as discrete areas for investigation. Systemic thinking, involving the dynamic use of the assessment triangle, is necessary to explore the interconnections and interactions between different pieces of information, rather than providing a static description. However, studies have shown that practitioners do not always give equal attention to all three domains of the Assessment Framework to get a balanced understanding of the child and family's situation. The transactional-ecological approach proposed by Brandon *et al.* (2008; Brandon, Bailey *et al.* 2009) offers a helpful way of thinking about the interconnecting risk and protective factors in families' lives. Other approaches to support analysis and decision making involve the use of decision trees (Munro 2008) or methods drawn from qualitative research (Holland 2010).

The role of analysis and the use of professional judgement

Good assessment is a complex activity. It involves the systematic and purposeful gathering of information but is more than simply a process of collecting 'facts' (which may, themselves, be disputed). The practitioner needs to know why they are seeking the information in the first place, and then be able to analyse and make sense of a mass of multi-faceted and sometimes contradictory material. Information needs to be 'processed' to allow the practitioner to come to a view about its meaning – including understanding its meaning to the parents and to the child – and decide how to proceed. This requires a range of knowledge and skills, including the use of analytical and critical approaches and the ability to reflect. Intuition also has a role to play and can, additionally, be helpful in establishing rapport and demonstrating empathy.

Critical and analytical thinking encourages the practitioner to process information rigorously and methodically and to question the reliability of both sources and content. Building reflection into practice allows for regular review of assumptions and formulations in the light of new information. Whilst intuition has a place in the reasoning processes that are needed, drawing as it does on the practitioner's life experience and practice knowledge, it is prone to bias, is not necessarily reliable and may lead to premature judgement. So intuition can be a good place to start but not to finish thinking, and its use should be tempered by both critical and analytical reasoning and reflection.

It is clear from the studies we reviewed that the analysis of information has continued to be problematic in practice, with assessment reports providing evidence of considerable effort in terms of collecting information but less consistent evidence of analysis and evaluation. Indeed, the increase in information collected may have made the task more difficult. Attention needs to be focused on strengthening this crucial aspect of the assessment process. This should include ensuring that social work education and training at all levels provide the learning required to support the development of analytical skills and their application in assessment. Methods of teaching and learning analysis in assessment are being developed and there are a number of useful research-based texts that provide additional advice and guidance for practitioners (Beesley 2010; Bentovim et al. 2009; Brown, Moore and Turney 2011; Dalzell and Sawyer 2007; Helm 2010; Holland 2010; Platt 2011).

A number of factors – practical, cognitive/psychological, emotional and systemic/organisational – can undermine the capacity to think purposefully and effectively. Reflective supervision, to which we turn in the next section, has a significant part to play in supporting and promoting this capacity.

Support, supervision and consultancy

Supervision has long been recognised as a cornerstone of professional practice. But evidence suggests that changes in organisational culture have affected the way social work practice is managed and have led to a prioritising of the administrative and performance management functions of supervision at the expense of the professional learning and development functions (Munro 2010). The priority of reflective, 'clinical' supervision has been reaffirmed in a number of recent guidance documents and reports (Barlow and Scott 2010; HM Government 2010a; Laming 2009; Social Work Reform Board 2010), in line with findings about the role and significance of this process for safe and effective practice.

Given the complexity of family situations, relationships and emotional dynamics, it is easy for practitioners working under pressure to lose focus or to get stuck in a particular way of thinking. And it is hard to challenge one's own patterns or habits of thought. So workers need a safe and 'containing' space to be able to think about what they are doing and how they make sense of the practical and emotional pressures of the work. Supervision also provides an opportunity for the practitioner to review and, if necessary, rethink their understanding of particular situations. Actively reviewing assessments is important for a number of reasons: new information may become available and needs to be rigorously assessed, particularly if it appears to be at odds with the prevailing understanding of the case, to avoid the danger of 'verificationism'; situations do not remain static and families and children change; and review allows the practitioner to check the accuracy of the original assessment – they may find they have jumped to the wrong conclusion.

The supervisor may need to use their view from 'outside' the case to challenge assumptions, prejudices and fixed thinking and to help the practitioner to remain open-minded. Analysis of serious case reviews has drawn attention to the danger of 'enmeshed interaction between overwhelmed families and overwhelmed professionals' (Brandon, Bailey *et al.* 2009) and the potential for this to contribute to a vulnerable child within the family being 'lost' or unseen. So it is essential that supervisors help practitioners to keep the child at the centre of their analysis.

When practitioners are working with complex emotional relationships, it is not uncommon for the worker/service user relationship to become reflected in the supervisor/practitioner relationship. So both practitioners and supervisors need some understanding of emotional dynamics and psychological processes – for example, mirroring, transference and over-identification – in order to manage these different relationships safely. Reflective supervision in such situations is itself a challenging task and one for which supervisors need to feel properly equipped. So it is important that the time, training and support that supervisors need to do the job properly are considered, along with their own levels of experience. Moreover, practitioners may also benefit from opportunities to learn by doing joint assessments alongside more experienced practitioners.

Team managers or senior practitioners are in a key position to offer supervision but they are not the only possible source of support. Peer-group or other forms of group supervision can provide valuable support and insights, and external consultancy can also be appropriate, especially in complex cases. There may also be a role for senior managers in auditing case files to review the quality of assessment as part of the 'organisational health checks' recommended by the Social Work Task Force (2009).

The use of questionnaires, measures and scales

One of the challenges highlighted by a number of studies is how to use standardised assessment tools in ways that support and inform the exercise of professional judgement.

Good assessment is likely to use a range of methods other than just interviewing to obtain information from a variety of sources. A number of tools can help, alongside more 'traditional' approaches to information gathering such as observation. (Child observation, itself a key skill, is included in some basic-level training and post-qualifying programmes but is not currently a requirement for social workers in training.) Validated assessment instruments may be useful for practice in some situations and with some user groups, and there are a range of questionnaires and scales to support the use of the Assessment Framework (Department of Health, Cox and Bentovim 2000). Some tools and measures require dedicated training before they can be used reliably and effectively, but others could be more easily introduced into practice and assist in understanding particular behaviours. For example, there is evidence that social workers have difficulty in assessing the extent of alcohol use – or how much of a problem it actually is. Tools such as the Alcohol Use Questionnaire (Department of Health, Cox and Bentovim 2000) or the screening questionnaires T-ACE and TWEAK (British Medical Association 2007) could therefore assist practitioners. However, the use of such instruments is still relatively rare in the UK, although the use of the Strengths and Difficulties Questionnaire (SDQ) has now been incorporated into routine practice with looked after children (DCSF 2009a).

Several studies in our sample cautioned against reliance on actuarial methods in relation to risk assessment. Such tools can play a part in case management, providing opportunities to develop shared standards between practitioners, but social workers should be cautious about the level of accuracy that can be achieved and not place undue reliance on these methods. Actuarial methods of assessing risk cannot provide certainty and, if used, should be part of a broader holistic assessment of the child's situation. The key message from the relevant studies is that they should be treated as an aid to professional judgement rather than as a substitute for it.

The regular use of scales, measures and questionnaires would involve a major culture shift within social work practice, with implications for professional education, training and supervision. Assessment 'cannot be replaced by "algorithms" for recognition' (Daniel *et al.* 2009, p.40), but it is not an option simply to ignore these various instruments or dismiss them as an unwelcome manifestation of a 'tick-box' culture. Judicious use of tools and measures could contribute to improved assessments, as part of the range of resources drawn on by practitioners to inform and support their exercise of professional judgement.

Relationship-based practice

Studies indicate that good assessment is grounded in a thorough understanding of the child and family's situation, needs and strengths, and, to gain this knowledge, practitioners need to work directly with the child and their family. This highlights the importance of the professional relationship and its role in the assessment process and for any subsequent intervention and future planning. While some studies have suggested improvements in relationships between social workers and parents in the UK between the 1990s and the 2000s, the research has also highlighted substantial complexities in managing relationships in practice.

The child's voice

Keeping the child or young person 'in view' is fundamental to good assessment, and failure to do so can have severe consequences as analyses of serious case reviews have consistently demonstrated. Good practice with children and young people includes taking time to build relationships, listening to and respecting them, giving information, providing support for them to understand assessment reports, and offering them real choices when possible. However, research continues to indicate that there are difficulties for many workers in making and sustaining relationships with children and with representing the child's voice in assessments. A number of personal and practical factors have been identified that affect the relationship between the practitioner and the child or young person. These include time constraints, insufficient skill or confidence in conducting direct work or undertaking child observations, and insufficient emotional support to ensure that workers do not become overwhelmed by such engagement. When children are seen, they do not always feel they can be open because of their concerns about confidentiality and the consequences for their parents of any disclosure.

Keeping the child at the centre of the assessment process can be a particular issue in relation to older young people. A number of studies commented on an apparent unwillingness to intervene with this group – in some cases because of a (possibly misplaced) reluctance to bring young people into the looked after children system, or in response to perceived pressures to ration resources. This lesser level of engagement may also reflect a misunderstanding of the vulnerability of older young people and a belief that they will sort things out for themselves – or that practitioners do not follow up contact with the young person, if initially rebuffed. However, evidence from serious case reviews has highlighted the vulnerability of these young people and indicated that suicide was a common cause of death within this group of 16- and 17-year-olds. It is important, therefore, that practitioners are aware of the potentially significant impact of neglect and abuse on these young people and that agencies have appropriate strategies and resources in place to address their needs.

Some parents make it difficult for workers to see the child and/ or overwhelm workers with their own difficulties. When workers over-identify with the parents or become desensitised over a period of time to low levels of care – as can happen, particularly in relation to chronic neglect – children's difficulties are less likely to receive adequate attention. These factors need to be considered by professionals and organisations to ensure that children are kept fully in view; clinical supervision has an important role to play here.

Relationships between social workers and parents

The relationships formed between social workers and parents during assessments serve a dual function of allowing the work to proceed, at the same time as providing relevant information. It is not always easy to establish good partnership or cooperative working and there is a degree of consensus about the characteristics of 'hard to help' parents. However, the research does not identify clearly the extent to which parental involvement and cooperation is affected by the skills of the social worker compared with other contributory influences, most importantly the attitudes and behaviour of the parents, and the organisational or managerial systems.

As a general point, the relationship between parental engagement and outcomes for children remains under-researched. However, there is considerable evidence that the nature of parental relationships with professionals affects decisions arising from assessments. Interventions tended to de-escalate where parents appeared cooperative (although there is evidence that cooperation, in itself, is not an adequate predictor of parents' abilities to change sufficiently to meet the needs of the child). More coercive intervention was likely where parental involvement was considered inadequate. It is concerning to note that in some instances an opposite effect occurred, and lack of parental engagement led to less intervention, because parental obstructiveness effectively restricted access to evidence.

Practitioners can find themselves trying to manage what may be contradictory imperatives: to maintain a central focus on the child, at the same time as trying to establish effective working relationships with parents, because without their active involvement the basis for intervention may dissolve. Clearly, cooperation and partnership working are not possible in all cases and parents may respond to professional concerns with denial and outright hostility. Situations can also occur where apparent cooperation and compliance disguise a lack of congruence between parental and professional perspectives. It is therefore important that practitioners have the knowledge, skills, time and support to work with non-compliant parents and to maintain an attitude of 'healthy scepticism' and 'respectful uncertainty' (Laming 2003, pp.322, 205).

There is evidence that the expectation to focus on the child can sometimes have a negative impact on social workers' engagement with parents. There is also evidence of practitioners becoming 'enmeshed' in chaotic family systems and finding their attention diverted away from the child by the pressures to work with often very needy parents. Managing this dilemma clearly requires good organisational support, supervision and time for reflection.

Working with parents who are misusing drugs or alcohol and where domestic violence is involved

A number of studies showed that problems with substance misuse are a feature of a significant proportion of cases dealt with by children's social care services. However, currently social workers are not always well equipped to deal with these issues. A clear message from the studies we reviewed was that children's social workers needed a broader understanding of how to assess and work with substance misuse and that appropriate training in this area should be included in social work education and in-service training. Working with specialist substance misuse workers can be helpful for children's social workers, although continuing differences, in professional perspective and approach to issues such as client confidentiality, may make this quite challenging.

Other studies pointed to the need to develop understanding of the impact of domestic violence on children and to work with specialist domestic violence services where appropriate, and highlighted the importance of taking account of the role of fathers and male partners, including those who live outside the family.

Effective assessment within a multi-agency or inter-professional group

The complex, multi-dimensional problems experienced by many families who come into contact with children's social care services are likely to require a range of knowledge, skills and expertise beyond that of a single professional, and there is evidence of the value of different professional inputs in the production of a holistic assessment of a child's needs. Studies found, for example, that psychological assessment could contribute helpfully to the process of family finding and matching children to potential adopters or foster carers, in particular early on when decisions were being made about whether or not to separate siblings. In neglect cases, psychological assessments in care proceedings were found to make a major contribution to decisions about whether or not a child could be returned to their parents.

More generally, there is evidence of the importance of coordinated multi-agency assessment for families with complex, entrenched and multiple difficulties and that children were more likely to be returned home safely where multi-agency assessments had been conducted. Good outcomes for children are likely to be enhanced in the context of a professional culture of good communication and information sharing and there are examples of successful practice in this regard using the Common Assessment Framework and the model of the 'team around the child' (TAC).

It seems clear that professionals should work together for the benefit of the child and there are policy imperatives to ensure that agencies work together to provide better services. However, doing so raises a number of challenges. One challenge lies in finding effective ways to manage different professional perspectives and cultures – for example, in relation to client confidentiality and boundaries around information sharing – and to promote 'joined up' working. Evidence suggests that organisational restructuring is not associated with better outcomes and, indeed, that *intra*-organisational factors – the 'climate' and culture within an organisation, which includes features such as cooperation, role clarity and low levels of conflict – may be more significant in promoting improvements in service delivery and outcomes for children than inter-organisational factors or major structural changes. In addition, successful 'joined up' working is supported by the establishment of effective relationships and trust between the front line and other practitioners in the agencies involved and it takes time, effort and personal and organisational commitment to develop these links.

A second challenge concerns the role of 'expert' assessments and how they relate to social work assessments, particularly in family court proceedings. As noted above, specialist assessment can be immensely helpful. But some studies suggest that a hierarchy can emerge in the court arena with 'higher status' professionals' assessments (usually medical or psychological) taking precedence over those of social workers. Furthermore, there is evidence that additional and/or repeated assessments may be used to defer difficult decisions and can increase delay in complex cases. So the potential for delay – and the costs – that can be introduced by commissioning additional assessments need to be weighed against the additional insights and guidance that they can offer for the management of the case. And alongside that, there is also a need to be clear about and value where *social work* expertise lies – for example, in terms of knowledge and skills about relationships, and knowledge of the child and family over time – and how this contributes to the assessment process.

Thresholds, early intervention and targeting assessments

Where thresholds are set to initiate an assessment depends on the interaction of a number of factors. Studies suggest that these include:

- the nature and quality of the information about the individual child/ren and family who are the subject of a referral

- the reasoning strategies employed by practitioners to assess that information and manage referrals

- systems and organisational factors (for example, the level of resources available, perceived pressures to ration demand for services, time constraints and the requirements of case management procedures and systems).

Limited resources and pressure of work generally result in a tendency to raise thresholds for access to services as a way of rationing responses. High thresholds may mean that children and families with substantial problems and high levels of need do not receive timely help, resulting in continuing distress and/or an increased likelihood of harm to children and families. This is particularly an issue in cases of child neglect and emotional abuse. However, in some circumstances, failure to receive a service does not lead to deterioration in the family's situation, probably related to the level of informal support available to them.

The importance of timely assessment is reflected in the current concern with very early or 'earlier' intervention. The rationale for this approach – that it is better to intervene early in the 'life course' of a problem, before difficulties become established and potentially more severe – is hard to challenge (see Allen 2011). It is also the case that costs are likely to escalate when assessment is either delayed, absent or of poor quality. However, some caution is needed. Considerably more assessment work (with its associated costs) would be necessary to ensure the maximum number of children requiring early intervention actually receive it. Also, early intervention depends on being able to identify additional need at an early stage and accurately assess the likelihood of particular types of harm. But in practice it is not always straightforward to ensure that the right individuals or groups are identified for intervention. Further research is needed to understand better what works, why and, more particularly, for whom, in supporting children with additional needs and their families.

However, at this stage, there is evidence to suggest some groups who may benefit from a targeted approach, for example young people who become looked after. It is known that children who are looked after have a higher prevalence of mental health problems than children in the community and that in most cases these conditions pre-exist the young person's entry to the looked after children system. Therefore, given the link between emotional and behavioural difficulties, the stability of placements and poorer long-term outcomes for young people, it is important that practitioners are alert to assessing these needs at or around entry to the looked after children system so that appropriate services can be accessed and foster carers prepared. As previously noted, the current statutory guidance on promoting the health and wellbeing of looked after children (DCSF 2009a) suggests the use of the Strengths and Difficulties Questionnaire (SDQ) as an early stage screening tool for this purpose and its use at entry to the looked after children system should be beneficial.

There is evidence to suggest that social workers may be relatively successful at identifying children at most risk of suffering significant harm but this does not mean that such children always receive further assessment or services since local thresholds for initiating core assessments or for holding initial child protection conferences have been found to vary greatly between local authorities. Moreover, the acceptance of referrals for further intervention will be affected by the 'speed practices' and short cuts to manage and deflect referrals which develop when referral levels are high, especially when performance targets mandate tight timescales.

As would be expected, practitioners are more willing to intervene to protect children under six than older children, but even for very young children a desire to give parents the benefit of the doubt even in the absence of any signs of change or capacity to parent adequately can lead to very delayed decision making about their future by practitioners and the courts. In addition, in longer-term work a range of factors may affect practitioners' ability to assess or see clearly what is happening, since they may become desensitised to abuse and neglect or have 'fixed ideas' about the case. This is compounded in cases of neglect by the difficulty of determining the threshold for decisive action based on an accumulation of concerns.

The research suggested a number of ways of assisting practitioners with these difficult issues. For example, the presence of a second worker on periodic visits to longer-term child protection cases might ensure that thresholds for intervention were reviewed (Farmer and Lutman 2009), and Forrester (2008) suggested that when two or more of four identified risk factors are evident these cases (which were at high risk of re-referral) might benefit from specific interventions targeted at key problems such as neglect, drugs misuse or parent–child relationship difficulties.

Research

A number of areas can be identified for further research and study, focusing on different elements of the assessment process. These include the following:

- The importance of involving children and young people in assessments has been noted in this report, but the perspectives of children and young people themselves on assessments have generally not been prominent in research. So this is an area for future research.

- A number of scales and measures were published alongside the Assessment Framework. However, use of the Family Pack of Questionnaires and Scales and other supporting instruments such as the HOME Inventory (Cox and Walker 2002) and the Family Assessment (Bentovim and Bingley Miller 2001) has remained limited. Currently, the Strengths and Difficulties Questionnaire (SDQ) is becoming more widely used but there are continuing difficulties in relation to the use of the other formal instruments and measures that accompany the Assessment Framework. This area would benefit from further study, perhaps building on the original pilot study that preceded the compilation of the *Family Pack of Questionnaires and Scales* (Department of Health 1999).

- In relation to early intervention, accurate targeting of services is not straightforward and further research is needed to understand better what works, why and for which children, in supporting children with additional needs and their families. Studies have highlighted the potential significance of social support for vulnerable families and further research into the role of informal support and its relationship with formal support might therefore be fruitful.

- Further research into assessing parental cooperation and engagement with social work and the relationship between parental engagement and outcomes for children would be helpful.

- There are likely to be benefits in identifying and sharing examples of good and innovative practice in assessment. So systematic evaluation of proactive approaches to in-service training and development (within local authority children's services or voluntary agencies) that appear to work well may lead to the development of good practice ideas/models that can be shared. Sharing examples of good practice in relation to supervision would also be helpful.

Quality in assessment

The research we reviewed gave evidence of considerable variation within and between local authorities in relation to the way different assessment reports are completed, with significant differences noted in terms of content, length and completeness of reports and their related documentation. This variation was found in a number of studies, with poor assessments identified across a range of different contexts. Shortcomings in relation to assessments of black and minority ethnic children, in particular, were noted. Studies continue to identify concerns with the quality of recording and highlight problems with missing assessments, gaps and inaccuracies in information recorded and 'cut and paste' strategies that lose the individuality of the child at the heart of the assessment process. At the same time, though, it is important to acknowledge that broader organisational issues – for example, time constraints and workload pressures, associated, in part, with a system of strict performance management – have a significant impact on assessment and recording practices.

The research reviewed suggested that poor quality assessments typically feature:

- gaps and inaccuracies in the information collected (or included in the file record)

- description rather than analysis of the information presented

- little or no indication of service user (including the child's) views.

Conversely, good quality assessments:

- ensure that the child remains central

- contain full, concise, relevant and accurate information

- include a chronology and/or family and social history

- make good use of information from a range of sources

- include analysis that makes clear links between the recorded information and plans for intervention (or decisions not to take any further action).

The importance of good knowledge of the case history – including the child's history and that of the parents, past events and interventions that have been tried before and their success or otherwise – was underlined by the research. This may be particularly important in long-term, chronic cases, such as those involving child neglect, to help avoid the 'start again syndrome' that has been identified.

Underpinning the notion of quality is an expectation that assessment should be both *purposeful* and *timely*. Practitioners need to know why they are undertaking an assessment and to think about what it is they are trying to achieve. The review highlighted the range of assessments that take place for children in need at different stages/times, for different reasons and with different outcomes. Whatever the format or circumstance, though, the *purpose* (and possible consequences) of the assessment should be clear – to the practitioner, to the agency and to the service user – and practitioners need to be able to use the assessment process to:

- identify needs, risk and protective factors

- come to a view about how far, or to what extent, change is possible for an individual, a family or a situation. As previously noted, this can sometimes be tested by using written agreements or similar methods which provide clarity about the changes expected and timescales and which allow practitioners and parents to review parental progress or lack of it.

An awareness of timeliness and purpose should also reduce the likelihood of (potentially unnecessary) repeat assessments. No assessment can guarantee certainty but it is important that repeated assessment is not used as a way of avoiding difficult decisions.

As can be seen, assessment is a complex activity and there are a number of factors that appear either to help or hinder practice.

Barriers to quality in assessment

Barriers can operate at a number of different levels:

- *Personal* – including whether or not the practitioner feels competent and confident to carry out the required tasks, and has the scope to do so within their individual caseload.

- *Inter-personal/relational* – including the range of activities involved in communicating with children and young people, parents, and other professionals.

- *Systems issues* – including increasing dependence on complex and sometimes unreliable or unwieldy procedures or IT systems and the sense of lack of time for face-to-face work as a result of time spent inputting data.

- *Organisational constraints* – including the organisational culture, for example whether or not there is a commitment to reflection and learning, management of workloads and so on, and level of resource. The outcomes of assessments often depend on there being adequate resources to implement plans.

But there are also positive indicators in terms of the climate or contextual factors affecting assessment, which are highlighted in the final section below.

Supporting quality in assessment practice

Drawing together the messages from this review, the following points describe the organisational and professional climate needed to support good assessment practice:

- A knowledgeable, highly skilled and confident workforce, supported by appropriate education, training and continuing professional development.

- A clear framework for reflective 'clinical' supervision (individual and/or group) and other forms of case-based consultation, including support for practitioners working directly with children.

- An adequate level of resource – in terms of time and staffing, as well as services – to allow practitioners to complete assessments and plan appropriate interventions in a thorough but timely manner.

- Good intra-organisational and inter-professional working relationships.

- An organisational culture that supports reflection and learning (not a 'blame culture').

- Electronic information management and recording systems that 'work with' practice, are reliable and not unnecessarily time-consuming.

- 'Organisational health checks' or audits of the quality of assessments undertaken.

As we have noted, a number of different reviews have been commissioned by government and, at the time of writing, there are still many changes ahead. The implementation strategies developed by the Social Work Reform Board are intended to bring about significant changes to social work education, training, practice and management, and the government has started to outline its plans for reform of child protection services following the completion of the Munro Review. It is to be hoped that these initiatives will give due focus to the development of assessment knowledge and skills.

Good assessment matters and is key to effective intervention and case management. It takes time and support to do it well, and getting it wrong may leave a vulnerable child in danger or a family without much needed support. We know from research studies, inquiries into child deaths and overviews of serious case reviews that assessment is an abidingly complex and challenging area of practice. However, there are clear messages from research about the factors that help to promote effective practice and improve the quality of assessments. These can be used to create a climate that supports practitioners to make the best assessments they can in order both to protect children from harm and to promote better outcomes.

Note

1 This is the subject of a forthcoming Department for Education research project.

METHOD

The study was commissioned to assemble the research findings in the field of children's social care published over the past decade that have provided information on all types of assessments of children in need. Much of the research during this period did not have a primary focus on assessment and consequently the task of this literature review was to find and draw out 'hidden' findings on assessment from a wide range of different reports and documents.

Objectives

The key objectives of the study were to obtain evidence from published research studies that would provide information on:

- the quality of the data populating initial, core and other types of assessments carried out for children in need, including looked after children and children placed for adoption
- the variation in the quality of assessments by local authority and by different groups of children
- the factors that assisted or acted as barriers to good-quality assessments of children in need
- to draw together findings on the thresholds operated by local authorities for responding to referrals, and the implications for outcomes for children in need and their families
- the extent to which professionals engaged with children, young people and their families to produce effective assessments
- the impact of the quality of assessments on decision making, planning, interventions and ultimately on children's and young people's short- and longer-term outcomes.

The review

This study involved analysis of published research addressing the topic of assessment of children in need. An initial search was conducted utilising a range of search terms and a number of literature databases and other sources to identify relevant material. The main search terms used are set out below and were intended to identify references to the assessment of children and young people in literature where this may not have been the primary focus of study. Other strategies employed to identify potentially 'hidden' data are described in the following sections.

Ethical approval for the study was obtained from the Ethics Committee of the University of Bristol's School for Policy Studies.

Defining 'assessments'

The range of assessment that might be included in a review of this kind is wide, and includes:

- initial and core assessments using the Framework for the Assessment of Children in Need and their Families (Department of Health *et al.* 2000)
- assessments carried out using the Common Assessment Framework
- other aspects of the Integrated Children's System, including arrangements for reviewing looked after children
- assessments under Regulations 28 and 39 of the Fostering Services Regulations
- Child Permanence Reports or Form E assessments of children to be placed for adoption
- health, education and other 'specialist' assessments.

Social workers also conduct other types of assessment, such as those that focus specifically on the assessment of adults: assessments of prospective adoptive/foster carers or assessments carried out in relation to Special Guardianship Orders. These were excluded from this review because the focus here was on assessments that are directly concerned with children in need.

Identification of relevant research and sources of 'hidden' data

The review process began with a systematic identification of research on children in need undertaken in the UK and published since 1 January 1999. The date of 1999 slightly precedes the introduction of the *Framework for the Assessment of Children in Need and their Families* (the Assessment Framework) (Department of Health *et al.* 2000) and allowed for the evaluation of assessments undertaken at the time when changes relevant to the Assessment Framework were being introduced in a number of local authorities. A number of approaches were employed to identify relevant material published within the target time period (1 January 1999–March 2010). These are outlined below.

1. Examining government research reviews and overview reports, overviews of serious case reviews and summaries of inspections

A number of key research initiatives were identified and these provided the starting point for the study. They were:

The Children Act Now: Messages from Research	10 studies (within the timeframe)
Supporting Parents: Messages from Research	14 studies
Fostering Now: Messages from Research	15 studies
Costs and Outcomes in Children's Social Care	14 studies
Quality Matters in Children's Services	9 studies
Adoption Research Initiative	9 studies
Safeguarding Children Research Initiative	11 studies
Total:	82 studies

2. Database search

A wide-ranging search strategy was employed to maximise data collection beyond the key material identified above and the following databases were searched:

- Applied Social Sciences Index and Abstracts (ASSIA) and Social Services Abstracts
- Cumulative Index to Nursing and Allied Health Literature (CINAHL)
- OpenSigle (System for Information on Grey Literature in Europe)
- Social Science Citation Index.

These databases were chosen to provide a focus on social work and social work-related material. A broader strategy – for example, involving detailed searching of databases covering the psychological and/or psychiatric literature – would no doubt have yielded interesting additional material, but was beyond the remit and timetable of this review.

Each of the databases identified above was searched using the following key words:

(child* or boy* or girl* or baby or babies or infant* or preschool* or pre-school* or schoolchild* or adolescen* or teen* or juvenile*)

AND

(youth work* or casework* or social work* or social service* or child welfare)

AND

(assess* or screen* or case management or evaluat* or apprais* or threshold*)

AND

(England or English or Wales or Welsh or Scotland or Scottish or Northern Ireland or Northern Irish)

Indexing/thesaurus terms for 'Children', 'Social work/ers', 'Evaluation/ Assessment' and 'United Kingdom' were used and exploded where available and appropriate.

Attention was focused on studies that were either based on research undertaken in England specifically or, if from elsewhere in the UK, had particular relevance for understanding issues of concern within the English system.

This search identified *1614 records*, with the results distributed as shown in Table A.1.

Table A.1 Preliminary search results

Source	Records
ASSIA	994
CINAHL	416
OpenSigle	11
Social Science Index	193

Once duplicates were removed, *1472 records* remained. EndNote reference managing software was used to import the records into an EndNote Library.

A search of Social Care Online was also undertaken using the terms 'assess*' + 'child*' + 'social work'. Once duplicates were removed, this identified a further *345* items and these were also imported into EndNote.

3. 'Snowballing' strategy

In addition, a 'snowballing' method was used to identify outlying studies that may not otherwise have come to light. This involved following up references known to team members, consulting the relevant academic community for information about studies bearing on assessment that should be included and searching the references of the main group of studies identified, along with those of other key publications such as text books on assessment. This 'snowballing' strategy generated a further *40* items; these included studies funded by government departments – the Department of Health (DH), Department for Education and Skills (DfES), Department for Children, Schools and Families (DCSF) or Department for Constitutional Affairs (DCA) – but which were outside the major initiatives listed, and studies conducted by a range of other bodies (Thomas Coram Research Unit, Nuffield, Joseph Rowntree Foundation, Centre for Excellence in Outcomes (C4EO), amongst others). This process also identified a number of peer-reviewed journal papers that addressed pertinent issues in relation to assessment.

4. Initial consultation with the academic community

The principal investigators for each of the studies within the six government-funded research initiatives and the fostering overview noted above were contacted by email to inform them of this literature review and request copies of any relevant reports. This process generated some significant additional source material (included in the 'snowballing' category above) as well as electronic copies of final and other reports. However, researchers were not able to identify any data pertaining to assessment that had not already been analysed. We were also assisted by members of the Steering Group and other colleagues who facilitated access to currently unpublished work and some additional material.

A total of 1939 reports and articles that needed to be screened for relevant information were identified.

The approach taken here was not that of a classic systematic review. Research in social care has generally not yet reached a stage that would meet the very specific requirements of a systematic review and most of the studies being included did not have assessment as their primary focus. Consequently, a systematic review would not have revealed sufficient information of value for the purposes of this study. We did nevertheless follow a rigorous approach to the identification of relevant research and to the reviewing process, and included a peer-monitoring procedure to enhance fairness and objectivity in the conclusions we drew.

Screening of research studies

The screening of each study was undertaken independently by two members of the team and studies that contained information on assessment were then shortlisted for detailed review. Flexible criteria were used in this process, to avoid eliminating studies that might have been primarily focused on another topic, but contained 'hidden' data on assessment.

Each report/article was assessed against the following criteria:

- published within the timeframe 1999–April 2010
- report/document discusses research concerned with practice in the UK
- indication of findings relating to assessment for children in contact with children's social care services.

This process resulted in the exclusion of 1804 references (see Table A.2).

As the concern of the review was with findings related to the assessment of children in need, items were excluded if the focus was on:

- evaluations of intervention/treatment
- adults (for example, foster carer or adopter assessments)
- parental need or specific parenting difficulties (for example, post-natal depression or parenting where alcohol abuse is a factor). However, as assessment of *parenting capacity* is clearly a significant part of any assessment of a child in need (Department of Health *et al.* 2000), studies addressing parenting capacity have been included
- the use/usefulness of different assessment tools and questionnaires/scales
- addressing factors that promote/inhibit access to services
- individual case studies.

Other relevant material

As part of the screening process, we were also able to identify a number of articles and books that contained useful conceptual or theoretical analysis, some of which has been drawn on to develop, or provide additional contextual material for, the discussion of the empirical findings. In the course of the review further new material meeting the criteria also became available and where possible this has been included. However, we also had to identify a cut-off point for data collection and therefore publications after April 2010 were excluded.

Second consultation with the academic community

A further consultation took place once the screening of studies had taken place. Feedback from the researchers originally consulted indicated that the range of material identified was broadly correct, but also included a small number of suggestions for additional material to consider. Each of these new references was scanned and included or excluded according to the criteria set out here. This gave a total of 135 items included in the review (see Table A.2).

Table A.2 The number of items included for review by source

	Number of records	Included items
Research Initiative Studies	82	50
Endnote records	1472	44
Social Care Online records	345	5
Additional material	40	36
Total	1939	135

Preparation of a pro forma for data extraction

Once reports had been screened as being likely to contain data on assessment, the next task was to extract the information. A pro forma was developed for extracting relevant information about assessment. In addition, it included brief consideration of the research methodology, its benefits, its limitations, and the consequent reliability and validity of the findings as relevant to the research aims.

Some reports and articles yielded significant amounts of data on assessment (in some cases, pro formas contained around 50 pages of material) while in others very small quantities of material were obtained. Serious case reviews and Ofsted reports were treated in a similar manner to the procedures outlined above. However, the focus was on summaries of reviews and inspections rather than on the original reviews or inspection reports themselves.

Coding and analysis of data

Once the data extraction had been completed, the material was imported into NVivo 8 (a software package for managing and analysing qualitative data) and the project team generated a number of broad themes for coding the data:

- analysis and critical thinking
- barriers to good assessment and enabling factors
- content of assessments
- inter-professional working
- outcomes
- professional relationships (i.e. between social workers and service users)
- quality of assessments
- systems, structures and organisational issues
- thresholds.

LIST OF EMPIRICAL STUDIES USED IN THIS REVIEW

Note that each study may have multiple outputs which, where used, are included in the references.

Author(s) and publication date	Primary aims of the study	Sample	Method
Aldgate J. and Bradley M. (1999) *Supporting Families through Short-term Fostering.* London: The Stationery Office.	To investigate the use of short-term fostering to support families and help prevent family breakdown.	60 children and their parents were recruited sequentially from 4 areas of the country	A 'before and after' study; interviews with parents, children, social workers and carers; standardised psychometric tests completed by parents and children.
Beckett, C. and McKeigue, B. (2003) 'Children in limbo: Cases where court decisions have taken two years or more.' *Adoption and Fostering* 27, 3, 31–40.	To identify reasons for long delays in child care proceedings and the consequences for the children.	All the cases in 1 local authority which took more than 2 years to resolve (6 cases involving 14 children)	A detailed examination of case files.
Bell, M. (2002) 'Promoting children's rights through the use of relationship.' *Child and Family Social Work* 7, 1–11.	To explore with children and young people their experiences of the child protection process, to what extent they felt involved and what helped or hindered this.	27 children and young people (aged 8–16) from 16 families involved in child protection cases in 1 northern local authority	Semi-structured interviews with the children and young people.
Bell, M., Shaw, I., Sinclair, I., Sloper, P. and Rafferty, J. (May 2007) *An Evaluation of the Integrated Children's System in Councils with Social Services Responsibilities.* Report to Department for Education and Skills and Welsh Assembly Government.	To assess how far ICS achieves its aim of generating accurate, reliable data for practitioners; enables monitoring and provides management information; to identify any constraints that limit effectiveness; to assess suitability of ICS for working with disabled children and their carers.	4 councils in England and Wales (only 1 had fully implemented the ICS system): 10 young people and 7 carers for a process study; 22 parents, their social workers and 7 disabled children	Qualitative and quantitative data from an audit of ICS records and responses of social workers and team leaders: interviews, postal questionnaires, audio diaries, documentary analysis and field logs.
Berridge, D., Beecham, J., Brodie, I., Cole, T., Daniels, H., Knapp, M. and MacNeill, V. (2002) *Costs and Consequences of Services for Troubled Adolescents: An Exploratory, Analytic Study.* Luton: University of Luton.	To learn more about 'difficult to manage' adolescents living in different forms of local authority care, the nature and costs of the services provided and consequences for young people; to develop methodology for estimating unit costs in a more substantial study.	257 adolescents (aged 13–18) living in children's homes, foster homes and residential special schools in 4 contrasting local authorities	An examination of case files and interviews with education and social services managers. Quantitative and qualitative data. 6 case studies were used to develop and pilot the qualitative methodology.
Berridge, D., Dance, C., Beecham, J. and Field, S. (2008) *Educating Difficult Adolescents: Effective Education for Children in Public Care.* London: Jessica Kingsley Publishers.	To evaluate the implementation of the *QP* education objectives by reviewing educational achievements, unauthorised absences and permanent exclusions in three contrasting Social Services and Education Departments.	150 adolescents with behavioural, emotional and social difficulties living in foster homes, residential children's homes or residential special schools	A detailed 9-month follow-up of care and educational experiences and outcomes, based on semi-structured interviews with young people, carers and teachers. An analysis of the costs and outcomes of placements.
Bichal, N. (2005) *Working with Adolescents. Supporting Families, Preventing Breakdown.* London: BAAF.	To compare the work of Specialist Adolescent Support Teams and mainstream social work with young people at risk of admission to care, and to estimate support package costs.	209 young people aged 11–16, of whom 144 were referred to support teams in 6 authorities, while 65 received the mainstream social work service in 3 authorities	Semi-structured interviews with young people and parents; 4 standardised measures of child and family wellbeing and a Severity of Difficulties measure; questionnaires completed by support workers, and in-depth interviews with a sub-sample of 50 families.

Author(s) and publication date	Primary aims of the study	Sample	Method
Boddy, J., Potts, P. and Statham, J. (2006) *Models of Good Practice in Joined-up Assessment: Working for Children with 'Significant and Complex Needs'*, Thomas Coram Research Unit, Institute of Education, University of London.	To provide an in-depth understanding of the different ways in which local authorities are seeking to join up assessment for children with significant and complex health needs and/or disabilities, and the issues they face.	6 local authorities chosen from 18 identified by a previous DfES scoping exercise as developing promising practice; 21 parents with experience of assessment	A case study of each local authority; review of key documents; open-ended interviews with over 50 professionals working in social care, education and health and with 21 parents; focus group discussions with parents.
Boddy, J., Statham, J., McQuail, S., Petrie, P. and Owen, C. (2009) *Working at the 'Edges' of Care? European Models of Support for Young People and Families.* Research Brief, DCSF-RBX-09-07. London: Thomas Coram Research Institute, Institute of Education, University of London.	To compare the support provided for young people and their families in England, Denmark, France and Germany.	Children in public care (in particular the 10–15 age group) in the 4 countries, and 105 respondents including policy makers in national and local government, service managers and practitioners	Experts in public care services in Denmark, France and Germany prepared knowledge reports on each country and facilitated interviews. Secondary analysis of population data on children in care and overview of whole population social indicators from EC data on social protection and social inclusion.
Booth, T. and Booth, W. (2004) *Parents with Learning Difficulties, Child Protection and the Courts.* A report to the Nuffield Foundation, Grant No. CPF/00151/G. Department of Sociological Studies, University of Sheffield.	An exploratory and descriptive study seeking to understand the position of parents with learning difficulties, who are navigating the child protection system and the courts.	All parents with learning difficulties involved in child protection cases in the Family Proceedings Court and County Court in Leeds and Sheffield in 2000. A purposive sample of legal and social work practitioners	Data was collected from court records for 437 public law applications and social services files for 310 cases, and additional data on 25 cases involving a parent with learning difficulties. In 12 cases proceedings were observed. 30 practitioners were interviewed and 31 took part in 8 group discussions. 25 parents and partners from 20 households were interviewed.
Brandon, M., Thoburn, J., Lewis, A. and Way, A. (1999) *Safeguarding Children with the Children Act 1989.* London: The Stationery Office.	To examine the place of the formal child protection system in protecting children, the thresholds for action, and whether the protection offered was appropriate.	4 local authorities; 105 cases were followed prospectively over 12 months, including 51 which were studied intensively, as parents agreed to take part	Quantitative and qualitative data. A template was used to collect data on from the key social worker in each case. Case records were viewed and most case conferences were attended. 51 parents were interviewed and 26 completed a standardised measure for health and wellbeing.
Brandon, M., Howe, A., Dagley, V., Salter, C., Warren, C. and Black, J. (2006) *Evaluating the Common Assessment Framework and Lead Professional Guidance and Implementation in 2005–6.* Research Report RR740. London DfES.	To evaluate practice and identify what helps or hinders practitioners in implementing the Common Assessment Framework and Lead Professional guidance.	12 local authorities in England; 114 respondents (mostly with direct knowledge of CAF and LP work)	The study used a 'constructive enquiry' approach, based on qualitative case studies with negotiated feedback from participants at regular intervals. A larger quantitative telephone survey was used to broaden and test the validity of earlier findings.
Brandon, M., Belderson, P., Warren, C., Howe, D., Gardner, R., Dodsworth, J., and Black, J. (2008) *Analysing Child Deaths and Serious Injury Through Abuse and Neglect: What Can We Learn? A Biennial Analysis of Serious Case Reviews 2003–2005*, London: DCSF.	To use the learning from serious case reviews to improve multi-agency practice at all levels of intervention; to identify ecological-transactional factors in the sub-sample; to provide practice tools for Local Safeguarding Children Boards.	A full sample of 161 cases, for which minimal notification data were available; 47 of these were studied intensively as detailed information was available	Review of case records, collecting quantitative and qualitative data. Cases and threshold patterns were analysed and grouped against common themes in the cases and key features in the child, the parents/carers and the community/environment of the family.
Brandon, M. and Thoburn, J. (2008) 'Safeguarding children in the UK: A longitudinal study of services to children suffering or likely to suffer significant harm.' *Child and Family Social Work* 13, 365–377.	To track the progress of children and young people identified as having suffered, or being likely to suffer, significant harm; to explore factors helping or hindering their capacity to deal with stress and adversity over 8 years, and the implications for policy and	4 English local authorities and 105 children and young people, of whom 77 were followed up 8–9 years later. This included an intensive study of 51 children, whose parents agreed to participate	This prospective longitudinal study collected quantitative and qualitative data from an examination of case files, interviews with children, family members and key professionals, and the use of standardised measures.

Author(s) and publication date	Primary aims of the study	Sample	Method
Brandon, M., Bailey, S., Belderson, P., Gardner, R., Sidebotham, P., Dodsworth, J., Warren, C. and Black, J. (2009) *Understanding Serious Case Reviews and their Impact: A Biennial Analysis of Serious Case Reviews 2005–07.* DCSF RR-129. London: DCSF.	To identify common themes and trends across review reports and the implications for policy and practice; to explore the classification of child deaths, the commissioning and scoping of reviews and the dissemination and implementation of findings.	A full sample of 189 cases and an intensive sub-sample of 40 cases. Comparisons were also made with the previous study (Brandon, Belderson *et al.* 2008), looking at a total of 350 cases over 4 years	This study uses similar methods to the Brandon, Belderson *et al.* 2008 study detailed above. Telephone interviews were held with members of the LSCBs and practitioners (a total of 24 from 17 cases) who had been involved with the serious case review or worked with the child or family at the time of the incident.
Brophy, J., Bates, P., Brown, L.., Cohen, S., Radcliffe, P. and Wale, C. (1999) *Expert Evidence in Child Protection Litigation: Where Do We Go from Here?* London: The Stationery Office.	To review public law Children Act cases in order to improve cross-government delivery of the core principles of the Children Act 1989 in line with the vision for children set out in the Green Paper *Every Child Matters.*	338 guardians (44% of the total workforce); 557 child care cases; a further 65 cases involving 114 children from 5 family proceedings courts and 1 care centre; 35 guardians and 17 purposively selected psychiatrists	This study included: a national random postal survey of guardians in England and Wales; mostly quantitative data from 557 child care cases involving expert evidence; an examination of 65 court files; and interviews with 35 guardians and 17 consultant child and adolescent psychiatrists
Butler, A.H. and Astbury, G.G. (2005) 'The caring child: An evaluative case study of the Cornwall young carers project.' *Children and Society* 19, 4, 292–303.	To evaluate the Children and Young Carers Project (CYCP) in Cornwall in order to provide a strong evidence base for additional funding.	202 referrals made to the CYCP over a 24-month period	A 'Theory of Change' approach was used. Methods included comparative national statistics, the collection of monthly and quarterly data, analysis of referrals and a service user focus group.
Carpenter, J., Tidmarsh, J., Slade, J., Schneider, J., Coolen-Schrijner, P. and Wooff, D. (2003) *Outcomes and Costs of Therapeutic Family Support Services for Vulnerable Families with Young Children.* Report to the Department of Health, University of Durham.	To evaluate costs and effectiveness of therapeutic family support services for 'high risk' families with children in need aged 12 and under.	188 staff in 27 family support projects in both statutory and voluntary agencies in England; 79 families took part, and 60 were followed up later	A wide-ranging mixed methods study, using questionnaires, standard measures, interviews with carers and the family's key worker; a 'theory of change' model of family support services and cost assessments.
Cemlyn, S., Greenfields, M., Burnett, S., Matthews, Z. And Whitwell, C. (2009) *Inequalities Experienced by Gypsy and Traveller Communities: A Review.* Equality and Human Rights Commission Report 12.	To compile and evaluate evidence of inequalities and discrimination from a wide range of Gypsies' and Travellers' experiences.	Gypsies and Traveller organisations and those working closely with them (16 responded)	Primarily a literature review, but also qualitative data from questionnaires to Gypsy and Traveller organisations and those working closely with them.
Cleaver, H. (2000) *Fostering Family Contact.* London: The Stationery Office.	To explore all forms of contact between foster children and their families in order to assess the impact of the Children Act 1989 on contact arrangements.	6 local authorities (over 300 social workers and managers took part); 152 foster children and a prospective sample of 33 foster children aged 5–12	Discussions with social workers and managers preceded a case file study. Interviews with children, key family members, foster carers and social workers took place 6 weeks after placement and 12 months later.
Cleaver, H. and Walker, S. with Meadows, P. (2004) *Assessing Children's Needs and Circumstances: The Impact of the Assessment Framework.* London: Jessica Kingsley Publishers.	To evaluate the implementation of the *Framework for the Assessment of Children in Need and their Families.*	24 English councils took part, and also parents, children over age 10 and social workers involved in 52 cases took part in a qualitative study	An audit of completed assessment records; postal questionnaires to practitioners and managers, and interviews with parents, children and social workers. A time record was also used to assess the time required.

Author(s) and publication date	Primary aims of the study	Sample	Method
Cleaver, H., Nicholson, D., Tarr, S. and Cleaver, D. (2007) *Child Protection, Domestic Violence and Parental Substance Misuse, Family Experiences and Effective Practice.* London: Jessica Kingsley Publishers.	To identify the factors that enable different agencies to work together successfully at the various stages of assessment, planning, service delivery and review.	6 local authorities took part in this study of 357 children referred to children's social care with safeguarding concerns and evidence of domestic violence and/or parental substance abuse	The study involved an analysis of agency plans, procedures and protocols, questionnaires from managers and training officers (78), a study of case files (357) and interviews with parents and professionals (17).
Cleaver, H. and Nicholson, D. (2007) *Parental Learning Disability and Children's Needs.* London: Jessica Kingsley Publishers.	To explore the needs and outcomes of children with a parent with learning disabilities, who are referred to children's social care, identifying factors that encourage or hamper involvement of parents with learning disabilities.	228 children living with a parent with learning difficulties	This 3-part study included: an examination of social work case files, qualitative interviews with parents and social workers, and a follow-up study of the children and families.
Cleaver, H., Walker, S., Scott, J., Cleaver, D., Rose, W., Ward, H. and Pithouse, A. (2008) *The Integrated Children's System: Enhancing Social Work and Inter-Agency Practice.* London: Jessica Kingsley Publishers.	To explore whether the ICS improves the quality of direct work with children and families and enables the achievement of better outcomes; to assess the impact of the ICS on the authorities' IT systems and the pros and cons of different approaches.	28 local authorities applied to take part in piloting the ICS and 4 were selected (a county council, a Welsh LA, a London borough and a unitary authority)	Qualitative and quantitative data were collected by: a scrutiny of documentary evidence; questionnaires and interviews with key service providers; and an audit of social work case files.
Clifford, D. and Burke, B. (2004) 'Moral and professional dilemmas in long-term assessment of children and families.' *Journal of Social Work 4*, 3, 305–321.	To identify factors that contributed to the variable use of voluntary adoption agencies by local authorities in the placement of looked after children.	Managers in adoption agencies in England and Wales; social workers in 4 local authorities in north-west England, which differed in type, size, demographics, practices and policies	Interviews with over 100 managers to gain an overview of policy and practice; 38 face-to-face in-depth interviews with social workers; focus group interview with 5 social workers in a local authority in the south of England to check for differences.
Corby, B., Millar, M. and Pope, A. (2002) 'Assessing children in need assessments – a parental perspective.' *Practice 14*, 4, 5–15.	To explore the experiences of parents whose children are being assessed and their perceptions of what works well or badly in the assessment process.	1 local authority area in the north-west of England	Interviews with 34 sets of parents (10 involved in initial assessments and 24 in core assessments), documentary information including reading case files; Questionnaires.
Corby, B. (2003) 'Supporting families and protecting children: Assisting child care professionals in initial decision-making and review of cases.' *Journal of Social Work 3*, 2, 195–210.	To establish if referrals were treated differently after a policy shift towards greater emphasis on family support; to evaluate social work decisions on whether to use a family-supportive or child protection approach.	400 child protection/children in need cases from before and after policy changes were implemented in a north-west local authority	A retrospective examination and analysis of case files.
Corlyon, J. and Clay, D. (2008) *Interventions for Children and Young People with Drug Misusing Carers.* Final Report to the Department of Health. London: Tavistock Institute.	To determine the range and type of services provided for the children of drug-misusing parents and to explore a number of projects in greater depth to establish the extent to which they met the needs of their clients.	66 services meeting the needs of children of drug misusers in England, and service providers in a sub-sample of 10 projects. 14 children/young people using the projects also took part	A scoping study generated a typology of services and interventions. An in-depth study of 10 services involved an interview with a service provider in each project, the collection of information about service users, and interviews with children and young people.

Author(s) and publication date	Primary aims of the study	Sample	Method
Dance, C., Ouwejan, D., Beecham J. and Farmer, E. (2010) *Adoption Agency Linking and Matching: A Survey of Adoption Agency Practice in England and Wales.* London: BAAF.	To identify variations in policy and practice in linking and matching in adoption in England and Wales.	168 local authorities and 29 voluntary adoption agencies	A self-completion questionnaire (done manually or on the internet) obtained both quantitative and qualitative data.
Daniel, B. (2000) 'Judgements about parenting: What do social workers think they are doing?' *Child Abuse Review 9*, 296–312.	To see whether there is consistency between what social workers believe to be the essential aspects of parenting and how they approach their decision making in child protection cases.	128 students on post-qualifying child protection courses run by Dundee University Social Work Department	Respondents indicated their subjective views and beliefs by scoring 50 statements about parenting, decision making and damaging environments (Q methodology).
Daniel, B. and Baldwin, N. (2001) 'Assessment practice in cases of child neglect: A developmental project.' *Practice 13*, 4, 21–38.	To examine current assessment practice in cases of neglect and to develop formal, flexible tools for the assessment of risk and need.	3 Scottish social services departments and Dundee University Social Work Department working in collaboration	A review of 10 case files from each authority (total of 30): questionnaires to all social workers involved in child care assessment (31 completed); a focus group in each authority (3).
Daniel, B. (2004) 'An overview of the Scottish multidisciplinary child protection review.' *Child and Family Social Work 9*, 3, 247–257.	To review child protection arrangements in Scotland following a child murder, and to involve not only the relevant authorities and agencies but also children and young people and the public.	Out of 5045 potential child protection cases, 188 were examined in depth. 438 professionals in 22 local authorities, 8 police areas and 13 health boards took part. 21 young people who had been abused and 74 children also took part	MORI Scotland was commissioned to carry out a public survey about child protection. Out of 1219 questionnaires, 109 were returned. Case files were audited. Professionals were interviewed and practice evaluated. 100 calls to Parentline and 216 calls to ChildLine were analysed. 74 children offered their views online.
Daniel, B. (2006) 'Operationalizing the concept of resilience in child neglect: Case study research.' *Child: Care, Health and Development 32*, 3, 303–309.	To explore the value of the concept of resilience as an aid to assessment and planning.	1 local authority in Scotland and 8 neglected children aged between 5 and 11	6 training days were provided. Social workers completed questionnaires. Semi-structured interviews were carried out with social workers, and assessment reports were analysed.
Dickens, J. (2007) 'Child neglect and the law: Catapults, thresholds and delay.' *Child Abuse Review 16*, 2, 77–92.	To investigate how social workers and solicitors work together in child care cases.	6 local authorities in England; a 'theoretically productive' sample of 23 cases of children involved court proceedings (selected in line with grounded theory)	A local authority solicitor and social worker were interviewed for each of the 23 cases (i.e. 46 interviews) and 8 managers provided an overview of inter-departmental relations (making a total of 54 interviews). Qualitative data.
Dunnett, K. and Payne, H. (2000) 'How can we make health assessments more acceptable to looked after young people of secondary school age?' *Adoption and Fostering 24*, 3, 83–84.	To evaluate a pilot project in Hertfordshire using school nurses to do the annual review health assessment for looked after children in their schools.	23 young people (in 21 placements), 17 of whom (14 boys and 3 girls) took part	Questionnaires were developed severally for young people aged 10 and over, carers, social workers and school nurses to evaluate the project.
Farmer, E., Moyers, S. and Lipscombe, J. (2004) *Fostering Adolescents.* London: Jessica Kingsley Publishers.	To analyse the parenting task for foster carers looking after adolescents with behavioural and emotional difficulties; to examine whether caring behaviours and skills contribute to good outcomes; to examine differences in the levels of formal support provided.	14 local authorities; 2 independent fostering agencies; a prospective sample of 68 newly placed young people aged 11–17	Quantitative and qualitative data from a review of case files, semi-structured interviews with the young people, their foster carers and social workers and the use of standardised measures.

Author(s) and publication date	Primary aims of the study	Sample	Method
Farmer, E. and Moyers, S. (2008) *Kinship Care: Fostering Effective Family and Friends Placements*. London: Jessica Kingsley Publishers.	To clarify and compare administrative and legal arrangements and outcomes for young people in kinship care placements and unrelated foster care placements.	4 local authorities from southern, Midland and northern England; 2240 children placed with unrelated foster carers or kin and a stratified random sub-sample of 270 children including 142 placed with kin	This study used a catch-up prospective design with a cross-section of children in placement on a set date. Quantitative and qualitative data from a review of case files and 70 interviews relating to 35 kinship care cases (32 with kin carers, 16 with children, 6 with parents and 16 with social workers).
Farmer, E., Sturgess, W. and O'Neill, T. (2008) *The Reunification of Looked After Children with Their Parents: Patterns, Interventions and Outcomes*. Report to DCSF; School for Policy Studies, University of Bristol.	To examine the patterns and outcomes of looked after children who were returned home; to investigate factors associated with successful and unsuccessful returns; and to explore the children and parents' experiences of reunification.	A consecutive sample of 180 children, aged 0–14, who were all returned home from care in 6 local authorities during a 1-year index period	Quantitative and qualitative data. Interviews were conducted relating to 37 (21%) of the cases – 34 with parents, 22 with social workers and team managers, and 19 with young people. Variables were analysed statistically against outcome.
Farmer, E. and Lutman, E. (2009) *Case Management and Outcomes for Neglected Children Returned to their Parent: A Five Year Follow-up Study*. Report to DCSF; School for Policy Studies, University of Bristol.	To examine the case management, interventions and outcomes of neglected children, who had been looked after and were all returned home during 2001.	110 neglected children from the reunification study (Farmer *et al.* 2011) and an additional 28 children from 7 local authorities (2 of the original ones and 1 extra)	Review of case files for 138 children 5 years after they returned home in 2001; semi-structured interviews with social work practitioners, and a small number of interviews with parents and children.
Farmer, E. and Dance, C. with Beecham, J., Bonin, E. and Ouwejan, D. (2010) *An Investigation of Family Finding and Matching in Adoption*. Report to the Department for Children, Schools and Families, School for Policy Studies, University of Bristol.	To examine the effectiveness, outcomes and costs of different family finding and matching practices and related decision-making processes.	10 local authorities in England; 149 cases (82 sampled retrospectively and 67 in real time) where the adoption panel had recommended that adoption should be the plan for the child	All 149 case files were reviewed. Interviews were conducted with social workers for children in the real time sample and also 27 adoptive parents after the match, and again with both 6 months into the adoptive placement. Periodic contact until the match was made. Costs were estimated.
Forrester, D. and Harwin, J. (2006) 'Parental substance misuse and child care social work: Findings from the first stage of a study of 100 families.' *Child and Family Social Work 11*, 325–335.	To describe the extent and nature of parental substance misuse in child care social work cases; to identify how social workers were assessing the families and intervening.	All 290 cases going for 'long-term allocation' in 4 London local authorities (3 whole LAs and one District in another) from Jan 2000 to April 2001	Quantitative and qualitative data were collected from a review of case files and interviews with 89 social workers.
Forrester, D. (2007) 'Patterns of re-referral to social services: A study of 400 closed cases.' *Child and Family Social Work 12*, 1, 11–21.	To investigate how many children were re-referred in the 27 months after their cases was closed, and to identify factors statistically associated with re-referrals.	3 local authorities in London; 400 referrals where a case was closed rather than going for long-term allocation	Children's files were studied in 2002, on average 27 months after the case had been closed. Logistic regression was used to analyse the results.
Forrester, D and Harwin, J. (2008) *Parents Who Misuse Drugs or Alcohol: Effective Interventions in Social Work and Child Protection*. Chichester: Wiley.	To report on placement and welfare outcomes for children allocated a social worker, where there was a concern about parental misuse of drugs or alcohol. This was a follow-up of the study by Forrester and Harwin in 2006.	100 families with 186 children, where parental substance misuse was mentioned as a concern in the earlier study	Case files were reviewed at allocation and 2 years post-referral.

Author(s) and publication date	Primary aims of the study	Sample	Method
Forrester, D., McCambridge, J., Waissbein, C. and Rollnick, S. (2008) 'How do child and family social workers talk to parents about child welfare concerns?' *Child Abuse Review* 17, 23–35.	To identify the skills social workers use to engage parents and work with resistance in child protection cases – the first part of a study to investigate the impact of training child and family social workers in Motivational Interviewing.	40 individual social workers from 7 London local authorities volunteered to take part in the study and to attend the training	Data was collected in a pre-training interview. Participants wrote down how they would respond to 6 client statements and also to 3 comments in a parental resistance vignette. Their responses were rated by researchers.
Franklin, A. and Sloper, P. (2005) *Participation of Disabled Children and Young People Under 'Quality Protects'*. Research Report, University of York. DfES 2119.	To improve knowledge about the effective participation of disabled children and young people under *Quality Protects* and the impact of their views on service development and/or tailoring of individual care packages and the impact on children themselves.	6 local authorities; 76 professionals; 24 parents/carers; 21 disabled children and young people and 2 siblings	Quantitative and qualitative data from an analysis of local authority GP Management Action Plans, a national survey of social services departments, case studies, and interviews with professionals, parents/carers and young people.
Gilligan, P. and Manby, M. (2008) 'The Common Assessment Framework: Does the reality match the rhetoric?' *Child and Family Social Work* 13, 2, 177–187.	To explore the extent to which the actions of practitioners and the experiences of service users with regard to the CAF reflect the content of government guidance and policy documents.	All CAF assessments done by 2 pilot projects in a northern town in England over 6 months; 17 practitioners; 4 parents; and 3 children and young people took part	Primarily qualitative: observations of 10 multi-agency meetings; interviews with practitioners, parents, children and young people, and focus group discussions with managers and practitioners and with young people.
Glaser, D., Prior, V. and Lynch, M. (2001) *Emotional Abuse: Suspicion, Investigation and Registration*. Great Ormond Street Hospital and United Medical and Dental Schools of Guy's and St Thomas' Hospitals, London. Department of Health.	To gather data about children registered for emotional abuse, including current and previous concerns, reasons for registration and outcomes.	4 local authorities; 94 children in 56 families, whose names were on child protection registers under the category of emotional abuse at 31 December 1994	Data were obtained from minutes (rendered anonymous) of the Child Protection Conferences at which the children were registered for emotional abuse, and from interviews with allocated social workers or social work supervisors.
Grant, C. and Hamlyn, B (2009) *Parental Experience of Services for Disabled Children*. London: Nuffield Foundation.	To generate an overall indicator and set of sub-indicators which measure parental views on the 5 elements of the *Core Offer* as set out in the government's report *Aiming High for Disabled Children*.	17,812 families with disabled children aged 0–19 were identified by a screening survey sent to households with school-aged children on the National Pupil Database	Postal questionnaires (1 for each disabled child) were sent to all parents with disabled children; 12,226 responses were received.
Harwin, J., and Forrester, D. (2002) *Parental Substance Misuse and Child Welfare: A Study of Social Work with Families in which Parents Misuse Drugs or Alcohol*. First Stage Report.	To collect detailed information on: families where substance misuse has been identified as an issue; incidence and patterns of substance misuse with child care concerns; assessments and the range of services and interventions offered; the involvement of other agencies; outcomes for children.	All cases (including substances misuse cases) going for long-term allocation in 3 London local authorities and 1 district within another London authority; a sample of c. 1000 closed referrals.	File studies of all cases going for long-term allocation and also the closed referrals to identify the extent and nature of substance misuse cases and patterns of re-referrals. Quantitative and qualitative analysis. (Parental interviews were dropped due to access difficulties.)
Harwin, J., Owen, M., Locke, R. and Forrester, D. (2003) *Making Care Orders Work: A Study of Care Plans and their Implementation*. London: The Stationery Office.	To evaluate the use of care plans under the Children Act 1989, assessing how far they contribute to proactive planning and good outcomes and exploring constraints and obstacles.	5 local authorities; a prospective sample of 100 children from 57 families, who were subject to care orders	An examination of court files and social services files; semi-structured interviews with social workers, guardians and LA solicitors, carers, children and birth parents; standard measures (SDQ and GHQ).

Author(s) and publication date	Primary aims of the study	Sample	Method
Harwin, J. and Ryan, M. (2007) 'The role of the court in cases concerning parental substance misuse and children at risk of harm.' *Journal of Social Work and Family Law 29*, 3–4, 277–292.	To examine practitioner and consumer views about the feasibility of a Family Drug and Alcohol Court, what it might achieve and likely challenges to its success.	Practitioners in adult and children's services in 3 London boroughs and a small number of mothers who had been or were using Class A drugs	57 semi-structured interviews with members of the steering group: representatives from government departments, CAFCASS, adult and children's services, solicitors.
Harwin, J. (2009) *Family Drug and Alcohol Court (FDAC) Interim Report.* Nuffield Foundation and Brunel University.	To evaluate the first pilot Family Drug and Alcohol Court (FDAC) in Britain.	37 families with 51 children involved in care proceedings due to parental substance misuse	Analysis of administrative child and parent file data; observation of court proceedings; interviews with parents, judges and the FDAC team; focus group with guardians.
Hatton, C., Akram, Y., Shah, R., Robertson, J. and Emerson, E. (2004) *Supporting South Asian Families with a Child with Severe Disabilities.* London: Jessica Kingsley Publishers.	To provide a comprehensive picture of the lives of UK South Asian families with a child with severe disabilities.	136 parents, sampled across five local authority areas	Quantitative data from structured interviews with 136 parents and qualitative data from semi-structured interviews at 2 time points with 26 parents. All interviews were conducted in the first language of the participant.
Hill, C. with Wright, V., Sampeys, C., Dunnett, K., Daniel, S., O'Dell, L. and Watkins, J. (2002) 'The emerging role of the specialist nurse: Promoting the health of looked after children.' *Adoption and Fostering 26*, 4, 35–43.	To review the role of the nurse in health assessment of looked after children, and to review the current professional status of looked after children's nurses in England and Wales.	49 LAC in Southampton, who had 2+ statutory medicals and 120 LAC assessed at a health project in Cardiff; 45 nurses, mostly specialist	Retrospective analysis of case notes and assessments; a survey of 45 nurses undertaken at the 2002 conference of the organisation Champions for Children and Young People in Care.
Holland, S. (2010) *Child and Family Assessment in Social Work Practice*, 2nd edn. London: Sage Publications.	To explore different approaches to assessment, outlining policy changes and their implications and focusing on planning assessment methods, analysis, reporting and critical evaluation.	35 children aged 0–12 and 1 unborn child involved in 20 child protection assessments, their social workers and a further 10 social workers from the 2 agencies taking part	Examination of assessments; in-depth interviews with each social worker; observation of video-taped assessment sessions; semi-structured interviews with 10 social workers. The analysis was critiqued by a focus group of social workers.
Holmes, L., McDermid, S., Jones, A. and Ward, H. (2009) *How Social Workers Spend Their Time.* Research Report DCSF-RR087. London: DCSF.	To gather activity data on the amount of time social workers typically spend on the 8 case management processes that support their work with looked after children.	Social work practitioners in 12 local authorities in England and Wales	A series of focus groups with social workers in 6 local authorities and in 6 different authorities about 6 years later. Unit costs for social care processes were calculated and key issues explored.
Hunt, J. and Macleod, A. (1999) *The Best-Laid Plans: Outcomes of Judicial Decisions in Child Protection Proceedings.* London: The Stationery Office.	To ascertain what happens to children subject to care proceedings, looking at the implementation of court orders, compliance, effectiveness and the degree to which children have been protected and their wellbeing promoted.	131 children from 81 families in 3 local authorities. 148 practitioners took part (60 social workers, 15 team managers, 16 local authority solicitors, 28 guardians-ad-litem and 29 private practice solicitors)	Both quantitative and qualitative data. Case files were examined. A self-completion questionnaire was posted to 137 social workers responsible for these cases and 60 responded. Interviews with team managers and local authority solicitors and either questionnaires or interviews with guardians and private practice solicitors.
Hunt, J., Waterhouse, S., and Lutman, E. (2009) *Keeping Them in the Family: Outcomes for Children Placed in Kinship Care through Care Proceedings.* London: BAAF.	To assess placement stability and welfare outcomes for children placed with kin as a result of care proceedings; to identify factors contributing to better or poorer outcomes; to record the views of carers, children and, if possible, parents.	A 6-year cohort sample of all the children from 2 local authorities placed with family members or friends (113) at the end of care proceedings. A comparison group of 31 children placed for adoption or fostering	Quantitative and qualitative data from an examination of case files, interviews with kinship carers (37), social workers (24), children and young people (14) and parents (2); standardised measures of wellbeing completed by carers and also teachers in relation to 25 children.

Author(s) and publication date	Primary aims of the study	Sample	Method
Iwaniec, D., Donaldson, T. and Martin, A. (2004) 'The plight of neglected children: Social work and judicial decision-making, and management of neglect cases.' *Child and Family Law Quarterly* 16, 4, 423–436.	To examine changes to the gateways to care under the Children (Northern Ireland) Order 1995, focusing on decision making and care outcomes for looked after children.	A cohort of 107 children who became looked after or accommodated by the local authority	A prospective study with case files being examined at 2 points in time. An in-depth qualitative study of 14 cases, including interviews with parents and social workers, observations of court proceedings and case conferences, and focus groups with court practitioners, social workers and health visitors.
Macdonald, G. and Williamson, E. (2002) *Against the Odds.* London: National Children's Bureau and Joseph Rowntree Foundation.	To provide a detailed picture of the recipients of Child and Family Support Services, the services provided and the outcomes (intended or unintended); to explore the scope for refocusing services on early prevention.	152 families, who had received help from the child and family support service in a city in the south-west of England	An analysis of case records, reviews and working agreements; interviews with social workers, service users and family centre staff; analysis of management information data to see what happened to the children.
Masson, J., Winn Oakley, M. and Pick, K. (2004) *Emergency Protection Order: Court Orders for Child Protection Crises.* Research Report. University of Warwick, School of Law.	To examine how EPO processes operate in local authorities and the courts and the extent to which practice secures the rights of parents and of children and good decision making.	All the EPOs made in a specific 12 month period in 6 local authorities within 3 Magistrates Courts Committee areas – 86 cases involving 127 children	A national survey of court practice was done by phone interviews with 45 legal advisors. Examination of court files and local authority files; interviews with 41 local authority staff, 24 private practice solicitors and 13 court staff; questionnaire and group discussion for children's guardians, and 2 focus groups.
Masson, J., Pearce, J. and Bader, K. with Joyner, O., Marsden, J. and Westlake, D. (2008) *Case Profiling Study,* Ministry of Justice Research Series.	To provide 'baseline data' on proceedings brought under the Children Act 1989, s.31 (care proceedings) against which reforms to the care proceedings system could be evaluated.	386 cases from 23 courts, drawn from applications made by 17 local authorities in 2004 under Children Act 1989, s.31	Data gathered from court files using a recording instrument with pre-coded categories; observation in court; 3 separate focus groups with solicitors, barristers and judges.
McMurray, I., Connolly, H., Preston-Shoot, M. and Wigley, V. (2008) 'Constructing resilience: Social workers' understandings and practice.' *Health and Social Care in the Community* 16, 3, 299–309.	To explore how social workers perceive resilience and seek to promote it with children and young people at risk. (This was part of a larger 3-phase study)	A purposive sample of 52 children and young people at risk of becoming looked after; 19 social workers	A longitudinal multiple case study; semi-structured interviews with social workers; use of standard measures (2 psycho-social measures and 1 screening for child psychiatric disorders).
Millar, M. and Corby, B. (2006) 'The Framework for the Assessment of Children in Need and their Families – A basis for a "therapeutic" encounter?' *British Journal of Social Work* 36, 6, 887–899.	To consider whether the Assessment Framework provides a basis for therapeutic social work. (This was part of a larger study)	1 local authority area; 34 sets of parents (but focusing mostly on 24 sets of parents involved in core assessments)	Qualitative data from semi-structured interviews with 24 sets of parents; some references to focus groups undertaken with 40 practitioners.
Mitchell, W. and Sloper, P. (2008) 'The Integrated Children's System and disabled children.' *Child and Family Social Work* 13, 3 274–285.	To explore the use of ICS with families of disabled children to see if it is sensitive and responsive to the needs of disabled children.	22 families with disabled children in 4 pilot local authorities and 16 social workers who had used ICS	Parents were interviewed at home. Social workers were interviewed and also completed a questionnaire about the exemplars they had used.
Ofsted (2008) *Learning Lessons, Taking Action: Ofsted's Evaluations of Serious Case Reviews 1 April 2007–31 March 2008.* London: Ofsted.	To evaluate 50 serious cases reviews and recommend ways of improving practice; to consider how the process of conducting SCRs could be improved.	50 serious case reviews carried out between 1 April 2007 and 31 March 2008	A quantitative and qualitative analysis of the key themes and messages emerging from the sample of serious case reviews.

Author(s) and publication date	Primary aims of the study	Sample	Method
Pithouse, A. (2006) 'A common assessment for children in need? Mixed messages from a pilot study in Wales.' *Child Care in Practice 12*, 3, 199–217.	To design, pilot and evaluate a common Assessment Framework (CAF) for referring children in need to social services.	2 social services departments and their partner agencies in neighbouring local authorities in South Wales, of which only one used a CAF	Action research comprising a semi-experimental quantitative comparative investigation supported by qualitative interviews, focus groups and content analysis of CAFs.
Platt, D. (2001) 'Refocusing children's services: Evaluation of an initial assessment process.' *Child and Family Social Work 6*, 2, 139–148.	To evaluate a pilot initial assessment process.	3 teams in 1 local authority; 47 cases with sub-sample of 10	Questionnaires to social workers and other professionals; examination of files for main sample; interviews of social workers and parents in sub-sample.
Platt, D. (2006) 'Threshold decisions: How social workers prioritise referrals of child concern.' *Child Abuse Review 15*, 1, 4–18.	In the context of the Refocusing Initiative, to identify the practice issues for social workers attempting an assessment of a child and family instead of an investigation of alleged child abuse or neglect.	2 local authorities; 23 cases on the borderline of the threshold for investigation of alleged abuse	Case study approach; qualitative interviews with social workers and parents 3–6 months after initial assessment or investigation.
Preston-Shoot, M. (2003) 'A matter of record?' *Practice 15*, 3, 31–50.	As part of a study of outcomes for children in need to evaluate the nature and quality of social work assessments and report young people's experiences of professional intervention.	58 randomly selected children in need cases in 1 local authority	Case file analysis; items evaluated according to Social Services Inspectorate standards.
Randall, J. (2009) 'Towards a better understanding of the needs of children currently adopted from care: An analysis of placements 2003–2005.' *Adoption and Fostering 32*, 4, 31–41.	To establish a firmer evidence base for practice in a voluntary adoption agency.	1 voluntary adoption agency in the south-west of England; a consecutive sample of 103 children placed for adoption from care between 2003 and 2005 from 41 local authorities	An analysis of case files, providing quantitative and qualitative data. The *Matching Services and Needs* methodology was used to collect data on the needs of the children, the services they received and their outcomes.
Reder, P. and Duncan, S. (1999) *Lost Innocents: A Follow-up Study of Fatal Child Abuse*. London and New York, NY: Routledge.	To provide an overview of fatal child abuse cases and to elicit lessons that could be applied by members of child protection networks in their everyday practice.	All serious case reviews submitted in 12 months before 31 March 1994, in which abuse directly caused the deaths of 35 children or was suspected of doing so in 14, while 6 other cases were abuse related	All cases were summarised and those containing evidence or suspicion of abuse were analysed in detail, using an interactional framework and compiling a genogram and chronology of events for each family in order to identify recurrent themes.
Roach, G. and Sanders, R. (2008) 'The best laid plans? Obstacles to the implementation of plans for children.' *Adoption and Fostering 32*, 4, 31–41.	To explore the obstacles to the implementation of plans for children in 1 local authority.	1 local authority in south Wales. The closed files of 20 children were selected sequentially (10 children on the Child Protection Register and 10 looked after children)	A case file study with an emphasis on manifest content. 2 separate content analysis schedules were developed for each group of children and used for quantitative analysis of the tasks specified in each file and in associated plans and reviews.
Rose, W. and Barnes, J. (2008) *Improving Safeguarding Practice: Study of Serious Case Reviews 2001–2003*. London: Department for Children, Schools and Families/Open University.	To prepare an overview of findings from a selection of serious case reviews, identifying any new emerging issues, patterns or themes and any changes in policy or practice.	The then Social Services Inspectorate supplied 45 out of an estimated 180 reports, so the sample of 40 reports was not representative	Analysis of documentary sources (reports on serious case reviews, action plans and progress reports on implementation); 10 telephone interviews with key staff, and an invited national study seminar.

Author(s) and publication date	Primary aims of the study	Sample	Method
Rushton, A. and Dance, C. (2005) 'Negative parental treatment of the singled-out child: The responses to the problems by Health Visitors, Social Services Departments and Child and Adolescent Mental Health Services.' *Clinical Child Psychology and Psychiatry* 10, 3, 413–428.	To attempt to understand the service response to children singled out for rejection in a follow-up exploratory study of a previous sequence of studies.	All referrals to Children's Services over a 3-month period in an inner and outer London borough to identify emotional abuse cases. Total referrals = 647 with 31 allegations of emotional abuse, of which 28 involved siblings	Semi-structured interviews to survey the views of 107 health visitors; case files studied and followed through for a year; face-to-face interviews with 53 CAMHS professionals.
Schofield, G. and Beek, M. (2005) 'Risk and resilience in long-term foster-care.' *British Journal of Social Work* 35, 8, 1283–1301.	To identify how children's needs for permanence, security and stability can be met across time in planned, long-term foster care.	A prospective sample of 53 children (aged 3–12) in long-term foster care recruited in 1997–8 from 5 local authorities (52 remained at Phase 2)	Phase 2 of this longitudinal study involved questionnaires for social workers, in-depth interviews with foster carers and children, and use of a standardised measure (SDQ).
Schofield, G. and Beek, M. (2009) 'Growing up in foster care: Providing a secure base through adolescence.' *Child and Family Social Work* 14, 3, 255–266.	To identify how children's needs for permanence, security and stability can be met across time in planned, long-term foster care.	Out of the original 53 children (see Schofield and Beek 2005), 36 were approached to take part in the follow-up	Phase 3 of this longitudinal study involved follow-up interviews with social workers, 32 foster carers and 20 young people. 3 young people with severe learning difficulties were observed.
Selwyn, J., Quinton, D., Sturgess, W. and Baxter, C. (2006) *Costs and Outcomes of Non-Infant Adoptions*. London: BAAF.	To examine why some children were more easily adopted than others; to estimate the unit costs for adoption; to consider the support needs of those adopting older more challenging children.	A complete population-based sample of 130 older children, who were approved for adoption in the early 1990s in 4 local authorities and 1 voluntary agency, when they were aged 3–11	This study had a catch-up prospective design. Case files were read. Full interview data (quantitative and qualitative) were obtained from adopters, foster carers and social workers for 87 children and outcome interview data (including SDQs) for a further 20. Costs were assessed.
Selwyn, J., Harris, P., Quinton, D., Nawaz, S., Wijedasa, D. and Wood, M. (2010) *Pathways to Permanence for Black, Asian and Mixed Ethnicity Children: Dilemmas, Decision making and Outcomes*. London: BAAF.	To answer questions about differences between white and minority ethnic children in their characteristics, entry to care, service use, decision making and placement outcomes.	3 local authorities in England; a random sample of looked after children (48 white and 54 minority ethnic); a complete sample of 120 minority ethnic children with an adoption recommendation, and a 'real time' sample of 50 minority ethnic children	Case files were read and quantitative and qualitative data collected. The social workers for the 50 'real time' cases were interviewed before the panel hearing then at monthly intervals to track the children's progress. A final phone call was made in July/August 2007 to see whether there had been any change of plan.
Sempik, J., Ward, H. and Darker, I. (2008) 'Emotional and behavioural difficulties of children and young people at entry into care.' *Clinical Child Psychology and Psychiatry* 13, 2, 221–233.	To explore the emotional difficulties of children at entry to care and to compare the findings with normative data for the general population and with data on the mental health of children already in care.	453 children (aged 0–16) in 6 local authorities (these children were part of a wider sample used for an earlier study)	Data were collected retrospectively from case files at entry to care and at annual intervals. 2 psychologists then used this data to assess the children's emotional and behavioural difficulties.
Sheppard, M. (2008) 'How important is prevention? High thresholds and outcomes for applicants refused by children's services: A six-month follow-up.' *British Journal of Social Work* 38, 7, 1268–1282.	To test the hypothesis that the denial of children's services because of high thresholds is likely to result in more serious problems later.	1 unitary authority in England identified families assessed for but denied children's services as problems were not deemed serious enough; 102 women took part and 69 were followed up	All participants were interviewed within 3 weeks of being referred to the study and 69 were interviewed 6 months later. Standardised measures including the Parent Concerns Questionnaire and Beck Depression Inventory were used at both stages.
Sinclair, R. and Bullock, R. (2002) *Learning from Past Experience – A Review of Serious Case Reviews*. London: Department of Health.	To draw out the key findings of a sample of serious case reviews and their implications for policy and practice.	A random sample of serious case reviews, 20 completed between 1998–9 and 20 between 2000–01.	All case review reports were read and analysed. 33 semi-structured interviews with key informants in selected cases and 3 interviews with Social Services Inspectorate staff.

Author(s) and publication date	Primary aims of the study	Sample	Method
Sinclair, I., Baker, C., Lee, J. and Gibbs, I. (2007) *The Pursuit of Permanence: A Study of the English Child Care System*. London: Jessica Kingsley Publishers.	To explore what kind of children are looked after, how and why they move into, out of and within the care system, and the extent to which different factors determine their chances of stability and wellbeing.	13 councils in England; all children looked after between 31 May 2003 and 30 June 2004 (n=7399)	Data on all children on the IT system; questionnaires completed by social workers on 4647 children and on 1585 foster households; 95 case studies based on interviews with young people and their social workers; 34 telephone interviews with heads of children's services and senior managers.
Sinclair, I., Baker, C., Wilson, K. and Gibbs, I. (2005) *Foster Children: Where They Go and How They Get On*. London: Jessica Kingsley Publishers.	To follow up children over 3 years in order to find out where they went, how they were doing and what explained these outcomes.	A cross-sectional sample of 596 foster children from 7 local authorities (who had taken part in an earlier study) was followed up over 3 years	Questionnaires were sent to the children's social workers and foster carers, to foster children and to young people now living independently. There were also 30 case studies.
Skuse, T. and Ward, H. (2003) *Outcomes for Looked After Children: Children's Views of Care and Accommodation*. An interim report to the Department of Health, Centre for Child and Family Research, Loughborough University.	One of a group of studies designed to help councils explore how information gathered in the course of social work interactions with looked after children can be brought together and used for more effective planning of services.	The full cohort consisted of 242 children and young people, who had been looked after by 6 local authorities. 49 took part in this study, having been looked after for an average of 29 months	Interviews with children and young people, whose social services case files had been previously studied as part of a much larger sample.
Stanley, N., Miller, P., Richardson Foster, H. and Thomson, G. (2010) *Children And Families Experiencing Domestic Violence: Police and Children's Social Services' Responses*. London: NSPCC.	To examine the police notification process and the service pathways of families brought to the attention of children's social services in this way; to explore the contributions of other agencies; to report the views of young people, survivors and perpetrators.	A cohort of 251 incidents in domestic violence cases at 2 sites in the north and south of England	Interviews with 40 young people, survivors and perpetrators; a retrospective review of police and CSS records tracking cases over 21 months; interviews with 58 practitioners; and a national survey of local safeguarding children boards to collect examples of innovative practice.
Thoburn, J., Wilding, J. and Watson, J. (2000) *Family Support in Cases of Emotional Maltreatment and Neglect*. London: The Stationery Office.	To explore the extent of emotional abuse and neglect in referrals to social services, how social workers assess such cases, what services are provided, the views and experiences of the families, and whether services are appropriate and cost-effective.	3 local authorities; 555 families referred over a 20–30-week period; a random sample of 180 families (123 referred because of neglect or emotional abuse and a comparison group of 57)	Basic data collected on 555 families; interviews with 112 families from the random sample, of whom 138 were re-interviewed a year later; examination of case files; interviews with groups of social workers and managers in each area; 13 interviews with social workers doing longer-term work with families.
Thomas, J. and Holland, S. (2010) 'Representing children's identities in core assessments.' *British Journal of Social Work 40, 8, 2617–2633.*	To find out how social workers assess and report on children's identities.	1 Welsh local authority; 26 core assessments concerning 32 children, completed over a 6-month period	A qualitative research study, involving the reading and analysis of assessment reports and interviews with the 13 social workers, who wrote them.
Tompsett, H., Ashworth, M., Atkins, C., Bell, L., Gallagher, A., Morgan, M. and Wainwright, P. (2009) *The Child, the Family and the GP*. DCSF-RBX-09-05 ES. London: Kingston University/St George's University of London.	To explore the nature and the consequences of tensions and conflicts of interest for GPs in safeguarding children, taking account of the doctor/patient relationship, family interests versus the child's interests, risk and confidentiality issues; and to evaluate responses.	GPs in 2 contrasting Primary Care Trusts (PCTs) in a shire county and South London; groups of GPs accessed through training events	Quantitative and qualitative data from policy statements and child protection data in the PCTs, 96 questionnaires with GPs, 3 focus groups with service users and 19 interviews with key stakeholders. A Delphi panel (n=25) was used to obtain a consensus view.

Author(s) and publication date	Primary aims of the study	Sample	Method
Triseliotis, J., Borland, M. and Hill, M. (2000) *Delivering Foster Care*. London: BAAF.	To examine the characteristics, motives, social circumstances and experiences of active and former foster carers, seeking reasons for their retention or loss; to identify the policies, structures and organisation of local authorities with respect to fostering.	822 current foster carers and 149 former foster carers in 7 Scottish regional authorities before local government reorganisation; then all 32 new local authorities	Postal questionnaires to active and former foster carers; interviews and group discussions with about 40 active carers and 27 former ones; a postal questionnaire to all the new authorities; a census of foster placements over 6 weeks in 30 of the new authorities.
Tunstill, J., and Aldgate, J. (2000) *Services for Children in Need: From Policy to Practice*. London: The Stationery Office.	To evaluate the provision of family support services to a group of children in need.	7 local authorities; a prospective sample of 93 children (excluding child protection cases)	Quantitative and qualitative data from interviews with 93 parents/carers and 41 children, and questionnaire to social workers.
Tunstill, J., Aldgate, J., and Hughes, M. (2007) *Improving Children's Services Networks: Lessons from Family Centres*. London: Jessica Kingsley Publishers.	To examine the potential of family centres to act as a gateway to family support services and to coordinate such services, and the extent to which they develop links with informal support networks in the community.	A survey sample of 559 family centres in England (415 took part) and a purposive sample of 40 family centres (38 took part)	Quantitative and qualitative data from postal questionnaires to family centres and external stakeholders, follow-up questionnaires, and in-depth interviews with managers and service users (parents) in 38 family centres.
Tunstill, J., and Allnock, D. (2007) *Understanding the Contribution of Sure Start Local Programmes to the Task of Safeguarding Children's Welfare*. Sure Start Report 026. London: DfES Publications.	To explore the contribution of SSLPs to the objective of *staying safe*; and to examine their strategic and operational relationships with social services; to identify good practice and how it can be developed within the context of Children's Centres.	8 Sure Start Local Programmes and 4 local authorities; a random sample of more than 143 referrals to SSLPs from social services	A focused case study of each area; analysis of documentation on policies and procedures; a case file study of referrals from social services, and interviews with programme managers, child protection coordinators, a sample of frontline social workers and other key personnel, e.g. teachers.
Wade, J., Mitchell, F. and Baylis, G. (2005) *Unaccompanied Asylum Seeking Children: The Response of Social Work Services*. London: BAAF.	To establish how unaccompanied asylum-seeking children are referred to social services, how their needs are assessed, what services are provided, and what limits or facilitates support.	All new referrals (212) of 'unaccompanied children who received some form of service from 3 local authorities over 18 months retrospectively	Quantitative and qualitative data from an examination of case files and interviews with 31 children and young people and 27 practitioners.
Wade, J., Dixon, J. and Richards, A. (2010) *Special Guardianship in Practice*. London: BAAF.	To describe different approaches to implementing special guardianship, identifying policy, procedure and resource issues, and to explore the characteristics and motivation of those seeking special guardianship and the experiences of carers, children and social workers.	81 carers caring for 120 children in 8 local authorities, and a sub-sample of 15 special guardians and 3 of their children	A policy study based on document analysis and interviews with 38 local authority managers and 10 informants from national child welfare and legal agencies; postal questionnaires to special guardianship applicants and their social workers; case study interviews with the sub-sample.
Wade, J., Biehal, N., Farrelly, N. and Sinclair, I. (2010) *Maltreated Children in the Looked After System: A Comparison of Outcomes for Those Who Go Home and Those Who Do Not*. Research Brief published August 2010: DFE-RBX-10-06. London: Department for Education.	To compare the care pathways and progress of maltreated children who returned home with those of children who remained looked after; to examine how the decision to reunify was made and supported over 6 months.	A census study of 3872 children looked after by 7 local authorities in 2003–4; a survey sample of 149 of these children	The census study used administrative data to track care pathways. Case files were examined and cases followed up retrospectively from the decision for or against reunification. Social workers and teachers completed a global outcome measure. 9 birth parents and 11 children were interviewed.

Author(s) and publication date	Primary aims of the study	Sample	Method
Walker, M., Hill, M. and Triseliotis, J. (2002) *Testing the Limits of Foster Care*. London, BAAF.	To examine the characteristics, motives and social circumstances of active and former foster carers in Scotland.	All 32 Scottish local authorities; all active and former foster carers in 7 out of 12 regional authorities before reorganisation; 27 randomly selected former foster carers.	Postal questionnaires to all 32 local authorities, 822 current foster carers and 96 former foster carers; interviews and group discussions with 40 active and 27 former foster carers; a census of all fostering placements in a 6 week period in 30 authorities; review of policy documents.
Ward, H., Munro, E. and Dearden, C. (2006) *Babies and Young Children in Care: Life Pathways, Decision-Making and Practice*. London: Jessica Kingsley Publishers.	To explore in-depth the life pathways of very young children and the decision making process that influenced their care experiences.	A prospective sample of 42 babies, who entered care before their first birthday (selected from all children who entered care or accommodation in 6 local authorities in a given period)	Quantitative and qualitative data from an examination of case files and semi-structured interviews with social workers, team leaders, family placement workers, children's guardians, parents and carers.
Ward, H., Holmes, L. and Soper, J. (2008) *Costs and Consequences of Placing Children in Care*. London: Jessica Kingsley Publishers.	To trace and explore the relationship between costs and experience for looked after children, and to develop a Cost Calculator for Children's Services.	A sample of 478 children looked after over a 20 month period in 6 local authorities. A seventh local authority piloted the Cost Calculator	An examination of case files and financial records; construction of a computer application to calculate costs; interviews with children and young people; group discussions with over 140 staff.
Ward, H. (2009) 'Patterns of instability: Moves within the care system, their reasons, contexts and consequences.' *Children and Youth Services 31*, 10, 1113–1118.	To examine the moves of children and young people in the care system and to identify reasons, contexts and consequences.	242 children, who came into the care of 6 local authorities in England between 1 April 1996 and 31 March 1997 and were looked after for a year or more	Quantitative and qualitative data from an examination of case files and interviews with a sub-sample of children and young people. Cases were studied longitudinally for a minimum of 3.5 years after entry to care.
Ward, H., Brown, R., Westlake, D. and Munro, E. (2010) *Infants Suffering, or Likely to Suffer, from Significant Harm: A Prospective Longitudinal Study*. Research Brief DFE-RB053. London: Department for Education.	To trace the decision-making process influencing the life pathways of very young children identified as suffering, or likely to suffer, from significant harm; to identify consequences, the weight given to risk and protective factors, and the roles participants including birth parents play in decision making.	A prospective sample of 57 babies, who were the subject of a core assessment, a s. 47 enquiry or became looked after before their first birthday	Quantitative data from case files; in-depth case-specific interviews with birth parents, carers, social workers, team managers; interviews with senior managers, judges, magistrates and local authority solicitors; focus groups with health visitors.
White, S., Wastell, D., Pithouse, A., Broadhurst, K., Hall, C., Peckover, S., Thompson, K. and Davey, D. (2009) *Error, Blame and Responsibility in Child Welfare: Problematics of Governance in an Invisible Trade*. End of Award Report. Lancaster University, University of Nottingham and Cardiff University.	To examine the impact of changes introduced in the context of New Labour's programme of modernisation on professional decision making, focusing particularly on patterns of error and the attribution of blame.	Social workers, team leaders, middle and senior management in 4 varied local authorities in England and 1 in Wales (2 of these authorities were ISA Trailblazers)	A mixed methods qualitative study, incorporating institutional ethnography, interviews (60+), focus groups (12+) documentary analysis, analysis of key indicators in the public domain, a quasi-experimental micro-world simulation and 280 days of observation of everyday practice in key decision-making loci.
Woodcock, J. (2003) 'The social work assessment of parenting: An exploration.' *British Journal of Social Work 33*, 87–106.	To explore social workers' construction of parenting and how this feeds into their practice with parents.	15 social workers from 2 child and family welfare teams in an urban local authority; 27 cases of parental behaviour towards children	In-depth semi-structured interviews with participants; also used analytic tactics of theoretical sampling and constant comparative analysis from the grounded theory approach.

REFERENCES

Advisory Council on the Misuse of Drugs (2003) *Hidden Harm: Responding to the Needs of Children of Problem Drug Users. Report of an Inquiry by the Advisory Council on the Misuse of Drugs.* London: ACMD/Home Office.

Aldgate, J. and Bradley, M. (1999) *Supporting Families through Short-Term Fostering.* London: The Stationery Office.

Aldgate, J., Jones, D., Rose, W. and Jeffery, C. (2006) *The Developing World of the Child.* London: Jessica Kingsley Publishers.

Aldgate, J. and Statham, J. (2001) *The Children Act Now: Messages from Research.* London: The Stationery Office.

Allen, G. (2011) *Early Intervention: The Next Steps. An Independent Report to Her Majesty's Government.* London: The Cabinet Office.

Allen, G. and Smith, I.D. (2008) *Early Intervention: Good Parents, Great Kids, Better Citizens.* London: Centre for Social Justice and the Smith Institute.

Anning, A., Cottrell, D., Frost, N., Green, J. and Robinson, M. (2006) *Developing Multi-Professional Teamwork for Integrated Children's Services.* Milton Keynes: Open University Press.

Ashley, C., Featherstone, B., Roskill, C., Ryan, M. and White, S. (2006) *Fathers Matter: Research Findings on Fathers and Their Involvement with Social Care Services.* London: Family Rights Group.

Audit Commission (2002) *Recruitment and Retention – A Public Service Workforce for the 21st Century.* London: The Stationery Office.

Barlow, J. and Schrader-MacMillan, A. (2009) *Safeguarding Children from Emotional Maltreatment: What Works?* London: Jessica Kingsley Publishers.

Barlow, J. and Scott, J. (2010) *Safeguarding in the 21st Century – Where to Now.* Dartington: Research in Practice.

Barry, M. (2007) *Effective Approaches to Risk Assessment in Social Work: An International Literature Review.* Scottish Executive Social Research, Research Findings No.31/2007. Available at www.scotland.gov.uk/Resource/Doc/194419/0052192.pdf, accessed June 2011.

Beckett, C. and McKeigue, B. (2003) 'Children in limbo cases where court decisions have taken two years or more.' *Adoption and Fostering 27,* 3, 39–40.

Beecham, J. and Sinclair, I. (2007) *Costs and Outcomes in Children's Social Care: Messages from Research.* London: Jessica Kingsley Publishers.

Beesley, P. (2010) *Making Good Assessment: A Practical Resource Guide,* 2nd edn. London: BAAF.

Bell, M. (1999) 'Working in partnership in child protection: The conflicts.' *British Journal of Social Work 29,* 437–455.

Bell, M. (2002) 'Promoting children's rights through the use of relationship.' *Child and Family Social Work 7,* 1–11.

Bell, M., Shaw, I., Sinclair, I., Sloper, P. and Rafferty, J. (2007) *An Evaluation of the Practice, Process and Consequences of the ICS in Councils with Social Services Responsibilities.* Report to Department for Education and Skills and Welsh Assembly Government. York: Department of Social Policy and Social Work, University of York.

Belsky, J. and Vondra, J. (1989) 'Lessons from Child Abuse: The Determinants of Parenting.' In D. Cichetti and V. Carlson (eds) *Child Maltreatment: Theory and Research on the Causes and Consequences of Child Abuse and Neglect.* Cambridge: Cambridge University Press.

Bentovim, A. and Bingley Miller, L. (2001) *The Family Assessment: Assessment of Family Competence, Strengths and Difficulties.* Brighton: Pavilion Publishing.

Bentovim, A., Cox, A., Bingley Miller, L. and Pizzey, S. (2009) *Safeguarding Children Living with Trauma and Family Violence: Evidence-Based Assessment, Analysis and Planning Interventions.* London: Jessica Kingsley Publishers.

Berridge, D. (2000) *Placement Stability.* Quality Protects Research Briefing 2. London: Department of Health.

Berridge, D., Beecham, J., Brodie, I., Cole, T., Daniels, H., Knapp, M. and MacNeill, V. (2002) *Costs and Consequences of Services for Troubled Adolescents: An Exploratory, Analytic Study.* Luton: University of Luton.

Berridge, D., Dance, C., Beecham, J. and Field, S. (eds) (2008) *Educating Difficult Adolescents: Effective Education for Children in Public Care or with Emotional and Behavioural Difficulties.* London: Jessica Kingsley Publishers.

Berridge, D., Henry, L., Jackson, S. and Turney, D. (2009) *Looked After and Learning: An Evaluation of the Virtual School Head for Looked After Children Local Authority Pilots.* Bristol: School for Policy Studies, University of Bristol.

Biehal, N. (2005) *Working with Adolescents: Supporting Families, Preventing Breakdown.* London: BAAF.

Biehal N. (2006) *Reuniting Looked After Children with their Families: A Review of the Research.* London: National Children's Bureau.

Biehal, N., Ellison, S., Baker, C. and Sinclair, I. (2010) *Belonging and Permanence: Outcomes in Long-Term Foster Care and Adoption.* London: BAAF.

Bifulco, A., Lillie, A., Ball, B. and Moran, P. (1998) *Attachment Style Interview (ASI, Training Manual).* London: Royal Holloway, University of London.

Blom-Cooper, L. (1985) *A Child in Trust: The Report of the Panel of Inquiry into the Circumstances surrounding the Death of Jasmine Beckford.* London: London Borough of Brent.

Boddy, J., Potts, P. and Statham, J. (2006) *Models of Good Practice in Joined-up Assessment: Working for Children with 'Significant and Complex Needs'.* London: Thomas Coram Research Unit, Institute of Education, University of London.

Boddy, J., Statham, J., McQuail, S., Petrie, P. and Owen, C. (2009) *Working at the 'Edges' of Care? European Models of Support for Young People and Families.* London: Thomas Coram Research Institute, Institute of Education, University of London.

Booth, T. and Booth, W. (2005) 'Parents with learning difficulties in the child protection system: Experiences and perspectives.' *Journal of Intellectual Disabilities 9,* 2, 109–129.

Booth, T., McConnell, D. and Booth, W. (2006) 'Temporal discrimination and parents with learning difficulties in the child protection system.' *British Journal of Social Work 36,* 6, 997–1015.

Bostock, L. (2004) *Promoting Resilience in Fostered Children and Young People.* SCIE Guide 6. London: Social Care Institute for Excellence.

Brandon, M., Anthony, R., Colquhoun, F. and Connolly, S. (2009) *Evaluating the Common Assessment Framework and Database in 2008.* Wales: Wales Assembly Government.

Brandon, M., Bailey, S. and Belderson, P. (2010) *Building on the Learning from Serious Case Reviews: A Two-Year Analysis of Child Protection Database Notifications 2007–2009.* DFE-RR-040, University of East Anglia. London: Department for Education.

Brandon, M., Bailey, S., Belderson, P., Gardner, R., Sidebotham, P., Dodsworth, J., Warren, C. and Black, J. (2009) *Understanding Serious Case Reviews and Their Impact: A Biennial Analysis of Serious Case Reviews 2005–07.* Research Report DCSF-RR129, University of East Anglia. London: Department for Education. Crown Copyright.

Brandon, M., Belderson, P., Warren, C., Howe, D., Gardner, R., Dodsworth, J. and Black, J. (2008) *Analysing Child Deaths and Serious Injury through Abuse and Neglect: What Can We Learn? A Biennial Analysis of Serious Case Reviews 2003–2005.* Research Report DCSF-RR023. University of East Anglia. London: Department for Education and Skills. Crown Copyright.

Brandon M., Howe, A. Dagley, V., Salter, C., Warren, C. and Black, J. (2006) *Evaluating the Common Assessment Framework and Lead Professional Guidance and Implementation in 2005–6.* Research Report RR740. London: Department for Education and Skills.

Brandon, M. and Thoburn, J. (2008) 'Safeguarding children in the UK: A longitudinal study of services to children suffering or likely to suffer significant harm.' *Child and Family Social Work 13*, 365–377.

Brandon, M., Thoburn, J., Lewis, A. and Way, A. (1999) *Safeguarding Children with the Children Act 1989.* London: The Stationery Office.

Bridge Child Care Consultancy (1995) *Paul: Death through Neglect.* London: The Bridge Consultancy Service.

British Medical Association (2007) *Fetal Alcohol Spectrum Disorders: A Guide for Healthcare Professionals.* London: BMA.

Britton R. (1981) 'Re-enactment as an Unwitting Professional Response to Family Dynamics.' In S. Box, B. Coply, J. Magagna and E. Moustaki (eds) *Psychotherapy with Families: An Analytic Approach.* London: Routledge and Kegan Paul.

Broadhurst, K., Wastell, D., White, S., Hall, C., Peckover, S., Thompson, K., Pithouse, A. and Davey, D. (2010) 'Performing "Initial Assessment": Identifying the latent conditions for error at the front-door of local authority children's services.' *British Journal of Social Work 40*, 352–370.

Broadhurst, K., White, S., Fish, S., Munro E., Fletcher K. and Lincoln H. (2010) *Ten Pitfalls and How to Avoid Them: What Research Tells Us.* London: NSPCC.

Brodie, I. (2009) *Improving Educational Outcomes for Looked-After Children and Young People.* London: Centre for Excellence and Outcomes in Children and Young People's Services.

Brophy, J. (2006) *Research Review: Child Care Proceedings under the Children Act 1989.* Department for Constitutional Affairs, DCA Research Series 5/06. Oxford: Oxford Centre for Family Law and Policy, University of Oxford.

Brown, L., Moore, S. and Turney, D. (2011) *Analytical and Critical Thinking in Assessment – Pilot Action Pack.* Dartington: Research in Practice.

Budd, K.S. (2005) 'Assessing parenting capacity in a child welfare context.' *Child and Youth Services Review 27*, 4, 429–444.

Burton, S. (2009) *The Oversight and Review of Cases in the Light of Changing Circumstances and New Information: How Do People Respond to New and Challenging Information?* Safeguarding: Briefing 3. London: Centre for Excellence and Outcomes in Children and Young People's Services.

Butler, A.H. and Astbury, G. (2005) 'The caring child: An evaluative case study of the Cornwall young carers project.' *Children and Society 19*, 4, 292–303.

Butler, I. and Williamson, H. (1994) *Children Speak: Children, Trauma and Social Work.* Harlow: Longman.

Cameron, A. and Lart, R. (2003) 'Factors promoting and obstacles hindering joint working: A systematic review of the evidence.' *Journal of Integrated Care 11*, 2, 9–17.

Campbell, S., Pierce, E.W., March, C.L. and Ewing, L.J. (1991) 'Non-compliant behaviour, overactivity and family stress as predictors of negative maternal control with preschool children.' *Development and Psychopathology 3*, 376–395.

Carpenter, J., Tidmarsh, J., Slade, J., Schneider, J., Coolen-Schrijner, P. and Wooff, D. (2003) *Outcomes and Costs of Therapeutic Family Support Services for Vulnerable Families with Young Children.* Research Report. London: Department of Health/Department for Education and Skills and Research in Practice, University of Durham.

Cemlyn, S., Greenfields, M., Burnett, S., Matthews, Z. and Whitwell, C. (2009) *Inequalities Experienced by Gypsy and Traveller Communities: A Review.* Equality and Human Rights Commission Report 12. London: Equality and Human Rights Commission.

Chand, A. (2005) 'Do you speak English? Language barriers in child protection work with minority ethnic families.' *British Journal of Social Work 35*, 807–821.

Children's Workforce Development Council (2009) *NQSW Guide for Supervisors. Newly Qualified Social Worker Pilot Programme 2009–2010.* Leeds: CWDC.

Clark, A. and Moss, P. (2001) *Listening to Young Children: The Mosaic Approach.* London: National Children's Bureau.

Cleaver, H. (2000) *Fostering Family Contact.* London: The Stationery Office.

Cleaver, H. and Freeman, P. (1995) *Parental Perspectives in Suspected Child Abuse.* London: HMSO.

Cleaver, H. and Nicholson, D. (2007) *Parental Learning Disability and Children's Needs.* London: Jessica Kingsley Publishers.

Cleaver, H., Nicholson, D., Tarr, S. and Cleaver, D. (2007) *Child Protection, Domestic Violence and Parental Substance Misuse: Family Experiences and Effective Practice.* London: Jessica Kingsley Publishers.

Cleaver, H., Unell, I. and Aldgate, J. (1999) *Children's Needs – Parenting Capacity: The Impact of Parental Mental Illness, Problem Alcohol and Drug Use, and Domestic Violence on Children's Behaviour.* London: The Stationery Office.

Cleaver, H., Unell, I. and Aldgate, J. (forthcoming) *Children's Needs – Parenting Capacity. Child Abuse: Parental Mental Illness, Learning Disability, Substance Misuse, and Domestic Violence.* 2nd edn. London: The Stationery Office.

Cleaver, H. and Walker, S. (2004) 'From policy to practice: The implementation of a new framework for social work assessments of children and families.' *Child and Family Social Work 9,* 1, 81–90.

Cleaver, H. and Walker, S. with Meadows, P. (2004) *Assessing Children's Needs and Circumstances: The Impact of the Assessment Framework.* London: Jessica Kingsley Publishers.

Cleaver, H., Walker, S., Scott, J., Cleaver, D., Rose, W., Ward, H. and Pithouse, A. (2008) *The Integrated Children's System: Enhancing Social Work and Inter-Agency Practice.* London: Jessica Kingsley Publishers.

Clifford, D. and Burke, B. (2004) 'Moral and professional dilemmas in long-term assessment of children and families.' *Journal of Social Work 4,* 3, 305–321.

Coleman, J.C. (1974) *Relationships in Adolescence.* London: Routledge and Kegan Paul.

Cooper, A. (2005) 'Surface and depth in the Victoria Climbié Inquiry Report.' *Child and Family Social Work 10,* 1, 1–9.

Cooper, A., Hetherington, R. and Katz, I. (2003) *The Risk Factor: Making the Child Protection System Work for Children.* London: Demos.

Corby, B. (2003) 'Supporting families and protecting children: Assisting child care professionals in initial decision-making and review of cases.' *Journal of Social Work 3,* 2, 195–210.

Corby, B., Millar, M. and Pope, A. (2002) 'Assessing children in need assessments – a parental perspective.' *Practice 14,* 4, 5–15.

Corlyon, J. and Clay, D. (2008) *Interventions for Children and Young People with Drug Misusing Carers. Final Report to the Department of Health.* London: The Tavistock Institute.

Cox, A. and Walker, S. (2002) *The HOME Inventory – Home Observation and Measurement of the Environment.* Brighton: Pavilion Publishers.

Crisp, B.R., Anderson, M.R., Orme, J. and Green Lister, P. (2007) 'Assessment frameworks: A critical reflection.' *British Journal of Social Work 37,* 6, 1059–1077.

Crittenden, P. (2005) *Using the CARE-Index for Screening, Intervention, and Research.* Available at www.patcrittenden.com, accessed 27 May 2011.

CSCI (Commission for Social Care Inspection) (2005) *Making Every Child Matter: Messages from Inspection of Children's Services.* London: Commission for Social Care Inspection.

CSCI (Commission for Social Care Inspection) (2006) *Supporting Parents, Safeguarding Children.* London: Commission for Social Care Inspection.

Dalzell, R. and Chamberlain, C. (2006) *Communicating with Children during Assessment. National Children's Bureau.* Available at http://resources.ncb.org.uk/resources/free-resources/communicating-with-children-during-assessment, accessed 3 June 2011.

Dalzell, R. and Sawyer, E. (2007) *Putting Analysis into Assessment: Undertaking Assessments of Need.* London: National Children's Bureau.

Dance, C., Ouwejan, D., Beecham, J. and Farmer, E. (2010) *Adoption Agency Linking and Matching: A Survey of Adoption Agency Practice in England and Wales.* London: BAAF.

Daniel, B. (2004) 'An overview of the Scottish multidisciplinary child protection review.' *Child and Family Social Work 9*, 3, 247–257.

Daniel, B. (2006) 'Operationalizing the concept of resilience in child neglect: Case study research.' *Child: Care, Health and Development 32*, 3, 303–309.

Daniel, B. and Baldwin, N. (2001) 'Assessment practice in cases of child neglect: A developmental project.' *Practice 13*, 4, 21–38.

Daniel, B., Taylor, J., Scott, J. and Barbour, M. (2009) *Noticing and Helping the Neglected Child: A Systematic Review of the Literature.* Unpublished report. Department for Children, Schools and Families.

Department for Children, Schools and Families (2008) *Care Matters: Time to Deliver for Children in Care.* London: DCSF.

Department for Children, Schools and Families (2009a) *Statutory Guidance on Promoting the Health and Well-being of Looked After Children.* London: DCSF.

Department for Children, Schools and Families (2009b) *Referrals, Assessment and Children and Young People Who Are the Subject of a Child Protection Plan, England – Year ending 31 March 2009.* London: DCSF.

Department for Children, Schools and Families (2009c) *LAC Circular Ref 1706090002* (June). London: DCSF.

Department for Children, Schools and Families (2010) *Common Assessment Framework.* London: DCSF.

Department for Education (2010a) *Children In Need in England, Including Their Characteristics and Further Information on Children Who Were the Subject of a Child Protection Plan (2009–10 Children In Need Census).* London: Department for Education. Available at www.education.gov.uk/rsgateway/DB/STR/d000970/index.shtml, accessed May 2011.

Department for Education (2010b) *Statistical First Release: Children Looked After in England (Including Adoption and Care Leavers) Year Ending 31 March 2010.* London: Department for Education. Available at www.dcsf.gov.uk/rsgateway/DB/SFR/s000960/index.shtml, accessed May 2011.

Department for Education and Skills (2006) *The Children Act 1989 Report 2004–2005.* London: DfES.

Department of Health (1988) *Protecting Children: A Guide for Social Workers Undertaking a Comprehensive Assessment.* London: HMSO.

Department of Health (1995) *Child Protection: Messages from Research.* London: HMSO.

Department of Health (1999) *Consultation Draft: Framework for the Assessment of Children in Need and Their Families.* London: Department of Health.

Department of Health, Cox, A. and Bentovim, A. (2000) *The Family Assessment Pack of Questionnaires and Scales.* London: The Stationery Office.

Department of Health, Department for Education and Employment, and Home Office (2000) *Framework for the Assessment of Children in Need and Their Families.* London: The Stationery Office.

Department of Health and Social Services Inspectorate (1995) *The Challenge of Partnership in Child Protection: Practice Guide.* London: HMSO.

Dickens, J. (2007) 'Child neglect and the law: Catapults, thresholds and delay.' *Child Abuse Review 16*, 2, 77–92.

Donald, T. and Jureidini, J. (2004) 'Parenting capacity.' *Child Abuse Review 13*, 5–17.

Dunnett, K. and Payne, H. (2000) 'How can we make health assessments more acceptable to looked after young people of secondary school age?' *Adoption and Fostering 24*, 3, 83–84.

Emery, P. (2006) 'Four years on: Lessons learnt from the implementation of an Integrated Care Pathway to address 'Promoting Health of LAC' guidance (2002) in an English local authority.' *Adoption and Fostering 30*, 2, 81–83.

Farmer, E. (1999) 'Holes in the safety net: The strengths and weaknesses of child protection procedures.' *Child and Family Social Work 4*, 293–302.

Farmer, E. (2009) 'Reunification with Birth Families.' In G. Schofield and J. Simmonds (eds) *The Child Placement Handbook: Research, Policy and Practice.* London: BAAF.

Farmer, E. and Dance, C. with Beecham, J., Bonin, E. and Ouwejan, D. (2010) *An Investigation of Family Finding and Matching in Adoption.* Report to the Department for Children, Schools and Families, School for Policy Studies, University of Bristol. London: Department for Education.

Farmer, E. and Lutman, E. (2009) *Case Management and Outcomes for Neglected Children Returned to Their Parents: A Five Year Follow-up Study.* Report to the Department for Children, Schools and Families, School for Policy Studies, University of Bristol. London: Department for Education.

Farmer, E. and Moyers, S. (2008) *Kinship Care: Fostering Effective Family and Friends Placements.* London: Jessica Kingsley Publishers.

Farmer, E., Moyers, S. and Lipscombe, J. (2004) *Fostering Adolescents.* London: Jessica Kingsley Publishers.

Farmer, E. (2009) 'Reunification with Birth Families.' In G. Schofield and J. Simmonds (eds) *The Child Placement Handbook.* London: BAAF.

Farmer, E., Sturgess, W., O'Neill, T. and Wijedasa, D. (2011) *Achieving Successful Returns from Care: What Makes Reunification Work?* London: BAAF.

Fauth, R., Jelicic, H., Hart, D., Burton, S. and Shemmings, D. with Bergeron, C., White, K. and Morris, M. (2010) *Effective Practice to Protect Children Living in 'Highly Resistant' Families.* London: Centre for Excellence and Outcomes in Children and Young People's Services.

Ferguson, H. (2005) 'Working with violence, the emotions and the psycho-social dynamics of child protection: Reflections on the Victoria Climbié case.' *Social Work Education 24,* 7, 781–795.

Forrester, D. (2007) 'Patterns of re-referral to social services: A study of 400 closed cases.' *Child and Family Social Work 12,* 1, 11–21.

Forrester, D. (2008) 'Child protection and re-referrals involving serious concerns: A follow-up study of 400 referrals closed by Social Services Departments.' *Child and Family Social Work 13,* 3, 286–299.

Forrester, D. and Harwin, J. (2006) 'Parental substance misuse and child care social work: Findings from the first stage of a study of 100 families.' *Child and Family Social Work 11,* 325–335.

Forrester, D. and Harwin, J. (2008) 'Parental substance misuse and child welfare: Outcomes for children two years after referral.' *British Journal of Social Work 38,* 1518–1535.

Forrester, D., McCambridge, J., Waissbein, C. and Rollnick, S. (2008) 'How do child and family social workers talk to parents about child welfare concerns?' *Child Abuse Review 17,* 23–35.

Franklin, A. and Sloper, P. (2005) *Participation of Disabled Children and Young People Under 'Quality Protects'.* Research Report. University of York. DfES 2119. London: Department for Education and Skills.

Frost, N. (2005) *Professionalism, Partnership and Joined-Up Thinking: A Research Review of Frontline Working with Children and Families.* Dartington: Research in Practice.

Fuller, T., Wells, S. and Cotton, E. (2001) 'Predictors of maltreatment recurrence at two milestones in the life of a case.' *Children and Youth Services Review 23,* 1, 49–78.

Furstenberg, F.F. and Hughes, M.E. (1995) 'Social capital and successful development among at-risk youth.' *Journal of Marriage and the Family 57,* 580–592.

Galanter, C. and Patel, V. (2005) 'Medical decision making: A selective review for child psychiatrists and psychologists.' *Journal of Child Psychology and Psychiatry 46,* 7, 675–689.

Gambrill, E. (1990) *Critical Thinking in Clinical Practice.* San Fransisco, CA: Jossey-Bass.

George, C., Kaplan, N. and Main, M. (1985) *The Adult Attachment Interview.* Unpublished manuscript, University of California at Berkeley, Department of Psychology.

General Social Care Council (2005) *Specialist Standards and Requirements for Post-Qualifying Programmes: Children and Young People, Their Families and Carers.* London: GSCC. Available at www.gscc.org.uk/cmsFiles/Education%20and%20Training/PQ%20documents/Children%20and%20young%20people%20their%20families%20and%20carers.pdf, accessed June 2011.

Ghate, D. and Hazel, N. (2002) *Parenting in Poor Environments: Stress, Support and Coping.* London: Jessica Kingsley Publishers.

Gilligan, P. and Manby, M. (2008) 'The Common Assessment Framework: Does the reality match the rhetoric?' *Child and Family Social Work 13*, 2, 177–187.

Gillingham, P. and Humphreys, C. (2010) 'Child protection practitioners and decision-making tools: Observations and reflections from the front line.' *British Journal of Social Work 40*, 8, 2598–2616.

Glaser, D., Prior, V. and Lynch, M. (2001) *Emotional Abuse: Suspicion, Investigation and Registration.* Great Ormond Street Hospital and United Medical and Dental Schools of Guy's and St Thomas' Hospitals, London. London: Department of Health.

Glisson, C. and Hemmelgarn, A. (1998) 'The effects of organizational climate and interorganizational coordination on the quality and outcomes of children's service systems.' *Child Abuse and Neglect 22*, 5, 401–421.

Grimshaw, R. with Berridge, D. (1994) *Educating Disruptive Children.* London: National Children's Bureau.

Gupta, A. and Blewettt, J. (2007) 'Change for children? The challenges and opportunities for the children's social work workforce.' *Child and Family Social Work 12*, 2, 172–181.

Hannon, C., Wood, C. and Bazalgette, L. (2010) *In Loco Parentis.* London: Demos.

Haringey LSCB (2008) *Serious Case Review: 'Child A'. Executive Summary.* London: Haringey Children's Services Department.

Haringey LSCB (2009) *Serious Case Review: Baby Peter. Executive Summary.* London: Haringey Children's Services Department.

Harwin, J. (2009) *The Family Drug and Alcohol Court (FDAC) Evaluation Project. Interim Report – Summary of Key Issues and Findings* (August). Prepared for the Nuffield Foundation and the Home Office. London: Nuffield Foundation.

Harwin, J. and Forrester, D. (2002) *Parental Substance Misuse and Child Welfare: A Study of Social Work with Families in which Parents Misuse Drugs or Alcohol.* Unpublished First Stage Report for the Nuffield Foundation.

Harwin, J., Owen, M., Locke, R. and Forrester, D. (2003) *Making Care Orders Work: A Study of Care Plans and their Implementation.* London: The Stationery Office.

Harwin, J. and Ryan, M. (2007) 'The role of the court in cases concerning parental substance misuse and children at risk of harm.' *Journal of Social Welfare and Family Law 29*, 3–4, 277–292.

Hatton, C., Akram, Y., Shah, R., Robertson, J. and Emerson, E. (2004) *Supporting South Asian Families with a Child with Severe Disabilities.* London: Jessica Kingsley Publishers.

Haveman, R., Wolfe, B. and Spaulding, J. (1991) 'Childhood events and circumstances influencing high school completion.' *Demography 28*, 133–157.

Helm, D. (2010) *Making Sense of Child and Family Assessment: How to Interpret Children's Needs.* London: Jessica Kingsley Publishers.

Hester, M., Pearson, C. and Harwin, N. with Abrahams, H. (2007) *Making an Impact: Children and Domestic Violence. A Reader*, 2nd edn. London: Jessica Kingsley Publishers.

Hicks, L. and Stein, M. (2009) *Neglect Matters: A Multi-Agency Guide for Professionals Working Together on Behalf of Teenagers.* London: Department for Children, Schools and Families. Reference DCSF-00247-2010. Available at www.education.gov.uk/publications/standard/publicationDetail/Page1/DCSF-00247-2010, accessed 1 June 2011.

Higgins, D.J. and McCabe, M.P. (2000) 'Multi-type maltreatment and the long-term adjustment of adults.' *Child Abuse Review 9*, 6–18.

Hill, C. with Wright, V., Sampeys, C., Dunnett, K., Daniel, S., O'Dell, L. and Watkins, J. (2002) 'The emerging role of the specialist nurse: Promoting the health of looked after children.' *Adoption and Fostering 26*, 4, 35–43.

Hindley, N., Ramchandani, P.G. and Jones, D.P.H. (2006) 'Risk factors for recurrence of maltreatment: A systematic review.' *Archives of Disease in Childhood 91*, 744–752.

HM Government (2004) *Every Child Matters: Change for Children.* London: Department for Education and Skills.

HM Government (2008) *Information Sharing: Guidance for Practitioners and Managers.* Available from www.education.gov.uk/publications/standard/publicationdetail/page1/DCSF-00807-2008, accessed 15 June 2011.

HM Government (2010a) *Working Together to Safeguard Children: A Guide to Inter-Agency Working to Safeguard and Promote the Welfare of Children.* London: Department for Children, Schools and Families.

HM Government (2010b) *The Children Act 1989 Guidance and Regulations. Volume 2: Care Planning, Placement and Case Review.* London: The Stationery Office.

Holland, S. (2010) *Child and Family Assessment in Social Work Practice,* 2nd edn. London: Sage Publications.

Holmes, L., McDermid, S., Jones, A. and Ward, H. (2009) *How Social Workers Spend Their Time: An Analysis of the Key Issues that Impact on Practice Pre- and Post Implementation of the Integrated Children's System.* Research Report DCSF-RR087. London: DCSF.

Horwath, J. (2002) 'Maintaining a focus on the child? First impressions of the Framework for the Assessment of Children in Need and their Families in cases of child neglect.' *Child Abuse Review 11,* 195–213.

Horwath, J. (2007) *Child Neglect: Identification and Assessment.* Basingstoke: Palgrave.

Horwath J. (2009) 'The Assessment Process: Making Sense of Information, Planning Interventions and Reviewing Progress.' In J. Horwath (ed.) *The Child's World: The Comprehensive Guide to Assessing Children in Need,* 2nd edn. London: Jessica Kingsley Publishers.

Howe, D. (2005) *Child Abuse and Neglect: Attachment, Development and Intervention.* London: Palgrave.

Hunt, J. and Macleod, A. (1999) *The Best-Laid Plans: Outcomes of Judicial Decisions in Child Protection Proceedings.* London: The Stationery Office.

Hunt, J., Waterhouse, S. and Lutman, E. (2009) 'Keeping them in the family: Outcomes for children placed in kinship care through care proceedings.' *British Journal of Social Work 38,* 8, 1659–1660.

Iwaniec, D. (2006) *The Emotionally Abused and Neglected Child: Identification, Assessment and Intervention,* 2nd edn. Chichester: Wiley.

Iwaniec, D., Donaldson, T. and Martin, A. (2004) 'The plight of neglected children: Social work and judicial decision-making, and management of neglect cases.' *Child and Family Law Quarterly 16,* 4, 423–436.

Jack, G. and Gill, O. (2003) *The Missing Side of the Triangle: Assessing the Importance of Family and Environmental Factors in the Lives of Children.* Ilford: Barnardos.

Jones, D.P.H. (2007) 'Making plans: Assessment, intervention and evaluating outcomes.' Paper presented at the 2nd International Conference, Child Abuse and Neglect: The Facts, Leuven, Belgium, 9–10 May.

Jones, D.P.H. (2009) 'Assessment of Parenting.' In J. Horwath (ed.) *The Child's World: The Comprehensive Guide to Assessing Children in Need,* 2nd edn. London: Jessica Kingsley Publishers.

Kaniuk, J., Steele, M. and Hodges, J. (2004) 'Report on a longitudinal research project, exploring the development of attachments between older, hard-to-place children and their adopters over the first two years of placement.' *Adoption and Fostering 28,* 61–67.

Kirklees Safeguarding Children Board (2010) *Serious Case Review – Executive Summary: Regarding safeguarding issues between 1995 and 2008 associated with five children in a family.* Kirklees Safeguarding Children Board. Available at www.nscb.norfolk.gov.uk/documents/Kirklees_5childreninafamily.pdf, accessed 12 June 2011.

Korbin, J. and Spilsbury, J. (1999) 'Cultural Competence and Child Neglect.' In H. Dubowitz (ed.) *Neglected Children: Research, Practice and Policy.* Thousand Oaks, CA: Sage Publications.

Laming, Lord (2003) *The Victoria Climbié Inquiry: Report of an Inquiry by Lord Laming.* London: HMSO.

Laming, Lord (2009) *The Protection of Children in England: A Progress Report.* London: The Stationery Office.

Laub, J.H., Nagin, D.S., and Sampson, R.J. (1998) 'Trajectories of change in criminal offending: Good marriages and the desistance process.' *American Sociological Review 63,* 225–238.

Laub, J.H. and Sampson, R.J. (1993) 'Turning points in the life course.' *Criminology 31,* 301–325.

Littlechild, B. (2005) 'The nature and effects of violence against child-protection social workers: Providing effective support.' *British Journal of Social Work 35*, 3, 387–401.

Logan, T. and Royse, D. (2001) 'Program Evaluation.' In B. Thyer (ed.) *The Handbook of Social Work Research Methods*. Thousand Oaks, CA: Sage Publications.

London Borough of Greenwich (1987) *A Child in Mind: Protection of Children in a Responsible Society. The Report of the Commission of Inquiry into the Circumstances Surrounding the Death of Kimberley Carlile*. London: London Borough of Greenwich.

London Borough of Newham (2002) *Area Child Protection Committee: Ainlee*. London: London Borough of Newham.

Long, A., McCarney, S., Smyth, G., Magorrian, N. and Dillon, A. (2001) 'The effectiveness of parenting programs facilitated by health visitors.' *Journal of Advanced Nursing 34*, 5, 611–620.

Lowe, N. and Murch, M., with Bader, K., Borkowski, M., Copner, R., Lisles, C. and Shearman, J. (2002) *The Plan for the Child: Adoption or Long-term Fostering*. London: BAAF.

Luckock, B. (2010) 'A "Whole System" for the Whole Child? Integrated Services, Interprofessional Working and the Development of Effective Practice with Children and Their Families.' In M. Robb and R. Thomson (eds) *Critical Practice with Children and Young People*. Bristol: Policy Press.

Macdonald, G. (2001) *Effective Interventions for Child Abuse and Neglect: An Evidence-Based Approach to Planning and Evaluating Interventions*. Chichester: John Wiley and Sons.

Macdonald, G. and Williamson, E. (2002) *Against the Odds: An Evaluation of Child and Family Support Services*. London: National Children's Bureau/Joseph Rowntree Foundation.

McGee, R., Partridge, F., Williams, S. and Silva, P.A. (1991) 'A twelve-year follow-up of preschool hyperactive children.' *Development and Psychopathology 3*, 175–190.

McGee, R., Wolfe, D., Yuen, S., Wilson, S. and Carnochan, J. (1995) 'The measurement of maltreatment: A comparison of approaches.' *Child Abuse and Neglect 19*, 2, 233–249.

McMurray, I., Connolly, H., Preston-Shoot, M. and Wigley, V. (2008) 'Constructing resilience: Social workers' understandings and practice.' *Health and Social Care in the Community 16*, 3, 299–309.

Malek, M. (1991) *Psychiatric Admissions: A Report on Young People Entering Residential Psychiatric Care*. London: Children's Society.

Marchant, R. and Jones, M. (2003) *Getting it Right: Involving Disabled Children and Young People in Assessment, Planning and Review Processes*. Brighton: Triangle.

Masson, J., Oakley, M. and Pick, K. (2004) *Emergency Protection Orders: Court Orders for Child Protection Crises*. Research Report, School of Law, Warwick University.

Masson, J., Pearce, J. and Bader, K., with Joyner, O., Marsden, J. and Westlake, D. (2008) *Care Profiling Study*. Ministry of Justice Research Series (March). Available at www.justice.gov.uk/publications/docs/care-profiling-study.pdf.

Masten, A.S. and Powell, J.L. (2003) 'A Resilience Framework for Research, Policy and Practice.' In S.S. Luthar (ed.) *Resilience and Vulnerability: Adaptation in the Context of Childhood Adversities*. New York, NY: Cambridge University Press.

Meltzer, H., Gatward, R., Corbin, T., Goodman, R. and Ford, T. (2003) *The Mental Health of Young People Looked After by Local Authorities in England*. London: The Stationery Office.

Millar, M. and Corby, B. (2006) 'The Framework for the Assessment of Children in Need and their Families – a basis for a "therapeutic" encounter?' *British Journal of Social Work 36*, 887–899.

Mitchell, W. and Sloper, P. (2008) 'The Integrated Children's System and disabled children.' *Child and Family Social Work 13*, 3, 274–285.

Morgan, R. (2010) *Children's Messages on Care 2010: A Report by the Children's Rights Director for England*. Manchester: Ofsted.

Morton, T. and Holder, W. (2000) *Issues and Strategies for Assessment: Approaches to Child Maltreatment*. Duluth, GA: National Resource Centre on Child Maltreatment.

Munro, E. (1998) 'Improving social workers' knowledge base in child protection.' *British Journal of Social Work 28*, 89–105.

Munro, E. (1999) 'Common errors of reasoning in child protection work.' *Child Abuse and Neglect 23*, 8, 745–758.

Munro, E. (2004) 'A simpler way to understand the results of risk assessment instruments.' *Children and Youth Services Review 56*, 26, 873–883.

Munro, E. (2005) 'Improving practice: Child protection as a systems problem.' *Children and Youth Services Review 27*, 4, 375–391.

Munro, E. (2008) *Effective Child Protection*, 2nd edn. London and Thousand Oaks, CA: Sage Publications.

Munro, E. (2010) *The Munro Review of Child Protection Part One: A Systems Analysis*. London. Department for Education.

Munro, E. (2011) *The Munro Review of Child Protection. Interim Report: The Child's Journey*. London: Department for Education.

Murray, M. and Osborne, C. (2009) *Safeguarding Disabled Children*. DCSF-00374-2009. London: DCSF.

National Children's Bureau (2011) *Care Planning for Looked After Children*. Available at www.ncb.org.uk/careplanning/index.html, accessed 3 June 2011.

Ofsted (2008) *Learning Lessons, Taking Action: Ofsted's Evaluations of Serious Case Reviews 1 April 2007–31 March 2008*. London: Ofsted.

Ofsted (2009) *Learning Lessons from Serious Case Reviews: Year 2. Ofsted's Second Year of Evaluating Serious Case Reviews: A Progress Report* (April 2008 to March 2009). Available at www.ofsted.gov.uk/Ofsted-home/Publications-and-research/Browse-all-by/Documents-by-type/Thematic-reports/Learning-lessons-from-serious-case-reviews-year-2, accessed 1 June 2011.

Pallett, C., Simmonds, J. and Warman, A. (2010) *Supporting Children's Learning: A Training Programme for Foster Carers*. London: BAAF.

Peckover, S., Hall, C. and White, S. (2009) 'From policy to practice: The implementation and negotiation of technologies in everyday child welfare.' *Children and Society 23*, 2, 136–148.

Pithouse, A. (2006) 'A common assessment for children in need? Mixed messages from a pilot study in Wales.' *Child Care in Practice 12*, 3, 199–217.

Pithouse, A., Hall, C., Peckover, S. and White, S. (2009) 'A tale of two CAFs: The impact of the electronic Common Assessment Framework.' *British Journal of Social Work 39*, 599–612.

Platt, D. (2005) 'Social workers' decision-making following initial assessments of children in need in the UK.' *International Journal of Child and Family Welfare 8*, 4, 177–190.

Platt, D. (2006a) 'Investigation or initial assessment of child concerns? The impact of the refocusing initiative on social work practice.' *British Journal of Social Work 36*, 267–281.

Platt, D. (2006b) 'Threshold decisions: How social workers prioritize referrals of child concern.' *Child Abuse Review 15*, 4–18.

Platt, D. (2007) 'Congruence and co-operation in social workers' assessments of children in need.' *Child and Family Social Work 12*, 326–335.

Platt, D. (2008) 'Care or control? The effects of investigations and initial assessments on the social worker–parent relationship.' *Journal of Social Work Practice 22*, 3, 301–315.

Platt D. (2011) 'Assessments of children and families: Learning and teaching the skills of analysis.' *Social Work Education 30*, 2, 157–169.

Preston-Shoot, M. (2003) 'A matter of record?' *Practice 15*, 3, 31–50.

Quinton, D. (2004) *Supporting Parents: Messages from Research*. London: Jessica Kingsley Publishers.

Quinton, D. (2006) 'Self-development.' In J. Aldgate, D. Jones, W. Rose and C. Jeffery (eds) *The Developing World of the Child*. London: Jessica Kingsley Publishers.

Quinton, D. (2009) *Matching Adoptions from Care: A Conceptual and Research Review*. Unpublished report to DCSF Adoption Research Initiative.

Quinton, D. and Murray, C. (2002) 'Assessing Emotional and Behavioural Development in Children Looked After Away from Home.' In H. Ward and W. Rose (eds) *Approaches to Needs Assessment in Children's Services*. London: Jessica Kingsley Publishers.

Quinton, D., Pickles, A., Maughan, B. and Rutter, M. (1993) 'Partners, peers and pathways: Assortative pairing and continuities in conduct disorder.' *Development and Psychopathology 5*, 763–783.

Quinton, D., Rushton, A., Dance, C. and Mayes, D. (1998) *Joining New Families: A Study of Adoption and Fostering in Middle Childhood.* Chichester: Wiley.

Randall, J. (2009) 'Towards a better understanding of the needs of children currently adopted from care: An analysis of placements 2003–2005.' *Adoption and Fostering 33*, 1, 44–55.

Reder, P. and Duncan, S. (1999) *Lost Innocents: A Follow-Up Study of Fatal Child Abuse.* London and New York, NY: Routledge.

Reder, P. and Duncan, S. (2004) 'Making the most of the Victoria Climbié Inquiry Report.' *Child Abuse Review 13*, 95–114.

Reder, P., Duncan, S. and Gray, M. (1993) *Beyond Blame: Child Abuse Tragedies Revisited.* London: Routledge.

Reder, P., Duncan, S. and Lucey, C. (2003) *Studies in the Assessment of Parenting.* London: Routledge.

Roach, G. and Sanders, R. (2008) 'The best laid plans? Obstacles to the implementation of plans for children.' *Adoption and Fostering 32*, 4, 31–41.

Rose, W. (2009) 'The Assessment Framework.' In J. Horwath (ed.) *The Child's World: The Comprehensive Guide to Assessing Children in Need*, 2nd edn. London: Jessica Kingsley Publishers.

Rose, W. and Barnes, J. (2008) *Improving Safeguarding Practice: Study of Serious Case Reviews 2001–2003.* DCSF/Open University. London: DCSF.

Rubin, D.M. (2007) 'The impact of placement stability on behavioural well-being for children in foster care.' *Paediatrics 119*, 336–344.

Ruch, G. (2007) 'Reflective practice in contemporary child-care social work: The role of containment.' *British Journal of Social Work 37*, 659–680.

Ruffolo, M.C., Thoburn, J. and Allen-Meares, P. (2009) 'Children, Young People and Families.' In I. Shaw, K. Briar-Lawson, J. Orme and R. Ruckdeschel (eds) *The Sage Handbook of Social Work Research.* London: Sage Publications.

Rushton, A. (2003) *Knowledge Review 2: Adoption of Looked After Children: A Scoping Review of Research.* London: Social Care Institute for Excellence.

Rushton, A. (2004) 'A scoping and scanning review of research on the adoption of children placed from public care.' *Clinical Child Psychology and Psychiatry 9*, 1, 89–106.

Rushton, A. and Dance, C. (2005) 'Negative parental treatment of the singled-out child: The responses to the problem by health visitors, social services departments and child and adolescent mental health services.' *Clinical Child Psychology and Psychiatry 10*, 3, 413–428.

Rushton, A., Dance, C., Quinton, D. and Mayes, D. (2001) *Siblings in Late Permanent Placements.* London: BAAF.

Rustin, M. (2005) 'Conceptual analysis of critical moments in Victoria Climbié's life.' *Child and Family Social Work 10*, 11–19.

Rutter, M. (2000) 'Resilience Reconsidered: Conceptual Considerations, Empirical Findings and Policy Implications.' In J.P. Shonkoff and S.J. Meisels (eds) *Handbook of Early Intervention.* New York, NY: Cambridge University Press.

Ryan, M., Harwin, J. and Chamberlain, C. (2006) *Report on the Feasibility of Establishing a Family Drug and Alcohol Court at Wells Street Family Proceedings Court.* Report prepared for LB Camden, LB Islington, LB Westminster, CAFCASS, Wells Street Inner London Family Proceedings Court and Brunel University. Available at www.brunel.ac.uk.7067.FDAC/FDACFeasibilityStudy.pdf, accessed July 2011.

Schön, D. (1983) *The Reflective Practitioner: How Professionals Think in Action.* New York, NY: Basic Books.

Schön, D. (1987) *Educating the Reflective Practitioner.* San Francisco, CA: Jossey-Bass.

Schofield, G. and Beek, M. (2005) 'Risk and resilience in long-term foster care.' *British Journal of Social Work 35*, 8, 1283–1301.

Schofield, G. and Beek, M. (2008) *Achieving Permanence in Foster Care.* London: BAAF.

Scourfield, J. (2003) *Gender and Child Protection.* London: Palgrave Macmillan.

Selwyn, J., Harris, P., Quinton, D., Nawaz, S., Wijedasa, D. and Wood, M. (2008) *Pathways to Permanence for Black, Asian and Mixed Ethnicity Children: Dilemmas, Decision Making and Outcomes. Research Brief DCSF-RBX-13-08.* London: Department for Children, Schools and Families.

Selwyn, J., Quinton, D., Sturgess, W. and Baxter, C. (2006) *Costs and Outcomes of Non-Infant Adoptions.* London: BAAF.

Selwyn, J., Harris, P., Quinton, D., Nawaz, S., Wijedasa, D. and Wood, M. (2010) *Pathways to Permanence for Black, Asian and Mixed Ethnicity Children.* London: BAAF.

Sempik, J., Ward, H. and Darker, I. (2008) 'Emotional and behavioural difficulties of children and young people at entry into care.' *Clinical Child Psychology and Psychiatry 13,* 2, 221–233.

Sheppard, M. (2008) 'How important is prevention? High thresholds and outcomes for applicants refused by children's services: A six-month follow-up.' *British Journal of Social Work 38,* 7, 1268–1282.

Sheppard, M. (2009a) 'Social support use as a parental coping strategy – its impact on outcome of child and parenting problems: A six-month follow-up.' *British Journal of Social Work 39,* 1427–1446.

Sheppard, M. (2009b) 'High thresholds and prevention in children's services – the impact of mothers' coping strategies on outcome of child and parenting problems: A six-month follow-up.' *British Journal of Social Work 39,* 1, 46–63.

Sinclair, I. (2005) *Fostering Now: Messages from Research.* London: Jessica Kingsley Publishers.

Sinclair, I., Baker, C., Lee, J. and Gibbs, I. (2007) *The Pursuit of Permanence: A Study of the English Care System.* London: Jessica Kingsley Publishers.

Sinclair, I., Baker, C., Wilson, K. and Gibbs, I. (2005) *Foster Children: Where They Go and How They Get On.* London: Jessica Kingsley Publishers.

Sinclair, R. and Bullock, R. (2002) *Learning from Past Experience – A Review of Serious Case Reviews.* London: Department of Health.

Sinclair, I., Wilson, K. and Gibbs, I. (2005) *Foster Placements: Why They Succeed and Why They Fail.* London: Jessica Kingsley Publishers.

Skuse, T. and Ward, H. (2003) *Outcomes for Looked After Children: Children's Views of Care and Accommodation. An Interim Report to the Department of Health.* Loughborough: Centre for Child and Family Research, Loughborough University.

Sloper, P. (2004) 'Facilitators and barriers for co-ordinated multi-agency services.' *Child: Care, Health and Development 30,* 6, 571–580.

Smale, G. and Tuson, G. with Biehal, N. and Marsh, P. (1993) *Empowerment, Assessment, Care Management and the Skilled Worker.* London: National Institute for Social Work.

Social Work Task Force (2009) *Building a Safe, Confident Future: The Final Report of the Social Work Task Force.* Research Report DCSF-01114-2009. London: DCSF. Available at www.education.gov.uk/publications/standard/publicationdetail/page1/DCSF-01114-2009, accessed May 2011.

Stanley, J. and Goddard, C. (2002) *In the Firing Line: Violence and Power in Child Protection Work.* Chichester: John Wiley and Sons.

Stanley, N., Miller, P., Richardson Foster, H. and Thomson, G. (2010a) *Children and Families Experiencing Domestic Violence: Police and Children's Social Services' Responses.* London: NSPCC.

Stanley, N., Miller, P., Richardson Foster, H. and Thomson, G. (2010b) 'A stop-start response: Social services interventions with children and families notified following domestic violence incidents.' *British Journal of Social Work,* Advance Access, 19 June 2010, doi:10.1093/bjsw/bcq071.

Statham, J. and Smith, M. (2010) *Issues in Earlier Intervention: Identifying and Supporting Children with Additional Needs.* Research Report DCSF-RR-205. London: DCSF.

Steele, M., Kaniuk, J., Hodges, J., Haworth, C. and Huss, S. (1999) 'The Use of the Adult Attachment Interview: Implications for Assessment in Adoption and Foster Care.' In BAAF (ed.) *Assessment, Preparation and Support: Implications from Research.* London: BAAF.

Stein, M. (2006) 'Young people leaving care.' *Child and Family Social Work 11,* 273–279.

Stein, M., Hicks, L., Rees, G. and Gorin, S. (2007) *A Review of the Literature on the Preparation of Guidance for Multi-Disciplinary Teams and a Guide for Young People.* (Confidential Draft)

Stein, M., Rees, G., Hicks, L. and Gorin, S. (2009) *Neglected Adolescents: Literature Review.* Research brief: DCSF-RBX-09-04. London: Department for Children, Schools and Families.

Stevenson, O. (2007) *Neglected Children and Their Families,* 2nd edn. Oxford: Blackwell.

Strivastava, O.P., Stewart, J., Fountain, R. and Ayre, P. (2003) 'Common Operational Approach Using the Graded Care Profile in Cases of Neglect.' In J. Taylor and B. Daniel (eds) (2005) *Child Neglect: Practice Issues for Health and Social Care.* London: Jessica Kingsley Publishers.

Tanner, K. and Turney, D. (2000) 'The role of observation in the assessment of child neglect.' *Child Abuse Review 9,* 337–348.

Tanner, K. and Turney, D. (2003) 'What do we know about child neglect? A critical review of the literature and its application to social work practice.' *Child and Family Social Work 8,* 25–34.

Tarleton, B., Ward, L. and Howarth, J. (2006) *Finding the Right Support? A Review of Issues and Positive Practice to Support Parents with Learning Difficulties and their Children.* London: Baring Foundation.

Tarren-Sweeney, M. (2010) Poster presentation at the International Conference of Adoption Research, Leiden, Netherlands.

Thoburn, J. and Making Research Count Consortium (2009) *Effective Interventions for Complex Families Where There Are Concerns about, or Evidence of, a Child Suffering Significant Harm.* C4EO Safeguarding Briefing 1. London: C4EO.

Thoburn, J., Lewis, A. and Shemmings, D. (1995) *Paternalism or Partnership? Family Involvement in the Child Protection Process.* London: HMSO.

Thoburn, J., Wilding, J. and Watson, J. (2000) *Family Support in Cases of Emotional Maltreatment and Neglect.* London: The Stationery Office.

Thomas, J. (2010) *Re-Constructing Children's Identities: Social Work Knowledge and Practice in the Assessment of Children's Identities.* Unpublished PhD thesis, Cardiff University School of Social Sciences.

Thomas, J. and Holland, S. (2010) 'Representing children's identities in Core Assessments.' *British Journal of Social Work 40,* 8, 2617–2633.

Thomas, N. (2000) *Children, Family and the State: Decision-Making and Child Participation.* Bristol: Policy Press.

Thompson, R.A. (1995) *Preventing Child Maltreatment through Social Support: A Critical Analysis.* London and Thousand Oaks, CA: Sage Publications.

Tompsett, H., Ashworth, M., Atkins, C., Bell, L., Gallagher, A., Morgan, M. and Wainwright, P. (2009) *The Child, the Family and the GP: Tensions and Conflicts of Interest in Safeguarding Children.* Research Report DCSF-RBX-09-05 ES. London: Kingston University/St George's University of London.

Triseliotis, J., Borland, M. and Hill, M. (2000) *Delivering Foster Care.* London: BAAF.

Trotter, C. (2002) 'Worker skill and client outcome in child protection.' *Child Abuse Review 11,* 1, 38–50.

Trotter, C. (2008) 'Involuntary Clients: A Review of the Literature.' In M. Calder (ed.) *The Carrot or the Stick? Towards Effective Practice with Involuntary Clients in Safeguarding Children Work.* Lyme Regis: Russell House.

Tunstill, J. and Aldgate, J. (2000) *Services for Children in Need: From Policy to Practice.* London: The Stationery Office.

Tunstill, J., Aldgate, J. and Hughes, M. (2007) *Improving Children's Services Networks: Lessons from Family Centres.* London: Jessica Kingsley Publishers.

Tunstill, J. and Allnock, D. (2007) *Understanding the Contribution of Sure Start Local Programmes to the Task of Safeguarding Children's Welfare.* Sure Start Report 026. London: Department for Education and Skills.

Turnell, A. and Edwards, S. (1997) 'Aspiring to partnership: The Signs of Safety approach to child protection.' *Child Abuse Review 6,* 3, 179–190.

Turnell, A. and Edwards, S. (1999), *Signs of Safety: A Solution and Safety Oriented Approach to Child Protection Casework.* New York, NY: W.W. Norton.

Turney, D. (2009) *Analysis and Critical Thinking in Assessment.* Dartington: Research in Practice.

Wade, J., Biehal, N., Farrelly, N. and Sinclair, I. (2010) *Outcomes for Children Looked After for Reasons of Abuse or Neglect: The Consequences of Staying in Care or Returning Home.* Research Report DFE-RBX-10-06. London: Department for Education.

Wade, J., Dixon, J. and Richards, A. (2010) *Special Guardianship in Practice.* London: BAAF.

Wade, J., Mitchell, F. and Baylis, G. (2005) *Unaccompanied Asylum Seeking Children: The Response of Social Work Services.* London: BAAF.

Walker, M., Hill, M. and Triseliotis, J. (2002) *Testing the Limits of Foster Care: Fostering as an Alternative to Secure Accommodation.* London: BAAF.

Ward, H., Brown, R., Westlake, D. and Munro, E. (2010) *Infants Suffering, or Likely to Suffer, Significant Harm: A Prospective Longitudinal Study.* Research Brief DFE-RB053. London: Department for Education.

Ward, H., Holmes, L. and Soper, J. (2008) *Costs and Consequences of Placing Children in Care.* London: Jessica Kingsley Publishers.

Ward, H., Munro, E.R. and Dearden, C. (2006) *Babies and Young Children in Care: Life Pathways, Decision-making and Practice.* London: Jessica Kingsley Publishers.

Ward, H., Munro, E., Dearden, C. and Nicholson, D. (2003) *Outcomes for Looked After Children: Life Pathways and Decision-Making for Very Young Children in Care or Accommodation.* Loughborough: Centre for Child and Family Research, Loughborough University.

Ward, H. and Peel, M. (2002) 'An Inter-Agency Approach to Needs Assessment.' In H. Ward and W. Rose (eds) *Approaches to Needs Assessment in Children's Services.* London: Jessica Kingsley Publishers.

Webster-Stratton, C. (1990) 'Long-term follow-up of families with young conduct-problem children: From preschool to grade school.' *Journal of Clinical Child Psychology 19*, 2, 144–149.

White, A. (2005) *Literature Review: Assessment of Parenting Capacity.* Ashfield, New South Wales: Centre for Parenting and Research, NSW Department of Community Services. Available at www.community.nsw.gov.au/docswr/_assets/main/documents/research_parenting_capacity.pdf, accessed May 2011.

White, A. and Walsh, P. (2006) *Risk Assessment in Child Welfare: An Issues Paper.* Ashfield: NSW Department of Community Services.

White, S. (1998) 'Time, temporality and child welfare: The ascent and durability of psycho-legalism.' *Sociological Review 46*, 2, 265–292.

White, S. (2009) *Error, Blame and Responsibility in Child Welfare: Problematics of Governance in an Invisible Trade.* End of Award Report. Lancaster University, University of Nottingham and Cardiff University.

White, S. and Featherstone, B. (2005) 'Communicating misunderstandings: Multi-agency work as social practice.' *Child and Family Social Work 10*, 3, 207–216.

White, S., Wastell, D., Pithouse, A., Broadhurst, K., Hall, C., Peckover, S., Thompson, K. and Davey, D. (2009) *Error, Blame and Responsibility in Child Welfare: Problematics of Governance in an Invisible Trade.* End of Award Report. Lancaster University, University of Nottingham and Cardiff University.

Woodcock, J. (2003) 'The social work assessment of parenting: An exploration.' *British Journal of Social Work 33*, 87–106.

Worrall-Davies, A. and Cottrell, D. (2009) 'Outcome research and interagency work with children: What does it tell us about what the CAMHS contribution should look like?' *Children and Society 23*, 336–346.

SUBJECT INDEX

AUTHOR INDEX